British History in Perspective
General Editor: Jeremy Black

PUBLISHED TITLES

Paul Seaward *The Restoration, 1660–1668*
John Stuart Shaw *The Political History of Eighteenth-Century Scotland*
W.M. Spellman *John Locke*
William Stafford *John Stuart Mill*
Robert Steward *Party and Politics, 1830–1852*
Bruce Webster *Medieval Scotland*
Ann Williams *Kingship and Government in Pre-Conquest England*
Ian S. Wood *Churchill*
John W. Young *Britain and European Unity, 1945–99* (second edition)
Michael B. Young *Charles I*

Please note that a sister series, *Social History in Perspective*, is now available.
It covers the key topics in social, cultural and religious history.

British History in Perspective
Series Standing Order
ISBN 0–333–71356–7 hardcover
ISBN 0–333–69331–0 paperback
(*outside North America only*)

You can receive future titles in this series as they are published by placing a standing order. Please contact your bookseller or, in case of difficulty, write to us at the address below with your name and address, the title of the series and the ISBN quoted above.

Customer Services Department, Macmillan Distribution Ltd
Houndmills, Basingstoke, Hampshire RG21 6XS, England

CHURCHILL

IAN S. WOOD

St. Martin's Press
New York

CHURCHILL

St. Martin's Press, Scholarly and Reference Division, 175 Fifth Avenue, New York, N. Y. 10010

First published in the United States of America in 2000

This book is printed on paper suitable for recycling and made from fully managed and sustained forest sources.

Printed in Hong Kong

ISBN 0–312–23061–3 clothbound
ISBN 0–312–23062–1 paperback

Library of Congress Cataloging-in-Publication Data

Wood, Ian S.
    Churchill / Ian S. Wood.
      p. cm. – (British history in perspective)
    Includes bibliographical references (p.) and index.
    ISBN 0–312–23061–3 – ISBN 0–312–23062–1 (pbk.)
    1. Churchill, Winston, Sir, 1874–1965. 2. Great Britain–Politics and government–20th century. 3. Great Britain–History, Military–20th century. 4. Prime ministers–Great Britain–Biography. L Title. II. Series.
DA566.9.C5 W65 2000
941.084′092–dc21

                                                              99–05476

To Helen, Ben, David and Robbie with love

CONTENTS

PREFACE

When a young Winston Churchill entered Parliament in 1900 he was following the example of at least five of his patrician ancestors, though at twenty-six he was still older than his father and grandfather had been when they were first elected. If self-destruction was in the family genes it missed a generation with Churchill, even if he came close to it in his political career. His upbringing was a privileged but often unhappy one and the disarray of his parents' finances required him to earn a living, first in the army, then as a writer, journalist and politician.

A steady income became a matter of greater urgency in 1908 when he began a long and happy marriage to Clementine Hozier. The life-style which he was able to provide for her and a growing family was always comfortable, though not lavish by aristocratic standards. Churchill, it appears, hardly ever had the need to use public transport, to make purchases in shops or even to run his own bath. He and Clementine had a son and four daughters, one of whom died in infancy. Despite sharing more time with them than he had received from his own parents, the dark shadow of Churchillian history cast itself across their lives. All of them except Mary, Lady Soames, became alcoholics, and one committed suicide.

Churchill's political career can usefully be divided into three phases. The first, from his election to Parliament until 1915, was one in which his star was ascendant. After he crossed from the Conservative to the Liberal benches of the Commons in 1904 and was aided by the Liberal landslide in the 1906 General Election, his rise to high office was rapid. He identified himself vigorously with a Liberal agenda of social and constitutional reform as well as Irish Home Rule. However, his fall from power in 1915 over the Dardanelles disaster confirmed what many thought to be his capacity for headstrong misjudgement as well as self-advertisement. Yet his furious and often egocentric relish for crisis which was apparent in these early years would be one of his greatest attributes when he was called upon to give truly national leadership to the peoples of these islands in 1940.

That seemed a remote prospect in 1915, yet he was back in office by July 1917 and only out of it for two years between then and May 1929. This second period of his public life, from 1915 to 1939, saw his return to the Conservative fold in 1924, closely followed by appointment to the highest position he had yet held, that of Chancellor of the Exchequer, under Baldwin. Even so, he still had to live with accusations of political opportunism dating back to his first years in Parliament, while his role in the 1926 General Strike reinforced his reputation, perhaps unfairly, for being a class warrior with a crudely confrontational view of organised labour. Suspicion of Churchill cut across party lines and contributed to the political isolation he achieved with his attacks, after 1930, on Conservative policy towards India. It also limited, at least until 1938, the impact of his critique of the National Government's appeasement of Nazi Germany.

The third and triumphant phase of a career which would still have been remarkable even had it ended sooner, came with renewed war in 1939 and what he saw as his own rendezvous with destiny in May of the following year. From then until his retirement from office in 1955, he dominated both British politics and for a time a wider stage as a war leader and statesman. His role was also decisive as a supporter of the historic post-war Conservative compromise with new social forces and aspirations, which found their voice in Labour's 1945 General Election victory.

Defining the beliefs which kept Churchill on course over a political career as long as it was colourful and tempestuous, is no easy task. Yet these beliefs retained a consistency even though he changed sides politically and was never a model team player in party terms. As Isaiah Berlin put it in a perceptive essay on Churchill in 1949: 'When biographers and historians come to describe and analyse his views on Europe or America, on the British Empire or Russia, on India or Palestine, or even on social and economic policy, they will find that his opinions on all these topics are set in fixed patterns, set early in life and later only reinforced.'[1] This still goes far to explain Churchill's failures as well as his infinitely greater achievements.

ACKNOWLEDGEMENTS

To write at all about as compelling and complex a figure as Winston Churchill is to take risks. This is not only because of the potent legend created by the man and his achievements but also because of the superb literature about him to which so many historians have now contributed. Any attempt at yet another biography seemed superfluous, so this book has settled for a thematic look at some of the major yet overlapping concerns of an extraordinary life. Churchill's life was driven by a deep belief in his own destiny and an essentially Anglo-centric race-patriotism which now inevitably has its critics in a multi-cultural Britain confronting important constitutional changes as well as closer relations with the European Union.

Any merits which this book may have owe much to the conversation, advice and good company of colleagues and friends. Among them, but in no particular order, I must mention John Brown, Henry Cowper, Paul Addison, Mario Relich, David Stafford, Gerry Douds, Victor Rothwell and Séan McKeown, also Norman Bonney, a head of department who has supported me in my preparation of this work.

Ms J. Tyler-Copper did indispensable work in converting a manuscript to a useable item for publication. Special thanks are due from me to Simon Winder, Jonathan Reeve, Gabriella Stiles and Terka Bagley at the publishers; to Juanita Bullough for her skilful copy-editing; and also to Edinburgh University's Kerr-Fry Research Trust for their welcome financial support.

CHRONOLOGY

1874	Born at Blenheim Palace, Oxfordshire, 30 November, to the former Jenny Jerome and Lord Randolph Churchill, third son of the seventh Duke of Marlborough
1888	Attends Harrow School
1893	Enters Royal Military Academy, Sandhurst
1895	Commissioned as an officer in the Fourth Hussars
1896–99	Active service on the North-West Frontier of India and in the Sudan
1899	Reports the war in South Africa for the *Morning Post* and escapes from a Boer prison camp
1900	Elected Conservative MP for Oldham, October
1904	Joins Liberal Party, May
1905	Appointed Parliamentary Under-Secretary for the Colonies, December
1908	President of the Board of Trade, defeated in Manchester North-West by-election, elected as Liberal MP for Dundee, marries Clementine Hozier, April
1910	Appointed Home Secretary, February
1911	Appointed First Lord of the Admiralty, October
1915	Naval attack on Dardanelles, transferred from Admiralty, May, with formation of Coalition Government, to Chancellorship of Duchy of Lancaster. Resigns office and joins army on Western Front, November
1916	Commands Sixth Battalion, Royal Scots Fusiliers, January–May
1917	Minister of Munitions, July
1919	Secretary of State for War and Air, January
1921	Secreatary of State for the Colonies (retaining Air Ministry until May 1921)

1

CHURCHILL THE WARRIOR

In May 1912, Violet Asquith, the daughter of Britain's Liberal Prime Minister, was one of Churchill's guests cruising with him on the naval yacht *Enchantress* which he could use in his capacity as First Lord of the Admiralty. Her diary recalled what began as an idyllic moment. 'As we leaned side by side against the taffrail, gliding past the lovely, smiling coastline of the Adriatic, bathed in sun, I remarked "How perfect!" He startled me by his reply: "Yes – range perfect – visibility perfect – If we had got some six-inch guns on board how easily we could bombard...." etc., etc. – and details followed showing how effectively we could lay waste the landscape and blow the nestling towns sky-high.'[1]

Churchill, it has often been said, derived a real excitement from war and preparation for it. 'Radiant, his face bright, his manner keen'[2] was how David Lloyd George described him when war came two years later. Yet it was a guilty excitement, as Churchill often made clear when he thought aloud about it, and he was never indifferent to war's implacable human price. As a young officer he had seen this at first hand and written of it too. His account of frontier warfare in India described cavalry pursuing rebels up a narrow valley: 'No quarter was given and every tribesman caught was speared or cut down at once. Their bodies lay thickly strewn about the fields, spotting with black and white patches the bright green of the rice crop. It was a terrible lesson and one which the inhabitants will never forget.'[3]

At Omdurman in the Sudan, a year later in 1898, Churchill was both combatant and chronicler of what he saw and felt as British firepower inflicted hideous carnage on Mahdist rebels. The defeated enemy appeared as 'grisly apparitions; horses spouting blood, struggling on three legs, men staggering on foot, men bleeding from terrible wounds, fish-hook spears stuck right through them, arms and faces cut to pieces, bowels protruding, men gasping, crying, collapsing, expiring. Our first task was to succour these.'[4] Danger, in actions such as these and then in South Africa, was something the young Churchill sought out, hoping always for recognition that would make him known at home and advance the political career for which he was already preparing himself.

His exploits in the Boer War secured him that recognition and helped earn him not just a seat in Parliament but ministerial office, once he crossed the floor of the Commons to join the Liberals. When Britain declared war in 1914, he held what for one of his temperament was the perfect position at the Admiralty, for this was an operational as well as a merely administrative department, where he could have a direct role in the deployment of the Royal Navy. On 1 August 1914, for example, he ordered full mobilisation of the fleet, without reference to the full Cabinet, which merely confirmed it the next day. The result was that 'every one of H. M. ships, including the ships in reserve, was already at war station or had her war orders, ready for all contingencies'.[5]

Churchill's espousal of the cause of a strong navy had been seen by his critics as yet another volte-face after his previous support for Lloyd George in Cabinet arguments about economies in naval expenditure. The enthusiasm with which he took on his responsibility for the navy at war did not silence them, partly because of the way in which he involved himself across the whole range of decisions which the war demanded of the Cabinet. This proved within a few months to be his undoing, because a maverick political record, which had earned him bitter enemies over issues like Irish Home Rule, had left him little political capital to draw upon once his harassment of senior naval officers and his generous interpretation of his ministerial brief became known to political opponents and hostile newspapers.

It probably could not have been otherwise, given that 'he saw the war as a fulfilment rather than as a frustration of his destiny and he did not pretend otherwise'.[6] This became vividly apparent when, on 2 October 1914, the Belgians announced that they would have to abandon Antwerp to the advancing Germans. With the Prime Minister, Asquith, out of London, Grey, the Foreign Secretary, called an emergency meeting of available ministers which Churchill joined at midnight. In response to his fervour, it was agreed that the Belgians be urged to hold the port and that the First Lord should proceed there at once. He arrived while Antwerp was under severe artillery attack and assumed very effective command of British forces there, including two ill-trained brigades of the Royal Naval Division.

A friend of the Asquith family who arrived from British headquarters at the same time as Churchill described his impact: 'He dominated the whole place – the King [of Belgium], Ministers, soldiers, sailors. So great was his influence that I am convinced that with 20,000 British troops he could have held Antwerp against almost any onslaught.'[7] It was not to be, for reinforcements were not available, but on 5 October he sent a bizarre communiqué to Asquith, offering to resign from the Admiralty and take command at Antwerp officially with appropriate rank. A good case can in fact be made for the defence of Antwerp, which significantly delayed the German advance to the Channel ports, and Churchill's personal intervention had been sanctioned by his Cabinet colleagues, as well as the Prime Minister and Kitchener, the Secretary of State for War.

Even so, his impetuosity and flamboyant behaviour gave another hostage to his enemies. The opposition press ridiculed him, the *Morning Post* blaming him for what it called 'an eccentric expedition' and asking whether it was right for him to treat 'the resources of the Admiralty as if he were personally responsible for naval operations'.[8] Friends also were perturbed by his readiness at short notice to give up his Cabinet role for the excitement of renewed action and command.

If Antwerp had thrown into sharp focus some of Churchill's weaknesses, it provided a reminder of his ability to lead troops under fire. He had the opportunity to prove this again eighteen months later when he served on the Western Front as a courageous and conscientious commanding officer of the 6th Battalion of the Royal Scots Fusiliers. This, however, was a period of enforced exile from high office after the bloody failure of a venture that would haunt him for decades, the Dardanelles expedition.

The period of Churchill's direct responsibility for operations in the Dardanelles was a very brief one, ending for all practical purposes after naval attacks on Turkish fortifications in the Straits were called off on 18 March 1915. Yet the subsequent commitment to battle of the Royal Naval Division, which he had been instrumental in raising and which he had been accused of deploying at Antwerp as his private army, made him think of the campaign as a personal enterprise. In a real sense it was. Lord Beaverbrook wrote of him preaching the case for it like a crusade[9] which would tilt the balance of war in Russia's favour and provide a dramatic alternative to stalemate in the West.

At the start of 1915, the Royal Navy's performance in the war, and by implication, Churchill's, was under severe criticism. Only one significant surface action had been won off the Falklands, and the First Lord's relations with the admirals were fractious. His most important naval ally was Admiral of the Fleet 'Jackie' Fisher, twenty years his senior and a choleric and, Churchill came to believe, unstable character, although he had restored him to the position of First Sea Lord the previous October. Fisher's initial support for a naval action to force a passage through the Straits greatly strengthened Churchill's hand against the doubters in the Cabinet. The trouble was that Fisher himself joined them once he became clear in his own mind that Churchill believed warships could do the job alone and without ground forces landing on the Turkish shore.

Some accounts of what followed suggest that an adequate force of capital ships, audaciously led, could have neutralised the Turks' ability to hold the Straits, but the naval operation, launched on 19 February and carried on over the next four weeks, faltered. Ships were lost and Fisher's doubts grew as his personal relationship with Churchill worsened, partly because of the latter's tactlessness. Kitchener, meanwhile, refused to authorise any immediate deployment of troops and Churchill's frustration increased when the naval commander in the Straits called off operations which, on 18 March, Churchill rightly believed had come close to success.

When a military expedition was in fact decided upon, with more than adequate time for Turkish forces on the Gallipoli peninsula to prepare, Churchill strongly supported it but had little control over it or the appalling losses of the troops who landed there in April 1915. Their sacrifice became a deathless legend, especially those of ANZAC forces, but a mill town such as Bury in Lancashire, with countless other localities, lived for generations afterwards with a sense of loss for its battalions slaughtered on Cape Helles.[10] Coincidental with these events was the final collapse of Churchill's relations with Fisher, who resigned as First Sea Lord on 15 May. This sealed Churchill's fate, for Asquith, under pressure from the opposition over shell shortages and costly stalemate on the Western Front, was facing up to the need for a coalition government in which, with Fisher gone, he would be unable to keep Churchill at the Admiralty.

All that Churchill was offered was relegation to the Chancellorship of the Duchy of Lancaster. He accepted, though his wife feared it would destroy him and Max Aitken, Conservative MP and press owner (soon to be made Lord Beaverbrook) described him as a 'lost soul' on the night of his demotion,[11] only resigning from the government in November once his sense of impotence had further deepened. Just as he opposed until near the end evacuation of the troops from Gallipoli, Churchill never retreated from his fundamental belief in the strategic case for the campaign and the naval operations which had preceded it.

It had more to commend it than some of the wilder schemes for landing troops on Germany's North Sea and Baltic coast which he and Fisher had toyed with in late 1914, but it has to be said that Churchill willed the end, a second front in the Near East which would defeat Turkey and rejuvenate Russia as an ally, without addressing the logistic means essential to its achievement. This charge, it is true, was brought against him more than once in the Second World War, but in his defence it can be said that the elaborate inter-service planning and co-ordination of resources and firepower essential to as big an operation as the Dardanelles campaign was in its infancy in 1915. The War Council, set up in November the previous year to replace the peacetime Committee of Imperial Defence, proved a cumbersome mechanism for resolving inter-service suspicions, earmarking troops and supplies and relaying intelligence to commanders such as Sir Ian Hamilton, who had to commit his men to battle in Gallipoli with minimal knowledge of the levels and dispositions of the enemy force.

Ever since the Dardanelles Committee condemned the whole venture both in its conception and execution in two reports in 1917 and 1918, the inquest has gone on, Churchill making his own case with superb eloquence in 1923 in his history of the war, *The World Crisis*. Since then, opinion has hardened against his claims that the campaign was a legitimate gamble. One of the finest accounts of these events sees the whole venture as having been driven ahead by Churchill without a full grasp of the problems involved, a card forced upon a government incapable of playing it.[12] The same account admits how close allied troops at times came to a breakout from the unyielding terrain of Helles and Suvla. It also defines the outcome as a tactical draw at terrible cost, but a strategic defeat.[13]

Even if the Turks had been defeated at the Dardanelles and a Black Sea supply route to Russian ports opened as a result, only aid on a huge scale could have altered the balance of the struggle on the Eastern Front. Turkey depended on German military aid, so its elimination from the war could well, as A. J. P. Taylor pointed out, have lessened Germany's burden and freed resources for use elsewhere.[14] Constantinople, had it been taken as a result of victory by the British, ANZAC and French forces, would only have been of use as a base from which to strike at German-dominated Central Europe. This would have been a hazardous undertaking, depending on extended lines of communication, and when a Balkan front was opened at Salonika in late 1915, little progress was made.

All that was left to Churchill in May 1915, apart from the minor office he had accepted in the coalition, was membership of the Dardanelles Committee which replaced the War Council. However, he quickly realised how marginal was his influence on it and was actually seeking a command in the field even before he learned of his exclusion from the new War Committee, which had superseded the Dardanelles Committee in November. This, along with the obvious prospect of the troops being evacuated from Gallipoli, prompted his resignation from office on 13 November. Typically, he at once sought to be made Governor-General of British East Africa with command of British and colonial troops there in the campaign against General von Lettow-Vorbeck, the formidable leader of a German and African guerilla force. This was refused him, but he had clearly lost none of his belief, in his own ability to make both strategic and tactical decisions.

Even when the command of a mere battalion came to him early in 1916, though he quickly earned the liking and respect of its officers and men and once more showed himself apparently fearless under fire, he still planned to return to the political fray, retaining his seat in Parliament and consuming avidly the political news sent to him in regular letters from his wife. The only quick return route for him to ministerial office lay in the unravelling of the Asquith coalition. When this took place, in December 1916, he had no influence upon events and was excluded from the new administration led by Lloyd George; a condition the Conservatives had imposed before they would serve under him.

Only when the Dardanelles Committee published its first report in March 1917, assigning as much blame to Kitchener and Asquith as to Churchill, did his return from the wilderness begin to be possible, and Lloyd George had to prepare the ground with care before bringing him back to office as Minister of Munitions four months later.

Conservative reaction was furious, and, as Beaverbrook wrote of the appointment, 'a stick had been thrust into the political beehive, and the rage of the drones and workers was terrible to behold'.[15]

His new ministry, while it involved Churchill in critical production decisions and negotiations with trade unions and employers over pay, conditions and the reductions of differential rates for skilled and semi-skilled workers, issues which had created high tension on the Clyde and elsewhere the previous year, also gave him opportunities to visit the Front. These, needless to say, he made full use of, and Lloyd George received many observations and much advice from him about the conduct of the war. His alternative 'Eastern' strategy may have collapsed at the Dardanelles, but the mounting cost of attritional offensives in the West appalled him. After writing a *Times* obituary of a friend killed in May 1917, he unburdened himself of his feelings by letter to his wife – 'Never for a moment does the thought of this carnage and ruin escape my mind'[16] – and later that year, he strongly opposed Haig's third Ypres offensive.

Haig became deeply suspicious of Churchill's trips to the Front, ostensibly to monitor the shell situation, thinking of him as a meddler and spy who would make adverse reports to Lloyd George.[17] Churchill, for his part, read the brutal stalemate that British strategy seemed merely to contribute to as proof of the need for a strong executive centre through which the civil power could impose its will on the military. Germany's major errors in the war, he argued, such as the unrestricted U-Boat Campaign, were a result of blinkered military professionals overriding the will of politicians, and he came close to despair at the weakness of a Prime Minister in relation to commanders in the field whom he could not dismiss. That was something Churchill would not flinch from in a later conflict, but long before that he had vowed never, because of the integral relationship between strategy and politics, to accept political responsibility in time of war without real power.[18]

Such power, had it been Churchill's to exercise in 1917 and 1918, might have been a counterweight to Haig's intransigence. It might also have led to the more innovative and destructive employment of the tank, a weapon whose development he had enthusiastically supported while still at the Admiralty. Haig has his defenders, and the November 1918 Armistice was a victory which he could claim had been secured by the methods with which he had perserved. Haig returned home to have the laurels of the victor heaped upon him, but not before he clashed with Churchill over the army mutinies prompted by ill-planned demobilisation procedures. Churchill, by January 1919, was the responsible minister, having been appointed Secretary of State for War and Air by Lloyd George after the coalition's election victory in December 1918, and was able to prevail over Haig's preference for the discipline of the firing squads to restore order.[19]

One of his first actions as Secretary of State for War was to circulate to all commanding officers a question as to how their men would react to the prospect of serving in Russia, where civil war was already raging between the Soviet state and its enemies. The question was a relevant one, given the recent mutinies over demobilisation and the fear of some senior officers that soldiers could be affected by the current level of unrest among industrial workers. A copy of the War Office document was leaked to and published by the *Daily Herald*, but the most common reply was that men would accept any overseas duties with the exception of Russia.[20] This effectively limited any British intervention to supplying funds and equipment and using only such troops as were already there, strengthened with volunteers.

The original deployment of close to 200 000 British and allied troops who were in Russia by the end of 1918 had not been influenced by Churchill, but it soon became clear that his conception of their role was different from that of Lloyd George and the Cabinet. On 31 December, ministers agreed that British troops should not take sides in the fighting, and that any active military tasks should be limited to the assistance of Baltic and Caucasus states with definite non-Russian majorities who felt under threat from the new Soviet regime.

Churchill's hatred of Bolshevism and his apocalyptic view of its threat both to democratic states and to the British Empire made it very hard for him to accept this decision. Within a month of his taking his new office, Lloyd George was being alerted to what seemed to be his collegue's intentions. 'I cannot conceal from you', the Prime Minister's personal secretary Philip Kerr, wrote to him, 'that Mr. Churchill is bent on forcing a campaign against Bolshevik Russia.... He is perfectly logical in his policy because he declares that the Bolsheviks are the enemies of the human race and must be put down at any cost.'[21] The Cabinet was never going to support such a venture and Lloyd George instead was close to accepting the case for withdrawing British troops, but each new speech and article by Churchill convinced press and public that he was trying to lead a war party within the Cabinet.

Lloyd George's many other preoccupations delayed a decision on British troop withdrawal until early March 1919, when the Cabinet agreed to it in principle, but this made little difference to Churchill. He clung tenaciously to the case for intervention, often with a disregard for the military implications of his case, which alarmed senior army officers who were no less anti-Bolshevik than he. One of these was Sir Henry Wilson, Chief of the Imperial General Staff. In a letter to a colleague serving in France in May 1919, Wilson described Churchill in terms that would have come easily to the Chiefs of Staff Committee in the Second World War: 'Do not take too seriously conversations with the Secretary of State. I do not mean by this to disparage what he says, but he has a habit of throwing out schemes in conversation and in writing which when examined are found in many cases to be unworkable and which he himself, when the counter-case is put to him, is the first to admit.'[22]

For an army demobilising while still trying to meet large commitments in Ireland, Egypt, Palestine and India as well as maintaining an occupation force in the Rhineland, intervention in Russia would have posed huge problems, even when the anti-Bolshevik forces rallied and went on to the offensive, as they did for a time in the summer and autumn of 1919. Even then, Churchill's passionate advocacy of their cause only convinced those close to him of his instability. Wilson wrote after meeting him at Chequers in late July that he had been 'very excited and talked of resigning',[23] while the press still had in its sights the man it blamed for the Dardanelles. 'The country is absolutely unwilling to make a great war in Russia,' declared the *Daily Express*. It went on to deride 'the megalomania of Mr. Winston Churchill the military gamester. Let us bring our men back – if we can.'[24]

Nonetheless, barely a year later, Lloyd George found himself still having to set out for Churchill's benefit the case against military support for the Polish republic in its war with the Soviet Union.[25] The whole episode opened a breach between them which proved hard to repair and, it has been said, brought Churchill 'little credit either outside or inside the Government' as well as 'effectively reviving the apprehensions of 1915 about his judgement and capacity'.[26]

Churchill remained at the War Office until the end of 1920, with cuts in expenditure biting increasingly into the army's manpower, but once appointed Colonial Secretary in January 1921, he initially retained responsibility for the Air Ministry and an air force of whose potential he had been an early champion. Its cost-effective role in the 'air policing' of territories mandated to Britain by the League of Nations, such as Palestine and Mesopotamia, commended itself to Churchill. However, he could still talk about policy decisions in terms deeply alarming to military men such as Sir Henry Wilson, who wrote of him on 10 December 1921: 'he seems to be getting wilder and wilder, according as he gets deeper into the bog. He is now proposing to withdraw our British troops from both Mesopotamia and Palestine, governing the former with "hot air, aeroplanes and Arabs" and the latter with "hot air, aeroplanes and Jews", with a backing of "Black and Tans".'[27]

The coalition's collapse in late 1922 removed Churchill from direct contact with the service departments, but his appointment by Baldwin as Chancellor of the Exchequer in his 1924 administration placed him almost immediately on a collision course with his old department, the Admiralty. 'That extraordinary fellow Winston has gone mad,' wrote Beatty, the First Sea Lord, in 1925, 'economically mad and no sacrifice is too great to achieve what in his short-sightedness is the panacea for all evil – to take a shilling off the Income Tax.'[28] The navy, he went on to argue, was faring worse under Churchill than it had under Labour in office. His incomprehension was deepened by the fact that his own career had owed much to Churchill, and also by the very recent support he had received from him during the post-war coalition period for an increased battleship-building programme.

Churchill, of course, was simply carrying out, with the tenacity he brought to every task, a Treasury brief to bring all expenditure under control. If that meant cutting back on a fleet which he had worked determinedly to expand before 1914, he was ready to live with the rage that resulted; and ready also to tell Baldwin that the admirals 'should be made to recast all their plans and scales and standards on the basis that no naval war against a first class Navy is likely to take place in the next twenty years'.[29] In this he failed but he was able, in 1928, to persuade the Committee of Imperial Defence that no major war needed to be anticipated over the next ten years. This was the Ten Year Rule, though the services accepted it only subject to annual review and it was abandoned within four years.

Churchill's role in these policy decisions has led some to call into question his later claims to have been a consistent critic of British foreign policy in the inter-war period. This belongs to the larger debate about Churchill's opposition to appeasement,[30] but it should not be assumed that his zeal for including the service departments in across-the-board economies was tantamount to any cooling of his interest in defence policy and matters military. Apart from completing his six-volume work on the war, *The World Crisis*, during his term as Chancellor of the Exchequer, he also began a biography of his ancestor, John Churchill, first Duke of Marlborough. Military historians still turn to this account, completed in 1938, for the insights it offers into the author's views on strategy and tactics.

His own service had long since persuaded him that command decisions did not belong to some esoteric art of which civilians could never be vouchsafed any understanding. That belief had a profound and in the main energising effect on his relationship with military commanders in the Second World War, but his life of Marlborough at more than one point focuses on the multiplicity of factors that determine defeat or victory – the number and quality of troops available, their morale, their weapons, their confidence in their leaders, terrain and communications. In his view it was 'the true comprehension at any given moment of the dynamic sum of all these constantly shifting forces that constitutes military genius'.[31]

Though out of office by this time and with little immediate prospect of resuming it, Churchill retained military interests that were much more than academic and historical. As the European situation deteriorated after Hitler took power in 1933, he kept himself well briefed on defence policy by serving officers and civil servants who, under the 1911 Official Secrets Act, took major risks in reporting to him regularly about what they believed to be the inadequate rate of British rearmament and shortcomings in the equipment of the RAF. One of these informants was Major Sir Desmond Morton, who was head of the government's Industrial Intelligence Centre, and whose help Churchill acknowledged publicly after the Second World War.[32] Apologists for the National Government have, however, argued that it knew of these leaks but did not find them unwelcome as a way of influencing an anti-war public opinion in favour of the level of rearmament which it had already sanctioned.[33]

If this was so, not everyone in senior positions was indifferent to Crown servants having their own special relationship with an out-of-office critic of government policy. In late 1937, one of Churchill's sources, Group Captain Lachlan MacLean of the RAF, warned Churchill of an impending visit to Britain by General Milch, the German Minister of Aviation, based on an itinerary which would in fact familiarise him with some of the very shortcomings in both air defence and aircraft production that were troubling Churchill. Churchill's response was to take MacLean's report, without his name on it, to Sir Maurice Hankey, the Cabinet Secretary, who was more shocked at the way this information had been acquired than by its content.[34] Such sources, it has been argued, gave a cutting edge to Churchill's criticisms of government policy as well as enabling him to return to office in 1939, fully conversant with a complex and ongoing debate about military and air preparedness.[35]

Other work on Churchill in this period has taken a more guarded view of the quality of advice and information that came to him from his private sources and, indeed, of his overall grasp of military development. In May 1937 he wrote of how the war in Spain showed the limitations of air power; in January 1938 he was arguing that 'the air menace against properly armed and protected ships of war will not be of a decisive character' and in March, that in any future war 'the armies will use their spades more often than they use their bayonets'.[36] Similarly, he was, on his own later admission, slow to recognise the potential of tank warfare and appears to have had little contact with its major prophet and analyst in Britain, Basil Liddell Hart.[37]

One of his closest relationships to take shape in the inter-war period was with the scientist Professor Frederick Lindemann, later Lord Cherwell. Much has been written of the rapport that grew between them, yet on the crucial matter of the development of radar for air defence, 'the Prof', as Churchill often called him, showed little belief in its potential at a time when vital decisions had to be made by the Air Defence Research Committee. Churchill had been on the Committee since 1935 and gave the appearance of supporting Lindemann's alternative set of priorities, which he argued for on its Technical Subcommittee.[38] Fortunately for Britain, work on a radar defence network went ahead anyhow and once Churchill became Prime Minister, he was quick to make every resource available to it.[39]

Whether the signal 'Winston is back' was ever sent out from the Admiralty to British ships on 3 September 1939 has never been substantiated. Churchill's return to the same office of state a quarter of a century after he had held it at the outbreak of an earlier war could not have failed to strike naval officers with some sense of their service's history. If it did, it may even have been as a warning to those old enough to know of the volatile and interventionist way that Churchill as First Lord had interpreted his relationship to the navy and its senior officers in 1914 and 1915.

From almost the first day of his return to the Admiralty, Churchill made it clear that he saw the fleet's role as an offensive one, regardless of the Sea Lords' doubts about its resources. Officers at the Admiralty who voiced anxiety about committing surface ships to action in the Baltic to cut off German access to Scandinavian resources such as iron ore were liable to find themselves quickly returned to seagoing duties. So too were those who questioned Churchill's consistently high figures for claimed U-boat sinkings over the winter of 1939–40; 'a political distortion of intelligence that could not last' is how one account of his tenure of the Admiralty describes this.[40]

On 24 October 1939, Churchill put it to the War Cabinet that Eire's neutrality should not stand in the way of the navy's needs where the so-called 'treaty ports' were concerned. After negotiations which Churchill had bitterly opposed from the Conservative backbenches in Parliament, these had been returned to the de Valera government's control in early 1938, mainly as a result of Chamberlain's correct judgement that Irish neutrality in time of war would be essentially benevolent to Britain. Churchill found himself losing the argument for plans to retake the ports, which would in any case have been of little strategic value after the fall of France and the consequent re-routeing of convoys to Britain around Ireland's northern coast.[41]

The Royal Navy had changed by 1939 and was an infinitely more complex service than it had been twenty-five years earlier. Its senior officers were conscious also of the time needed to build up its fighting strength after a period of economies of which Churchill in office had been a conspicuous supporter. But he, it has been argued, had not changed, still being a heroic and impetuous figure who wanted others to be like him. Nowhere was this clearer than in his continuing advocacy of major naval action in Scandinavian waters[42] and in early April 1940, he moved closer to this when the Cabinet's Military Co-ordination Committee, of which Chamberlain had made him chairman, authorised mine-laying operations off the Norwegian coast.

This was rapidly overtaken by Hitler's decision to invade Denmark and Norway, which in turn led to a large naval force and an ill-organised military expedition being sent to take on the German forces. The burden of criticism for what followed fell upon Chamberlain rather than Churchill, who had favoured action off Scandinavia since September 1939. Royal Navy losses were heavy and a grim reminder of the vulnerability of surface ships to air attack, but so too were Germany's, its fleet losing the major part of its surface strength, something it was never able fully to replace. On the other hand, Hitler secured important bases for air and U-boat attacks on Britain, as well as substantial supplies of Swedish and Norwegian ore, once the port of Narvik was operating again.[43] When, on 7 May 1940, the House of Commons debated the failure to hold Narvik, it was hard for ministers to represent the campaign as anything less than a defeat, although Churchill loyally defended the government on the second day of the debate.

Before Churchill spoke, he was warned by Lloyd George that he 'must not allow himself to be converted into an air-raid shelter to keep the splinters from hitting his colleagues'.[44] When he was called by the Speaker, he accepted his full share of responsibility for operations in Norway. 'He made a dashing, vigorous speech, a magnificent piece of oratory', wrote the pro-Chamberlain Conservative and diarist, Sir Henry Channon: 'Winston told the story of the Norwegian campaign, justified it and trounced the Opposition.'[45] It was not, of course, enough to save Chamberlain, who resigned after his normal majority of 250 fell to 81 in the division on the adjournment motion which closed the debate.

'Thereupon the people picked a leader nearer to their mood, Churchill, who was at any rate able to grasp that wars are not won without fighting. Later perhaps, they will pick another leader who can grasp that only Socialist nations can fight effectively.'[46] This was George Orwell's response to what followed the Narvik debate, and it has been described in many different acounts. It remains important to stress that Churchill was not swept into Downing Street by any great groundswell of public opinion. Chamberlain at first believed he could remain Prime Minister of a coalition which Labour and the Liberals would join, but when it became clear that they would not, he had to decide whom he should recommend to the monarch as his replacement. His preference was for the Foreign Secretary, Lord Halifax, 'prince of appeasers yet adroitly free from blame',[47] as A. J. P. Taylor categorised him, but Churchill's clear unwillingness to serve under him, whatever he may previously have said, led the Labour leaders to withdraw their initial support for Halifax, subject to the backing of their party's National Executive, then meeting at Bournemouth in readiness for its annual conference. This backing came clearly and, along with the insistence of his Chancellor of the Exchequer, Sir Kingsley Wood, that he should go, sealed Chamberlain's fate.

2

NATIONAL LEADER, 1940–1945

Churchill was called to Buckingham Palace on 10 May 1940 and invited by a monarch deeply reluctant to part with Chamberlain to form a new administration. His recollection of events has been challenged, especially his claim to have maintained a dramatic two-minute silence on the previous day when, in Halifax's presence, Chamberlain asked Churchill whether he would serve under him.[1] This, if it ever happened, was of less importance than Halifax's own disinclination to become Prime Minister. The latter factor undermines assertions that Churchill carried out a coup,[2] but the argument matters less than the immediate reality of Guderian's Panzer divisions carrying all before them in Hitler's invasion of the West and of Churchill's own serene sense of purpose after he had become Prime Minister: 'At last I had the authority to give directions over the whole scene. I felt as if I were walking with destiny and that all my past life had been but a preparation for this hour and for this trial.'[3]

The way they feared this authority might be used heightened the venom felt at the turn of events by some of those close to Chamberlain. 'We drank in champagne the health of the "king over the water" (not King Leopold of Belgium, but Mr. Chamberlain)', wrote one Downing Street civil servant in his diary on 10 May 1940. 'Rab [R. A. Butler, then a junior minister at the Foreign Office] said he thought that the good clean tradition of English politics, that of Pitt as opposed to Fox, had been sold to the greatest adventurer of modern political history.' The entry goes on to quote Butler's description of Churchill as a 'half-bred American supported by a rabble'.[4]

'Seldom can a Prime Minister have taken office with "the Establish-
ment", as it would now be called, so dubious of the choice and so
prepared to find its doubts justified',[5] the same diarist wrote nearly
thirty years later. Yet in his next sentence he recorded the following:

> Within a fortnight all was changed. I doubt if there has ever been such
> a rapid transformation of opinion in Whitehall and of the tempo at
> which business was conducted.... Government Departments which
> under Neville Chamberlain had continued to work at much the same
> speed as in peacetime awoke to the realities of war. A sense of urgency
> was created in the course of a very few days and respectable civil
> servants were actually to be seen running along the corridors.[6]

Few people working in government in 1940 were untouched by this
dramatic injection of energy into the conduct of the war. It was, of
course, an extension of Churchill's own extraordinary self-belief and
also of his highly coloured vision of the history of an island race capable
of matching all its ingenuity and courage to the dangers of the hour.
For a time at least, and when it mattered most, he was able to commun-
icate his belief in them, to a wide range of people drawn into Britain's
war effort. Personal contact with him, R. V. Jones, the scientist, wrote,
could give 'the feeling of being recharged with a source of living
power'.[7]

   Alongside the incalculable importance of these personal qualities was
the machinery that Churchill developed through which to conduct the
war. Initially, his most important step was taking for himself the title of
Minister of Defence. He did this with the King's blessing but with no
mandate from Parliament. There was no Ministry as such, but what this
appointment signified was his determination to exercise an overall
control of decisions in a way that would minimise tensions between
policy and strategy. A key figure was Major-General Hastings Ismay,
Churchill's representative on the Chiefs of Staff Committee, who would
brief him on its decisions if or when he was not himself able to attend its
meetings.

   Senior to it, however, was the Defence Committee (Operations),
chaired by Churchill, usually attended by the service ministers and
Chiefs of Staff. The Foreign Secretary was also a member, and it has
been widely regarded as the focal point for bringing together the
political and military elements of grand strategy. Churchill also chaired
the Defence Committee (Supplies), whose remit was to handle logistic

issues but which kept in constant contact with the other committee. It was a system which let him exercise a continuous supervision over both policy formulation and military operations. Even when the Defence Committee (Operations) met less frequently as the war went on, it was still there as an outlet for doubts and dissent. As major decisions emerged increasingly from the Prime Minister's consultation with the Chiefs of Staff, the Defence Committee has been called part of the mechanism of restraint that operated to control Churchill.

Some of his wilder strategic notions needed control, but ultimately Churchill respected the system he had done so much to devise, even when his own eloquence and powers of persuasion and sometimes of intimidation had failed to win an argument. He bore few grudges against those who stood up to him openly and put their case clearly and without excessive deference, while his restless search for answers to new problems could be accommodated by a flexible system which allowed him to create new ad hoc committees to focus in a dramatic way on a particular aspect of the war.

A striking example of this was in late June 1940, when it was brought to his notice that the Germans had learned how to use radio beams to direct their aircraft to precise targets throughout the British Isles. The key figure was R. V. Jones, the young scientist seconded to the Air Ministry, who was at once invited by Churchill to address a special meeting of ministers and service chiefs on the implications for British air defence. Churchill listened, then acted decisively, according every resource needed by Jones and his colleagues to locate and then 'bend' the beam. 'Being master and not having to argue too much, once I was convinced about the principles of this queer and deadly game,' Churchill later wrote, 'I gave all the necessary orders that very day in June for the existence of the beam to be assumed and for all counter-measures to receive absolute priority.'[8]

The results were incalculable in their importance for the period of air warfare over British cities which lay ahead, proof of the way Churchill valued science and technology at something close to their true worth and of how he was ready to harness them fully to the war effort. Similar proof was apparent only three months later. Churchill again acted decisively when he set up a new ad hoc Cabinet committee on U-boat warfare and the Battle of the Atlantic, the latter a stirring phrase he himself had coined. With Churchill the driving force from the Chair, service chiefs and scientists could bring under review every aspect of the fight to keep the sea lanes open, settling inter-service disagreements and assessing expert evidence. The outcome has been described as 'an anti-submarine campaign waged under closer scientific control than any other campaign in the history of the British armed forces'.[9] Vital to both the war at sea and in the air was Britain's ability from quite early on to interpret or decrypt Germany's Enigma machines through which doubly encoded messages were sent by radio to commanders in the field. Although Churchill could not say so in his own history of the war, this was how the Air Ministry had learned of the Luftwaffe's use of the radio beam in 1940. By June the following year, these 'Ultra' intercepts, made possible by specialist cryptographers at Bletchley Park, alerted Stalin to his country's imminent invasion, though he did little with the information, and in February 1942, Britain and her allies had penetrated the codes through which orders went out to Admiral Doenitz's U-boat commanders in the Atlantic.

Intelligence gathering had always fascinated Churchill and as far back as 1920 he had called for the creation of a single intelligence service. Once in power he achieved some rationalisation out of which grew the Joint Intelligence Committee that co-ordinated, assessed and disseminated strategic intelligence. The vital Ultra intercepts were, however, known only to a few people such as the Chiefs of Staff and heads of the intelligence services. Even Churchill's Principal Private Secretary did not know the contents of the special yellow boxes delivered to him several times a day and to which he alone in Downing Street had a key. Churchill loved the drama of all this and his interaction with the intelligence services has been described as 'almost continuous'.[10] No British leader in modern times, it has been said, equalled him in his passion for secret intelligence and how to use it.[11]

Intelligence, in whatever form it is acquired, is only as good as the way in which it is interpreted and applied. As early as January 1941 Churchill had access to an Ultra intercept warning of German plans to invade Greece, though with no precise timetable of their movements. The force which finally sailed from Cairo in early March was inadequate to the task of countering the actual German invasion and the decision to send it denuded the North African theatre of vital units. Similarly with Crete, time provided by British intelligence was wasted, no measures being taken to defend the island effectively or to deny the invaders the use of its single airfield. Accounts of these campaigns tend not to blame Churchill for the way good intelligence was not exploited, making the point that Sir Archibald Wavell, the British

Commander-in-Chief in the Middle East, endorsed intervention in the Balkans if Hitler invaded. There was a logistic case against it which Wavell can be accused of failing to make because of the abrasive treatment he had already received over what Churchill saw as his overcautious leadership in North Africa[12] and also Abyssinia.

Churchill's relations with Wavell, a fine soldier and a scholarly but taciturn man with whom he achieved no personal rapport, is often cited as proof of the friction created by his highly personal and interventionist conception of his role in the military conduct of the war. Both Wavell and his successor in the Middle East Command, Sir Claude Auchinleck, were dismissed by Churchill in June 1941 and July 1942 respectively. Recent work on these commanders[13] shows the constant pressure they were under from Churchill, but then both his temperament and indomitable will for British survival and ultimate victory 'impelled him into a degree of civilian control of a war effort not seen since the days of Pitt'.[14]

This was also a product of a long-held enthusiasm for weaponry and logistics, but he sometimes showed little patience with generals and commanders who were, in his view, slow to use material with which he felt he had been instrumental in providing them.[15] Sometimes this was true but new tanks, just shipped over to Egypt, could not be used in battle right away. They often needed modification for desert conditions and re-servicing, while crews needed time to practise handling them. All this involved vital technical and support units which Churchill misrepresented as a drain upon the army's combat troops. At one meeting with service chiefs, Churchill petulantly declared that 'the army is like a peacock – nearly all tail', to which Sir Alan Brooke, Chairman of the Chiefs of Staff Committee, replied: 'The peacock would be a very badly balanced bird without its tail.'[16]

Brooke was right, as he often was, but Churchill, in an increasingly technological war in which effective support and supply units were essential, kept up his accusation that the army was overmanning its non-combat units.[17] This was one reason why he was so attracted to the role of special forces and commando units, as well as to the potential of resistance movements in Nazi-occupied territory 'to set Europe ablaze'. When, moreover, relatively junior officers of charm and proven courage, such as Lord Louis Mountbatten, met Churchill, their rise could be meteoric, especially if they could make a fluent case for operations that represented a bold alternative to the caution of the service hierarchy. Mountbatten has been claimed as an example of

Churchill's propensity to promote those with style and panache above the level of their real ability,[18] and the Dieppe raid of 1942 is still central to this debate.

Churchill's own account of events at Dieppe on 19 August 1942 is a bland one. He described it as 'a costly but not unfruitful reconnaissance in force'[19] and claimed that useful tactical lessons had been learned. In fact a British and Canadian force, without adequate air support or naval fire to help them, were flung against strongly defended German positions. The cost was more than 4000 casualties, many of the Canadians being cut down by a torrent of enemy fire in the surf, mere yards from their landing craft. Only one objective was taken by Lord Lovat's No. 4 Commando and survivors had to be taken off in a hazardous rescue operation. Mountbatten, promoted from being captain of a destroyer flotilla to the rank of Vice-Admiral in charge of combined operations, wanted to prove himself and reactivated an assault plan abandoned the previous month owing to bad weather and also through growing fears for its likely cost. He went ahead with the operation while Churchill and Brooke were abroad and all Churchill had agreed to was continued cross-Channel raiding as and when appropriate targets were available. What authorisation he had for his decision remains unclear.

Dieppe was not so much a target as a death-trap for those who landed there, yet Mountbatten justified it in terms of the need to show Roosevelt, and especially Stalin, that Britain could engage German troops in mainland Europe. Whatever the truth of the mission's authorisation, the prime responsibility was his, since he could have called the operation off once it was clear to him that the First Sea Lord, Sir Dudley Pound, was not going to make a single ship available to shell the target, while Sir Arthur Harris of Bomber Command refused to commit any of his crews to neutralising the German shore guns.[20] Eight years later, however, when Churchill wrote of this disaster, he did so as an opposition leader who knew that a future government led by him would need Mountbatten. His version was influenced by Mountbatten, and as a major Canadian account of the Dieppe raid has put it, 'Churchill the politician triumphed over Churchill the historian.'[21]

A much greater catastrophe than Dieppe had been the loss of Singapore to the Japanese in February of the same year. In a BBC broadcast on its surrender, Churchill spoke with eloquence of what such a loss meant, coming as it did hard upon serious reverses in North Africa and the Atlantic as well as what seemed a relentless German advance across

Russia.[22] Privately, he blamed Australia and its Prime Minister, John Curtin, whom he disliked, for insisting on reinforcing the Singapore garrison beyond the point where it could be defended and when he himself was thinking in terms of trying to hold off the Japanese in Burma. At this time of multiplying crises, his tendency may well have been, in the words of an Australian historian, 'as each domino fell to extol the strength of the next one in the line'.[23] For Australians, however, Singapore seemed, after Pearl Harbor, to be the domino that mattered if a southward advance by the Japanese was to be halted. Its loss was a traumatic blow for them, which put the dominion on a full war footing as its people's deepest racial fears of invasion and occupation took on vivid shape.

Churchill fell into the trap of equating Singapore's role as a naval base with its potential as a fortress, but the resources for a sustained defence were simply not there. Contrary to legend, some of its shore guns did point north across the narrow Johore Strait but lacked adequate ammunition, while many more were sited uselessly, pointing in the opposite direction from which the attack came. Worse than that, at the very point in January 1942 when Churchill was demanding the island's all-out defence,[24] it had hardly any prepared defensive positions or minefields. Thousands of British and allied troops paid the price, either of death in battle or brutal captivity in Japanese hands. Churchill accepted his responsibility in his history of the war, writing of 'the hideous spectacle of an almost naked island', and declared: 'I ought to have known. My advisers ought to have known and I ought to have been told. I ought to have asked.'[25]

George Orwell predicted correctly that Churchill would survive the political fallout from Singapore,[26] but it is also true that, between its surrender and the loss of Tobruk on 20 June 1942, criticism of him in Parliament grew to the point where he did have to face a no-confidence motion on 2 July. It failed, partly because the two principal supporters of the motion, Sir John Wardlaw-Milne and Admiral of the Fleet, Sir Roger Keyes, advanced conflicting arguments, the former calling for the Prime Minister to be relieved of his defence responsibilities, while the latter wanted more powers given him. Only twenty-five members voted for the motion, with another twenty-seven abstaining, after a powerful defence by Churchill of his conduct of the war. Perhaps a more serious portent for him should have been the coalition's defeat at the Maldon, Essex by-election by the left-wing Beaverbrook journalist

Tom Driberg, but any immediate challenge from Parliament had been safely contained.

This period was one in which, according to Gallup polls, approval ratings of the government dropped below 50 per cent, but Churchill's personal rating remained consistently higher than that, proof that in the public mind he had no preferred successor. He was, moreover, adept at securing his own position. After the fall of Singapore, he had consolidated the coalition's relationship with Labour by making Attlee his deputy, while in June, prior to a hazardous flight to the United States to meet Roosevelt, he let the Foreign Secretary, Eden, know he had advised the King that in the event of his death, Eden should be his successor. This neutralised any possible threat from that quarter, while the patrician Socialist, Sir Stafford Cripps, who handled difficult missions for the government both to the Soviet Union and to India, and who was made Leader of the Commons in February 1942, failed to become a real threat to Churchill even though he pressured him over matters which the War Cabinet had preferred to leave to the Prime Minister. When Churchill dismissed him from the War Cabinet in November, Cripps found he had no real support to call upon.[27]

By then, Churchill had been to Moscow on a delicate mission to explain to Stalin why no Second Front could be started by the Allies in Europe in 1942. It was a task which few of his critics would have relished, yet he accomplished it while managing to create a relationship with the Russian leader that was to remain important until the end of the war. This, along with the Eighth Army's victory over Rommel at El Alamein, put him beyond the reach of his political opponents for the duration of hostilities in Europe. Telegraphing Roosevelt on 17 August that year, Churchill had written of his Moscow visit: 'They have swallowed this bitter pill. Everything for us now turns on hastening "Torch" and defeating Rommel.'[28]

'Torch' was the Allies' code name for the large-scale landings at Casablanca, Oran and Algiers in November 1942, an operation which would not have taken place if Roosevelt had not been won over by Churchill's recommendation of it as a way to tighten the noose round the Axis powers in the Mediterranean and to support the British advance from Egypt.[29] Dwight Eisenhower, who accepted command of the Torch landing forces, was nonetheless uneasy about Churchill's advocacy of a course of action which, in his view, would divert resources from a 1943 landing in Europe as well as committing the Allies to an extended Mediterranean campaign in Sicily and Italy.

A decisive consideration was the President's acceptance of the political need to have American troops in action against the Germans soon, though casualties were inevitably higher than foreseen once Hitler resolved that his forces should fight along a line between Bizerta and Tunis. The Allies, it has been said, 'landed in North Africa ill-adapted to tackle anything but the most limited resistance',[30] but the fact that they did so at all was a measure of the leverage Churchill could exercise in Britain's relations with the United States. This leverage was to last until near the end of the following year, but even after that Churchill, despite worsening disagreements between the British and American Chiefs of Staff over the priority to be accorded an invasion of Europe, could still influence the course of operations and exercise a degree of control over them.

A striking example of this is the Allies' landing at Anzio in January 1944, behind the German lines in Italy, in order to achieve a link-up with the Eighth Army at Monte Cassino which would open the road to Rome. The hoped-for breakout came many weeks later at a cost to many British battalions comparable with battles on the Western Front in 1916 and 1917. Churchill justified the venture in his history of the war in terms reminiscent of his earlier defence of the Gallipoli campaign, calling it 'a story of high opportunity and shattered hopes, of skilful inception on our part and swift recovery by the enemy'.[31] The decisions which led to Operation Shingle, as Anzio was called, were dominated by Churchill as he convalesced in North Africa from serious illness. He was watched by his doctor, Lord Moran, who measured his patient's recovery by the way he absorbed himself in the planning of a bold move to end the stalemate in Italy.[32]

Carlo D'Este, in his history of the campaign, describes Churchill overruling American doubts, rescuing the operation from 'the wastebasket of discarded plans'[33] and arguing that prime responsibility for Mediterranean theatre decisions lay with the British Chiefs of Staff. At some points, D'Este claims, Churchill was close to fulfilling a lifelong fantasy by taking overall charge of a large military operation.[34] This was partly because of the absence of the restraining presence of Brooke, who was in London working on Operation Overlord, the Allies' landing in France, though Brooke was in fact a well-wisher to his Prime Minister's belief that success at Anzio 'would be a cure-all for the ills besetting the Italian campaign'.[35] With more resources and more audacious leadership, the Anzio landing force might indeed have breached the Germans' Gustav line and isolated their position at

Monte Cassino. Churchill was not alone in seeing these possibilities and not to blame for the attritional outcome, although important German divisions were tied down at Anzio, as well as Allied ones.

Right up to and beyond the Normandy landings, Churchill remained tenacious in his belief in the Italian campaign. Victory there could, in his view, take the Allied armies through the Ljubljana gap and into the Danube basin to avert a post-war Soviet occupation of Austria and Czechoslovakia. It is a view which has gained some merit in retrospect but it is more likely that such an effort would have weakened the Allies elsewhere. Brooke, always a vital restraining influence upon Churchill, opposed this totally, arguing that to put it to the Americans would reinforce their doubts about British willingness to fight in the West.[36] Eisenhower understood Churchill's Mediterranean preoccupations but was always clear in his own mind that they could not divert him from the overriding priority of Overlord, the code name for the 1944 landings planned in France. As he and Churchill drew closer, the latter revealed his fear of failure there. 'How often I heard him say,' Eisenhower wrote later, 'we must take care that the tides do not run red with the blood of American and British youth or the beaches be choked with their bodies.'[37] Many were indeed to die landing in Normandy, and Churchill was never callous about the human price of grand strategy. His fears were real, but by June 1944 he had overcome them after many months during which he had backed up all the doubts of his Chiefs of Staff about a Second Front in France.

Eisenhower's personal relationship with Churchill was always amicable, but his patience was further tested over the British Prime Minister's opposition to the decision to land a sizeable Allied force in the South of France in August 1944. Both Roosevelt and Eisenhower saw this as a means to liberate more of France as well as drawing German units into battle away from the Normandy front. However, Operation Anvil, as it was originally code named, seemed to Churchill, from its inception, a diversion of resources from the Italian front. He predicted that the Rhône valley would prove a bloody cul-de-sac and was unjustly dismissive of the quality of French troops, especially North African units, who were to be committed to the campaign.

As the launch of the operation, renamed Dragoon, grew imminent, Churchill went over Eisenhower's head with his opposition, seeking in vain to influence Roosevelt himself against it.[38] When this predictably failed, he then tried to talk Eisenhower round to the case for an alternative landing in Brittany to secure a second port for the Allied armies struggling to break out from Normandy. Eisenhower described this as his most protracted disagreement with Churchill: 'As usual the Prime Minister pursued the argument up to the very moment of execution. As usual, also, the second that he saw he could not gain his own way, he threw everything he had into support of the operation.'[39] Typically, Churchill flew out to the Mediterranean to witness the landing and was actually on board a destroyer to observe the supporting bombardment.

Episodes such as this, consuming hours in argument and straining the patience of allies, pose major questions about Churchill as a strategist. His continuing belief in the importance of the Mediterranean theatre should not, however, simply be cited as proof of his limitations. In 1940, as John Keegan has argued,[40] when military orthodoxy pointed to concentrating all resources on the defence of Britain and its home waters, Churchill identified the Mediterranean and North Africa as the area where the Axis powers could be hit where they were weakest. Spectacular and morale-raising victories were achieved there against Mussolini's armies and his fleet but at the price of much more formidable German forces being deployed in their support. The survival of any Mediterranean strategy came to hinge upon the defence of Malta, while victory on land over the Afrika Korps might have been denied Britain if so many German troops had not been committed to the Russian front after June 1941.

There was always, of course, a political dimension to Churchill's Mediterranean priorities, as Eisenhower and Roosevelt could see. It involved important calculations about the likely balance of Soviet and Western influence and power in post-war Greece, the Balkans and Central Europe and until the end of 1943 he was able to get, if not a free hand, then at least Washington's acquiescence in applying this strategy. That changed once a date for the invasion of Western Europe was finally agreed on at the Teheran Conference that November. 'From that moment onwards,' Keegan has said, 'Churchill's ability to deflect the course of Allied strategy from anything but an all-out battle with the Wehrmacht in the heartland of Europe withered away.'[41] Churchill may have bridled at the growing ascendancy of the United States in the wartime alliance, but he had always seen how vital was its entry into the war. On the night of Pearl Harbor he stayed up late to send off many telegrams and talk to Roosevelt on the telephone. When he finally went to bed, he 'slept the sleep of the saved and the thankful'.[42]

He saw, too, the turning-point represented by Hitler's invasion of the Soviet Union, though welcoming it as an ally required his grasp of strategic necessity to override deep-seated ideological aversion to Stalin's regime. For him, the Soviet cause at once became Britain's, as he told listeners to his 22 June 1941 broadcast. He also told them that the Red Army's defeat would directly imperil Britain and that Hitler would reactivate the invasion plans of 1940 with troops released by victory in the East: 'He wishes to destroy the Russian power because he hopes that if he succeeds in this, he will be able to bring back the main strength of his army and air force from the East and hurl it upon this island, which he knows he must conquer or suffer the penalty of his crimes.'[43] Right-wing historians now dispute this, blaming Churchill for not seeking terms from Hitler in 1940, a refusal they claim led inevitably to the political price that had to be paid for accepting Stalin as an ally.[44]

Their case is part of a larger exercise in dismantling Churchill's reputation and it will be considered elsewhere in this book. Contrary to some of their accusations, Churchill knew well the risks of a Soviet alliance, despite the personal rapport with Stalin which he achieved at their wartime meetings. With rather more clarity than is credited to him in recent hostile work, Churchill saw the choice in 1941 as either allowing a German victory to leave all of Europe under Nazi domination, or, as the price of crushing Hitler, accepting Soviet domination of its Eastern half.[45] In November 1944, in conversation with General de Gaulle in liberated Paris, Churchill admitted to his fears of Soviet ambitions and of the need to alert Washington more fully to them.

> At present Russia is a great beast which has been starved for a long time. It is not possible to keep her from eating, especially since she now lies in the middle of the herd of her victims. The question is whether she can be kept from devouring all of them. I am trying to restrain Stalin, who has an enormous appetite but also has a great deal of common sense. After a meal comes the period of digestion. When it is time to digest, the surfeited Russians will have their difficult moments.[46]

Churchill lived long enough to see the first evidence of these digestive troubles, in the form of the East Berlin strikes of 1953 and the Hungarian uprising three years later.

If the Soviet alliance, with all its hazards, was one part of the price Churchill was ready to pay in order to defeat Hitler, another part of it lay in having to accept the increasingly brutal conduct of a war in which firepower became relentlessly more destructive and indiscriminate. Nowhere was this more apparent than in an air war in which the bombing of German cities developed as Britain's only means of offensive action against the Reich prior to the June 1944 invasion of Europe. Churchill's horror at what the German Blitz did to London and other cities was genuine, but he has been accused of complicity in the way that this brutality was matched and surpassed by the RAF once the striking power became available to hit major urban targets.

He had little to say in his history of the war about the awful firestorm unleashed over Dresden on 14–15 February 1945, which to many is still the climactic horror of the area bombing of Germany. In fact, worse fire raids had already taken place, notably on Hamburg in July and August 1943, and other cities had felt the enhanced power of Bomber Command as the Lancaster aircraft came into full production. As early as July 1940, Churchill had written to Lord Beaverbrook, his minister for aircraft production, on the case for 'devastating, exterminating attack upon the Nazi homeland',[47] and in September, when 100 bombers were launched against Berlin, his reaction was to say 'Never maltreat the enemy by halves.'[48]

These early attacks achieved little, but once the Soviet Union was an ally, the best case had to be made for what RAF bombers could do. Talking to Stalin in August 1942, two months after the first 1000-bomber raid on Cologne, Churchill claimed much for the effects more raids could have on the German population: 'We look upon its morale as a military target. We sought no mercy and we would show no mercy.'[49] Defenders of Bomber Command and its Commander-in-Chief, Sir Arthur Harris, are thus justified in arguing that the air war over German cities was not waged in some moral context unacceptable to Churchill and his ministers, and this was precisely the case that Harris was quick to put once the war was over.[50]

Churchill's moral doubts about the way RAF air power was being used came late in the war but grew to the point where he was clearly anxious not to be too much associated with Bomber Command, a matter for resentment even yet among its survivors. That troubled him, too, as he much later told his Private Secretary: 'Of course Harris was under-recognised at the end and so were his gallant men who suffered the heaviest casualties of all. I did something for him when I got back to power, but it wasn't much.'[51] (The last sentence was a reference to the baronetcy for Harris which Churchill was able to have included in the 1953 Honours List.) Where Churchill disagreed with Harris was in seeing Bomber Command's role as a means, of itself, to deliver victory. Too much has been claimed for the influence of his scientific adviser, Professor Lindemann, in making this case to Churchill. Alongside the sometimes combative way he endorsed Harris's operations he could admit to doubts also, and was doing so before Harris took over Bomber Command. On 27 September 1941, in reply to the Chief of the Air Staff's advocacy of intensified attacks on Germany, Churchill replied: 'It is very doubtful whether bombing will be a decisive factor in the present war',[52] and he went on to sound a note of caution over its potential to destroy both Germany's industry and its morale. He continued to support Bomber Command and the aircraft industry upon which it depended, but he saw clearly that there was no single panacea strategy with which to bring the Third Reich to its knees.

Churchill's five years as Prime Minister, from May 1940 to July 1945, are still a defining period of modern British history. His 1940 speeches and broadcasts move those born long afterwards and are woven into the potent images of an offshore island of Europe confronting, alone and defiant, a victorious Third Reich. The enduring power of such images and Churchill's part in shaping them has prompted revisionist historians to try and strip away layers of what they see as sacrosanct myth masking economic decline, dependence upon America and acquiescence in the creation of a Soviet empire in Europe. Britain's sacrifices, they argue, especially of its great power status, were out of proportion to what was actually won in 1945. The critique can become banal in its expression, as when John Charmley writes that in 1945, Britain 'had nothing save the aim articulated by Churchill in 1940: victory over Nazi Germany. This was a great achievement but it buttered no parsnips.'[53]

Charmley argues that Churchill's historic error lay in his determination to fight on in 1940, rather than seeking terms with Hitler and letting the German and Soviet armies destroy each other. That there was indeed a peace party in Britain in 1940 which had support within Churchill's government is now well documented, and recent work has seized upon Churchill's knowledge of it to take further the dismantling of heroic legend.[54] Yet in May 1940 Churchill had little choice but to retain appeasers such as Chamberlain and Halifax in his Cabinet, and was initially in no position to prevent the consideration of the possibility of defeat, as well as the case for pre-empting it by some sort of agreement with Hitler. Exactly this was discussed on the afternoon of 28 May as news of the Dunkirk evacuation was coming in. Lord Halifax made the case for Italian mediation as the basis for a cessation of hostilities with Hitler and Chamberlain supported him.

Churchill opposed them, and in a five-man War Cabinet, it was his Labour colleagues Attlee and Greenwood who backed him unequivocally in what have been called 'the two most crucial hours in modern Cabinet history'.[55] At 6 p.m., twenty-five senior ministers not in the War Cabinet came in to be briefed by their Prime Minister, and gave a tumultuous reception to a defiant speech by him. Three weeks later, France had fallen and Britain was alone, but even before then Berlin had guessed Churchill's position was not secure. One of its sources in London was Bjorn Prytz, the Swedish Ambassador. On 18 June, the very day of Churchill's speech to Parliament urging British people to be worthy of their finest hour, Prytz had a chance meeting with R. A. Butler, a junior Foreign Office minister and Chamberlain supporter. Butler was called out during the talk that followed to see the Foreign Secretary, returning to pass on to Prytz the message that 'common sense, not bravado' would shape British policy.[56]

Little came of this episode except some embarrassment for Butler, though there appear to be gaps in its documentation in the Public Record Office. For Churchill, the Battle of Britain, then the Luftwaffe's Blitz on London and other cities, came to his rescue and he was able to isolate pro-peace feeling in high places by both tapping into and voicing a powerful popular patriotism manifested by the one and a half million men who joined the Local Defence Volunteers (LDV) in late May and June. The LDV, or Home Guard, as it later became, may have entered into the comic folklore of wartime Britain, but the huge inflow of recruits to it was not a sign of defeatism, given what was likely to await them if a German landing took place.

No more so were the population movements out of bombed cities, often the immediate reaction to attack, especially in areas where shelter provision was inadequate and emergency services overstretched. Negatives can be selected and emphasised to support the view that Churchill led a people less heroic than he claimed they were in his speeches. Yet, as Tom Harrison showed in his book on the Blitz,[57] air attack, after its initial horror, taught people to adapt and endure and in many industrial target areas, output in fact rose after major raids. Churchill himself has been described as often moved and overwhelmed by the reception he received in such places.[58] The morale of civilians under attack is no more a bottomless well to be drawn upon indefinitely than that of soldiers in battle, but Churchill was justified in 1940 and 1941 in thinking of British morale as something more than the mere creation of propagandists. As he put it many years later in a speech to mark his eightieth birthday: 'It was the nation and race dwelling all around the globe that had the lion's heart. I had the luck to be called upon to give the roar.'[59]

Even a lion's heart needed the hope of ultimate salvation, which Churchill knew Britain alone could not achieve, and from early in his premiership some of his greatest speeches were targeted to an American as well as a British audience. In his 4 June 1940 Dunkirk speech, for example, he told the House of Commons how, even if Britain were invaded and occupied, he would carry on the fight 'until, in God's good time, the New World, with all its power and might, steps forth to the rescue and liberation of the Old'.[60] His critics argue that it was in fact Japan, and not Churchill, who brought the United States into the war, and that the flow of American machine tools to British aircraft plants in 1940 was simply part of the process by which a once great economy lost its independence to the new power of America.[61]

The 'special relationship' with the United States may already have been showing in 1940 and 1941 that Britain as a great power was living on borrowed time. What mattered for Churchill and his aircraft production minister, Beaverbrook, was that American lathes and power tools helped factories and their workers keep fighter aircraft rolling off the production lines. As Peter Hennessy has recently put it, 'if a great nation is engaged in what might be its, and democratic Europe's last throw, the manufacturing process, chemical composition and countries of origin of the dice's raw materials are not the main issue. Survival is.'[62]

Survival and victory for Britain and its peoples were Churchill's guiding priorities even as he grieved for what total war was costing them. He was seen to weep at the sight of London's East-Enders queuing to buy canary seed in what remained of their streets during a lull in the 1940 Blitz, and often admitted to guilt at his own exhilaration in the conflict and his power to direct it. His rapport with those he led, while it lasted, involved no condescension to them, and he brought a highly coloured, passionate vision of history to the task of rallying them to the struggle. 'For a time in the 1940s, by dramatising their lives and making them seem to themselves and to each other as acting appropriately for a great historic moment, Churchill transformed the British people into a collective, romantic and heroic whole.'[63]

Finally, it needs to be said that Churchill's determination to fight on against Hitler whatever the risks was influenced profoundly by his knowledge of the Nazi Holocaust against Europe's Jews. From the moment he was first aware of it he condemned it and gave the highest priority to bringing those responsible for it to justice. After reading reports, in July 1944, of the mass murder of Jews at Auschwitz, he minuted to Eden: 'this is probably the greatest and most horrible crime ever committed in the whole history of the world',[64] and in the same month he supported the Jewish Agency for Palestine's demand that Allied air power be used to disrupt the rail links that were critical to the logistics of the Final Solution. That this did not happen was not Churchill's fault,[65] but without his indomitable will to wage war on Hitler until victory was won, countless more Jews would have died in the Third Reich's concentration camps.

3

CHURCHILL AND THE UNITED STATES

Around midnight on 4 March 1946, on a long train journey from Washington to Fulton, Missouri, where he would make a speech that was to acquire a symbolic place in Cold War history, Churchill played poker with President Truman and some of his staff. According to one player, at about 2.30 a.m., Churchill put down his cards and declared: 'If I were to be born again, there is one country in which I would want to be a citizen. There is one country where a man knows he has an unbounded future.' Churchill was asked to name this country and replied: 'The USA, even though I deplore some of your customs.' When asked which customs, his answer was prompt: 'You stop drinking with your meals.'[1]

The humour of his answer of course stemmed from an affection for the United States which Churchill had long felt, for by birth he was half-American. His father Lord Randolph's marriage to Jenny Jerome in 1874 was one of many fashionable Anglo-American unions in the later nineteenth century, but he himself did not visit her homeland until his twenty-second year. This was in 1896, en route to observe the Spanish-American war in Cuba, and he returned late in 1900 to give paid lectures on his experiences in the Boer War. He encountered some pro-Boer and anti-British feeling,[2] and commented in private about the brashness of a young and arrivist nation,[3] but was careful to be diplomatic in public. Good relations between Britain and America were important to Churchill from early in his political career, and at the height of the Home Rule crisis in February 1912, he warned a nationalist audience in West Belfast of the damage a hostile Irish-American population could do to Britain's friendship with the United States.[4]

He was eloquent in acclaiming America's entry into the First World War. Recognition of America's war effort did not, however, blind Churchill to some of what he saw as its post-war misjudgements, especially the rapidity with which war loans were called in. Churchill supported the Lloyd George coalition's abortive policy of securing an agreed all-round cancellation of war debts and took a bleak view of the December 1922 agreement reached by Stanley Baldwin, Chancellor of the Exchequer in the Bonar Law government, with President Harding. In Churchill's view, this had a knock-on effect on every debtor state which responded to the demands of American policy on repayment by tightening the screw on Germany: 'The enforcement of the Baldwin-Harding debt settlement', he wrote later, 'is a recognisable factor in the economic collapse which was presently to overwhelm the world, to prevent its recovery and inflame its hatreds.'[5]

As Chancellor of the Exchequer after 1924, Churchill drove through substantial and controversial cuts in Britain's naval building budget, but took pains to argue that these would not enable the United States to challenge the Royal Navy's global power. This was not a prospect he would have countenanced, because in this period he often expressed suspicion of America's intentions and what he saw as its always latent hostility to the British Empire. After the Baldwin government's defeat in 1929 he resumed direct personal contact with the United States through journalism as well as lecture tours to meet growing financial commitments, but he became increasingly fearful of American isolationism. This seemed to him to define both the Hoover administration's response to the Wall Street crash, which included a huge array of import duty increases and he was shaken, too, by how Roosevelt, after his presidential victory in 1932, seemed to acquiesce in his country cutting itself off from the European economy. The June 1933 World Economic Conference in London was for all practical purposes wrecked by Roosevelt's message to it rejecting any currency stabilisation agreement. Churchill was shocked at this, though of course the National Government formed in August 1931 had some share of the blame for obstructing moves to economic co-operation in Europe by abandoning the Gold Standard and enacting tariffs. America's leaders could also see Britain's commitment to a protected system of imperial preferences and the sterling area, created in the Depression years, as impediments to world trade and a trade agreement between the two countries in 1938 did little to reduce these tensions.

Even so, Churchill was attracted to the vigour with which Roosevelt attacked America's economic problems and in October 1933, although he had only once met him briefly in 1918, he sent the President a signed copy of the first volume of his life of the Duke of Marlborough, his great ancestor. The inscription on it read: 'With best wishes for the success of the greatest crusade of modern times',[6] but his doubts about the new administration's readiness to react to events in Europe grew once Hitler began to show his hand on the international stage.

In a changing world Churchill could see that a separate American agenda could develop. 'Although the ideals of the two countries are similar,' he wrote in 1937, 'their interests are in many ways divergent',[7] but he still underestimated Roosevelt's problems where foreign policy was concerned. Intervention in the First World War had cost America serious casualties and had scarred it in ways which reinforced isolationism, in that Roosevelt had little choice but to buy agreement on his domestic programme by a turning away from an active international role. This was not enough for those whose distrust of foreign commitments made them press Congress for neutrality legislation in 1935, forbidding either loans or arms sales to any belligerent state, and in May 1937, Roosevelt had to accept a permanent Neutrality Act.

Churchill, however, remained an optimist about American intentions and was critical of the Chamberlain government's negative response to Roosevelt's plan, in January 1938, to issue a general appeal to the major powers to agree on some basic rules of international conduct. He had in mind also a conference on world economic problems which could negotiate commodity-trading agreements provided the states who attended consented to armaments limitation as well. The President made his initial approach to Chamberlain, making it clear he would only proceed with British support.

This was not forthcoming, for Chamberlain thought little of the plan, which seemed to him an inopportune diversion from his own efforts to reach agreement with the European dictators. His response angered Eden, his Foreign Secretary, who felt he had not been fully consulted. In fact, Eden resigned from the Cabinet in February 1938 over other issues but Churchill, in the ensuing debate, argued that serious damage had been done to Britain's relations with the United States.

Ten years later, he did not retreat from this view when in his war memoirs he wrote: 'that Mr Chamberlain, with his limited outlook and inexperience of the European scene, should have possessed the self-sufficiency to wave away the profferred hand stretched out across the Atlantic leaves one, even at this date, breathless with amazement'.[8]

Within a week of Britain going to war, Churchill wrote to Roosevelt, although they had not met since 1918, and stressed their shared naval interests, for the President had been Secretary for the Navy in the previous conflict. 'What I want you and the Prime Minister to know', he went on, 'is that I shall at all times welcome it if you will keep me in touch personally with anything you want me to know about.'[9] This was the start of what became a prolific correspondence between the two leaders, consisting ultimately of nearly 2000 communications. When published in 1984, they offered unique insight into the conduct of the war, though Churchill had made selective use of them in his own history of the war.

This correspondence and other sources show us just how much a 'special relationship' with the United States mattered to Churchill. It would have done, anyway, because of his own origins and from a vision that always sustained him of the English-speaking world as a force for good, but he was always clear in his own mind that the war could not be won without American intervention. For at least his first year as Prime Minister he overestimated the prospects of this happening but once it did he was able, where the conduct of the war was concerned, to get much of what he wanted from Roosevelt, a relationship that only began to change towards the end of 1943. The change became perceptible at the Teheran Conference in November of that year, but Churchill still gave priority to Britain's partnership with America even as British influence within the relationship began to slip.

On 15 May 1940, as German Panzer divisions raced across the Low Countries and Northern France, Churchill sent his first telegram as Prime Minister to Roosevelt. It is clear from it that he was already anticipating a French defeat: 'If necessary, we shall continue the war alone and we are not afraid of that,' he wrote, 'but I trust you realise, Mr. President, that the voice and force of the United States may count for nothing if they are withheld too long. You may have a completely subjugated Nazified Europe established with astonishing swiftness and the weight may be more than we can bear.'[10] What followed was an appeal for all aid America could provide short of actually committing its own forces. Roosevelt's response was noncommittal, particularly where the loan of warships was concerned, a matter which would require Congressional authorisation.

Four weeks later, Churchill reiterated his plea in another telegram, but even as it was drafted on 15 June, the Treasury was making known to him the rate at which Britain's gold reserves were being depleted by desperately needed arms purchases. There were further warnings, and at a Cabinet meeting on 22 August, Sir Kingsley Wood, the Chancellor of the Exchequer, presented a paper on gold reserves and overseas assets. By the end of the year, Wood calculated, Britain would no longer be able to fund the war from its own resources. American aid was the only alternative to a compromise peace, but this was not discussed and no minister present dissented from the Chancellor's analysis of the situation.

Help on the scale needed from America could only come after the November Presidential election and one minister, Lord Beaverbrook, argued that Britain's best interim course was to step up orders from American factories so as to tie its industry closer to the war effort, and he is cited in some recent writing as representative of the view that the Prime Minister could drive a harder bargain with Roosevelt. 'Given Churchill's obsession with defeating Germany and his need for American aid in this task, this was like putting a spine into a jellyfish',[11] John Charmley has written, giving away something of his own prejudices with his use of the word 'obsession' in such a context. So too does Clive Ponting in his book on 1940 when he writes that 'the country no longer had the resources to continue the war. Its fate would be decided by another nation.'[12] Neither author sees fit to discuss whether it was better that this other nation be a liberal democracy led by Roosevelt or Nazi Germany.

Once Roosevelt had been re-elected, Churchill prepared a new approach, circulating to the War Cabinet for comment two drafts of a letter which finally went to Washington as a telegram on 7 December 1940. It has been described as 'the most carefully drafted and re-drafted message in the entire Churchill–Roosevelt correspondence',[13] and it set out Britain's plight in graphic terms with the words: 'the moment approaches when we shall no longer be able to pay cash for shipping and other supplies'.[14] Lord Lothian, the British Ambassador in Washington, had a key role in persuading Churchill to lay the financial facts before the President because he was confident of his willingness to help Britain without incurring the political risks of being drawn into the conflict.

Roosevelt's answer came at a Press conference on 17 December when he announced that fifty American destroyers recently taken out of service would be made available to the Royal Navy. The ships, in fact, were old and only thirty were ready for operational service by May 1941, yet the gesture was of immense symbolic importance. Even more dramatic was the President's radio broadcast of 29 December, when he called upon his country to become 'a great arsenal of democracy' and promised his support for a huge programme to supply Britain with weapons, machine tools and food under what became known as Lend-Lease.

Between the enactment of this legislation and the war's end Britain received aid worth over £5000 million, a life support system for its war effort even if an initial down payment was required from what remained of its gold reserves. Exactly what alternative Churchill had other than seeking peace on Hitler's terms remains unclear from the work of writers who see Lend-Lease as part of an American strategy to end Britain's role as an imperial power by exploiting the financial crisis the war had created for it.[15] Churchill saw no conflict between accepting American help and Britain maintaining an imperial presence in the world, which indeed it did do for some years after 1945, with the support of American administrations who, it has been forcefully argued, were quick to see that the Cold War's imperatives must give priority to anti-Communism over anti-Imperialism[16] if there had to be a choice between the two.

Lend-Lease represented in an 'American Century' the final end of Britain's role as paymaster to its wartime allies and the terms on which it was enacted added up to a hard bargain. In its ultimate legislative form there were no concessions on payments due by Britain on arms orders already placed in the United States and in December 1940, an American destroyer was sent to Cape Town to collect the last £50 million of British gold reserves as part-payment for existing orders. Churchill brooded privately over the effect this might have on British opinion at the height of the German Blitz on London and other major cities, and put his anxieties in writing for Roosevelt's attention but never sent them.[17] Privately, too, he wrote to Chancellor Wood that 'we are not only to be skinned but flayed to the bone',[18] yet in public he was right to be generous about Lend-Lease simply because Britain could not have stayed in the war without it. 'Overseas finance was Britain's wartime Achilles heel',[19] it has been said, and the drying up of its gold and dollar reserves had been inevitable once Churchill's intention to fight on was clear.

While the Lend-Lease legislation was going through Congress, emissaries of Roosevelt such as Harry Hopkins and Averill Harriman arrived in London to assess both Britain's needs and its morale. Churchill took them into his confidence[20] at once and Hopkins was soon reporting back to the President that 'Churchill *is* the government in every sense of the word.'[21] Late in January 1941, while Hopkins was still in Britain, joint Staff Conversations opened in Washington, a crucial start to the process of preparing for a joint war effort, though Churchill of course had to keep a tight rein on his hopes of America joining the war even, and perhaps especially, after the high excitement of his August 1941 meeting with Roosevelt on the battleship *Prince of Wales* off Newfoundland.

Moving film footage survives of Churchill and Roosevelt singing hymns together at a deck service and flanked by a ship's company of whom hundreds would die within a few months when the *Prince of Wales* was sunk off Malaya by Japanese aircraft. It remains a symbol of British and American amity at a critical point in the war, as does the Atlantic Charter, the declaration of common purpose agreed to by the two leaders. It was a declaration, just that, for Roosevelt could not have contemplated singing a treaty which would then have had to be ratified by Congress, and he returned to Washington believing he still had a free hand. This has led some historians to represent the meeting and its outcome as part of the Churchillian myth of the 'special relationship'. 'For the British,' one has written, 'the Atlantic Charter lasted scarcely longer than the battleship on which it was signed.'[22]

The content of the Charter contributed to the rhetoric of the Allies' cause, pledging as it did its signatories to principles such as territorial changes and forms of government being conditional upon the consent of peoples concerned; freedom of the seas and of world trade, long-term world disarmament and a permanent system of security with which to outlaw war. Churchill, however, was quick to see the implications of the Charter's third article on the rights of all people to self-determination. Eight days after the signing he wrote to Leo Amery, his Secretary of State for India, that Article Three did not mean 'that the natives of Nigeria or of East Africa could by a majority vote choose the form of Government under which they live, or the Arabs by such a vote expel the Jews from Palestine'.[23] A year later, on the first anniversary of the Charter, he communicated the same reservations to a Roosevelt leading a nation at war.

Churchill knew the Charter was no substitute for an American declaration of war and returned to London still perplexed as to how this could be brought about. He conveyed many of his worries in a letter in late August 1941 to his son Randolph, stressing that Hitler would provide no help by attacking American ships until victory on the Eastern Front was within his reach. He was wrong about this because serious incidents involving American ships and German submarines occurred in the autumn of that year. They provide part of the explanation for Hitler's readiness to declare war on America after Pearl Harbor. In the same letter, he said: 'the President, for all his warm heart and good intentions, is thought by many of his admirers to move with public opinion rather than to lead and form it. I thank God, however, that he is where he is.'[24]

Churchill's anxiety over American intentions was well understood by members of Roosevelt's staff such as Hopkins who could see that the British public needed to believe that his country would join them at some point in the war. If, he wrote, they 'ever reached the conclusion that this was not to be the case that would be a very critical moment in the war and the British appeasers might then have some influence on Churchill'.[25] Such a crisis was of course averted by Pearl Harbor and Hitler's declaration of war upon the United States which followed it.

Over the next two years, certainly until the latter part of 1943, Churchill had good reason to think of his country's relationship with the United States as one of equality. In September of that year, in accepting an honorary degree from Harvard University, he brought all his eloquence to bear upon the two English-speaking democracies' shared commitment to a fight for world order against moral anarchy. 'Tyranny is our foe,' he declared, 'whatever trappings or disguise it wears, whatever language it speaks, be it external or internal, we must forever be on our guard, ever mobilised, ever vigilant, always ready to spring at its throat. In all this, we march together.'[26]

He went on in this speech to look to a post-war world in which real peace and security would depend on the continuance of the two nations' wartime alliance. Yet disagreements well before this had surfaced within the relationship which Churchill had celebrated at Harvard. As early as February 1942, the State Department had added to the original Lend-Lease agreement an article seeking to pledge Britain to end discriminatory trade practices. There was a certain irony in this given that it was the United States' departure from it that had wrecked the June 1933 World Economic Conference on trade liberalisation.

Churchill drafted a reply to Roosevelt, which was sent in a shortened and modified form, stressing Britain's long history as a Free Trade country and warning of the danger of anyone taking a prescriptive view of what British post-war economic policy should be.[27]

His position, like that of Britain itself, was of course a weak one, because America was not demanding financial recompense from Lend-Lease, but repayment in the form of a phasing out of sterling controls and imperial preference to help American exports, as well as preparing the way for a multilateral post-war world economy. In talks about this, Churchill was reluctant to yield much ground and his ministerial colleague Amery was strongly committed to the goal of an imperial trading bloc, as was the Conservative right wing as a whole. Eventually, in July 1944, the Bretton Woods Conference agreed on the principle of a post-war system of freed exchange rates, with an International Monetary Fund substantially supported by the United States to help countries with balance of payments problems, but Churchill's government had still not ratified this when the war in Europe ended.[28]

India was another issue which soon generated tension between the two allies. Some of Roosevelt's advisers were hostile to British rule there and they influenced his reaction to the failure of the 1942 mission to India by Sir Stafford Cripps. In April of that year, talks broke down between him and the Indian National Congress over what he had hoped might be a constitutional package they could accept. Cripps in fact had offered them rather more than either Churchill or the Viceroy, Lord Linlithgow, would have agreed to, but Roosevelt's response was to write to the Prime Minister urging the importance of a new British initiative based upon the promise of real self-government.

Hopkins witnessed what he called an explosive reaction to this by Churchill, who talked of resigning. Premature concessions to Congress, in his view, would enable Hindus to dominate India with effects on the country's communal relations damaging to its war effort.[29] He drafted an irate reply to Roosevelt which was later considerably modified in tone and tension eased, but he had to accept the need to improve Britain's standing on Indian policy in American eyes.[30]

Divergent British and American priorities in the conduct of the war are discussed in another chapter. They involved often intense and exhausting argument, with Churchill getting initially much of what he wanted. A fundamental issue from the outset was how to help the Soviet Union break the back of Hitler's armies while also striking effectively at Japan. Agreement was reached on a 'Europe first' strategy, but Churchill always saw merit in engaging German forces on the periphery of Hitler's 'fortress Europe' while Americans such as Marshall and Eisenhower believed that large-scale landings in France were essential.

Once they accepted his case against a premature landing in Europe, it fell to Churchill to tell Stalin, in August 1942, that there would be no invasion that year. With this done (see Chapter 4), he could press harder the merits of the Mediterranean and North African theatre, though he was greatly aided by Roosevelt's willingness to overrule Eisenhower on the November 1942 landings in Tunisia, Algeria and Morocco. American support was also needed for an invasion of Sicily once North Africa had been secured and this was forthcoming at the January 1943 Casablanca Conference, an occasion of great Anglo-American bonhomie.[31]

Others had their doubts. One of them was Brooke, who although he saw operations on Sicily and mainland Italy as being a useful means both of drawing German units into battle and securing airfields from which the Reich could be more deeply penetrated, recognised that the real priority lay with landings on North-Western Europe. In May 1943, in conference with the American Chiefs of Staff, he sensed their unease. 'We are a long way apart in our strategy in the European theatre', he confided to his diary, and went on to express the view that they felt Churchill had misled them in securing their agreement to the Sicily landing. 'They do not intend to be led astray again',[32] Brooke concluded.

His assessment was correct, although when the allies met again in Cairo in November 1943, Churchill still held out for a Mediterranean strategy. He hoped to do so at Teheran at the end of the month but Stalin dominated the proceedings, insisting from the start that all other operations must be subordinated to a European invasion. Churchill had little option but to accept, with some flexibility conceded as to the precise date, in May 1944. He also had to agree to Roosevelt's decision to land a major force in the South of France simultaneously with or close to the main invasion, with all the implications this had for the Italian front.

Stalin's tactics at Teheran have been described as 'political karate' exploiting British and American disagreements to drive through the decision he wanted on the invasion of Europe.[33] The conference was a turning-point in the war, with Stalin making a promise, which he kept, of a massive Red Army offensive to back up the Allies' 1944 landing in

France. It was also a watershed in Churchill's relations with Roosevelt, who had clearly arrived at Teheran determined to talk directly to Stalin on his terms, not Churchill's. His resolve to do this without Churchill present, and the latter's reactions, receive much comment in Lord Moran's account of the conference though Harry Hopkins, who was also there, sought to reassure Moran with the thought that the President did not want 'an impression to get abroad that he and Winston are putting their heads together to plan Stalin's discomfiture'.[34]

These strategic debates, of course, had a bearing upon the shape of any post-war settlement and Roosevelt was more sensitive to how this should accommodate British interests than were some of his advisers. Even when the President showed this, as when in March 1944 he gave clear assurances that the United States had no designs upon Britain's sources of oil in the Middle East, Churchill's response could be prickly: 'Great Britain', he wrote in reply, 'seeks no advantage, territorial or otherwise, as a result of the war. On the other hand, she will not be deprived of anything which rightly belongs to her after giving her best service to the good cause – at least not so long as your humble servant is entrusted with the conduct of her affairs.'[35]

Behind this robust language was a real determination by Churchill to fight Britain's corner, even if this meant talking directly to Stalin without an American presence. With the Warsaw rising crushed and most of Poland and much of Germany under threat of Soviet control, he went to Moscow in October 1944 to salvage what he could for Britain in the Balkans. Concern for Britain's influence there had motivated much of his Mediterranean strategy and on 5 October he and Stalin reached on a sheet of paper their famous 'percentages' agreement, according each other agreed levels of interest in post-war Greece, Yugoslavia, Hungary, Romania and Bulgaria. Churchill did not immediately tell Roosevelt about this, informing him only of his anxiety to secure a 'full meeting of minds' with Stalin over the Balkans.[36]

Harriman, the American Ambassador in Moscow, had guessed Churchill's and Stalin's intentions and in fact learned of the agreement a week later. He was quick to warn Churchill that Roosevelt would not support formal representations to Stalin being based upon it. Churchill accepted this and never sent on a letter he had drafted to the Soviet leader filling out the 'percentage' terms, and the telegram he sent to Roosevelt after his 5 October talk with Stalin made no reference to what type of agreement they had in mind on the Balkans.[37] His unease over the episode is clear in his own account of it[38] and on 11 October he wrote to Stalin that the Moscow 'percentages' were only a very general guide for the conduct of British and Soviet affairs. Inevitably, some State Department officials reacted by questioning whether American troops were being sacrificed in Europe 'so that Britain and Russia could divide the spoils of war'.[39] The Moscow agreement did, however, secure Churchill a free hand from Stalin to use British troops in Athens in December 1944 against ELAS, the left-wing Greek guerrilla force. Roosevelt and his advisers were unhappy about this, too, but when the three leaders met together for the last time at Yalta the following February, the 'percentages' agreement was never mentioned.

What appeared to be important agreements were reached at Yalta about the creation of a United Nations organisation and on policy towards a defeated Germany. These generated much optimism in the West, especially Stalin's signature to the Three Power Declaration on liberated Europe. Roosevelt was terminally ill by the time the conference met and barely able to take part in all the negotiating sessions, let alone to react effectively to Stalin's evasiveness over Poland's post-war future being based upon democratic elections. Churchill was deeply troubled by this but in equally little doubt that Roosevelt would not risk a breach with Stalin at the very point when, with no final decisions made about the use of the atomic bomb, he was hoping for the Soviet Union's early entry into the war against Japan. Churchill's report on his return home to Parliament on his and Roosevelt's dealings with Stalin was approved with no dissenting voices. The next occasion when he spoke to it of Roosevelt was on 17 April 1945, when he paid a heartfelt tribute to an ally who had died five days earlier, describing him as 'the greatest American friend we have ever known and the greatest champion of freedom who has ever brought help and comfort from the New World to the Old'.[40]

Churchill's wartime relationship with Roosevelt has been called 'probably the most remarkable alliance of modern history'.[41] Yet the author who makes this claim has to concede that much of what was hoped for from it, like the shared development of atomic power and the creation of a multilateral world economy, did not come to pass. At the outset of their wartime partnership, Britain and the United States were closer to each other in military power than would ever be possible in a post-war world in which, despite the Cold War, the complexity of their interests made each a less essential partner of the other. This was an altered reality hard for Churchill to accept.

One product of the wartime special relationship of which the new President, Harry Truman, knew almost nothing before taking office was the atomic weapons development programme. It was Churchill's decision that the pioneering research findings of British scientists should be shared with the United States. Agreement on this was reached in June 1942 and Churchill's later recollection was that 'everything was on the basis of fully sharing the results as equal partners'.[42] He soon, however, had to accept that work on the project would be on such a scale that it would have to be done in America, and in the view of the principal historian of British atomic and nuclear energy development, he and his government soon became junior partners in the project they had been instrumental in creating.[43]

Within only a few months, however, Sir John Anderson, Lord President of the Council, who had been much involved in contacts with America over the project, was advising the Prime Minister that strict limits were being placed upon the exchange of information by the military authorities in Washington who had assumed almost complete control. 'We hope you will be able to prevail upon the President to put matters right',[44] Anderson minuted to Churchill in January 1943. Churchill made representations to American contacts such as Hopkins but also asked Anderson for a feasibility report on an independent British atomic weapons programme. The reality of American control of Canadian uranium and heavy water resources made this impossible, but four months later, Churchill did at least secure agreement from Roosevelt on the resumption of full exchanges of information on atomic weapons research.

The issue was raised again at the Quebec Conference in August of that year, when 'full and effective collaboration' was agreed upon but with the actual manufacture of atomic bombs to be in the United States. An agreed memorandum emphasised that it was a joint project with no secrets withheld by either side, and it was further decided that atomic weapons would never be used by Britain and the United States against third parties without mutual consent. A year later the two leaders again met at Quebec and then at Roosevelt's Hyde Park home. Both of them by then knew how far the bomb had developed and that it might be used against Japan, but post-war collaboration was also agreed upon for both military and commercial purposes 'until terminated by joint agreement'.[45]

Churchill gave his consent at the Potsdam Conference on 4 July to the use of the bomb against Japan, but the final decision was Truman's.

'I never doubted that it would be,' he later wrote, 'nor have I ever since doubted that he was right.'[46] He was out of office by the time the two bombs were actually dropped, and the period which followed proved to be one in which Britain was effectively excluded from the further development of an awesome new weapon. This in turn led to the Labour Government's decision to build a British atomic bomb. Ill-advisedly, when back in power after the October 1951 election, Churchill attacked Labour for failing to capitalise on Britain's status as a supposedly equal partner in atomic and nuclear weapons policy, notably in an acrimonious debate in Parliament in April 1954, on the news of the first American hydrogen bomb test.[47]

Although in opposition after July 1945, Churchill still saw himself as the custodian of what could remain a special relationship with America. His meeting with Truman at the Potsdam Conference at least gave him time before his election defeat to establish a good working relationship with him, although the new President was a little sceptical of the flow of rhetoric on British and American amity which he had to listen to on that occasion. Writing in his diary, Truman described how Churchill 'gave me a lot of hooey about how great my country is and how he loved Roosevelt and how he intended to love me, etc., etc. Well, I am sure we can get along fine if he doesn't try to give me too much soft soap.'[48]

Churchill's concern that Britain's wartime co-operation with America should continue was already apparent and in November 1945 he put his thoughts confidentially to the Labour Foreign Secretary, Ernest Bevin. This was partly to voice his unease over the Foreign Office's failure to secure a joint British role in the occupation of Japan, but also to make the more general case for any British government to work closely with the United States. 'With that,' he declared, 'there can be no war. Without it there can be no peace',[49] and he pressed upon Bevin the importance of keeping in being the wartime Combined Chiefs of Staff Committee and the continued sharing of military and scientific data.

Western leaders and diplomats were still divided in their reading of Soviet intentions at that time and this was still so after a major speech by Stalin on 9 February 1946 in which he seemed to restate the notion of socialism in one country and closing the door on any continued co-operation with the West. It was a speech isolationist as much as aggressive in content, but it prompted the famous 'long telegram' to the State Department by George Kennan which called into question the durability of the Soviet system but also set out the case for its 'containment' by the West through strategies that were as much political as military.[50]

Kennan's 1947 analysis probably did more to influence American policy than Churchill's famous speech at Fulton, Missouri, some months earlier on 5 March 1946, but it was delivered privately and only appeared anonymously in the journal *Foreign Affairs* the following year. Churchill's oratory at Fulton was as resonant as ever and drew an ovation from the audience in which Truman was seen to join. It also went out live on American radio, but it tends now to be interpreted not so much as a turning-point in the West's Cold War policy but as an event highlighting the Truman administration's ambivalence about relations with the post-war Soviet Union. Truman in fact saw the text on the train journey to Fulton with Churchill, as did Lord Halifax, the British Ambassador, whose advice to tone down the content Churchill declined to take.

The speech has always been best remembered for one dramatic sentence: 'From Stettin in the Baltic to Trieste in the Adriatic an iron curtain has descended across the Continent.'[51] Churchill had no copyright on this phrase but he used it with effect, arguing that from behind this curtain the Soviet Union sought 'the fruits of war and the indefinite expansion of their power and doctrines',[52] but he was also emphatic that this was not tantamount to a desire for war with the West. Peace could be maintained, he stressed, by a strong United Nations supported to the full by Britain and the United States. Much of the American press nonetheless reacted with hostility, the *Nation* and the *Wall Street Journal* condemning the speech outright, while the respected columnist Walter Lippman called it 'an almost catastrophic blunder'.[53]

Editorials accused Churchill of poisoning already tense American–Soviet relations and of trying to pre-empt the administration's foreign policy. Truman, who, once back in Washington, had to disclaim prior knowledge of the speech to distance himself from it, told Dean Acheson, Under-Secretary at the State Department, not to attend a reception for Churchill in New York. To placate Stalin, he wrote offering him passage to America on the battleship *Missouri* to deliver a speech of his own at Fulton, but the invitation was declined.[54] Other American commentators, however, sensed that the speech reflected much of what Truman was still inhibited from saying himself. *Time Magazine* wrote of it as a 'magnificent trial balloon'[55] which the White House was using to test public opinion.

In London, *The Times* ran a leader critical of Churchill on the grounds that Russian fears might be reinforced by his Fulton speech,[56] but the leading members of the Labour Cabinet agreed with its general argument, especially the Foreign Secretary, Bevin. He took a much more imperial view of Britain's post-war role than Attlee and felt that American support would be vital in sustaining it.[57] This certainly also influenced Churchill's thinking and some recent work on British foreign policy after 1945 takes the view that the urgency of a new American alliance signalled at Fulton was driven as much by fear for the future of an empire which could only be held together with American support, or at least acquiescence, as by fear of the Soviet Union.[58]

Growing domestic anti-Communism and spy hysteria could have altered the direction of American policy without Churchill's Fulton speech and James Byrnes, Truman's Secretary of State, even before the speech, had been having doubts over his own earlier optimism about Soviet intentions and may have been thinking about the world situation requiring an active American role.[59] So, despite the lukewarm and even hostile reaction in the United States to what Churchill said at Fulton, the speech may still have helped to prepare American opinion for the interventionist role in Europe embodied in dramatic form two years later by the Marshall Plan.

Churchill welcomed this American initiative but did not seem to grasp that a revitalised and democratic Western Europe was seen by Washington as having the potential to be as important a partner as Britain alone. The Marshall Plan and the beginnings of movement towards closer economic and political relationships among European states were developments Churchill could applaud, but no more than the Attlee government did he seem able to see a role for Britain in the emergence of a new Western European grouping of states. This will be explored more fully in a separate chapter, but in the light of recent work vilifying Churchill for supposedly failing to see clearly American intentions to marginalise Britain's role as a major power, it is important to quote Roosevelt at Teheran in November 1943: 'I do not want the United States to have the post-war burden of reconstituting France, Italy and the Balkans. This is not our natural task at a distance of 3,500 miles. It is definitely a British task in which the British are far more vitally interested than we are.'[60]

If Churchill neglected Europe in his opposition years, he used them to give continued support to the United States as Cold War tension heightened, and when he returned to office in October 1951 he wasted little time in announcing a visit to Washington. At a dinner there, on 6 January 1952, he told his host that 'you, more than any other man, have saved Western civilisation'.[61] Hyperbole it may have been, but Truman, despite himself, was moved and also heartened, after a thankless period during which a costly war in Korea had dragged on and public confidence in his administration had slipped.

Behind tributes such as these Churchill was privately lamenting that he could no longer go to Washington as an equal. Britain's dollar reserves were falling fast and the burden of rearmament since the Korean War started had been a heavy one. Even with it, the Royal Navy was no longer such a power that it could dispute Eisenhower's decision, as NATO Supreme Commander in Europe, to place its ships under an American admiral. Churchill fretted over it but knew that he had to accept it[62] and it was still all-important to him to stress the primacy of the American alliance. In Washington, on the other hand, Truman's advisers were urging upon him the tactical course of agreeing in general terms with Churchill, even as they argued that the two countries could work best as allies through multilateral structures such as NATO.

Whatever his broodings over Britain's declining influence within the 'special relationship', Churchill still set much store by it. This was clear in his response to the election as President, in November 1952, of Eisenhower, whom he still saw as a comrade-in-arms from a heroic and recent past. He hoped that the new Republican administration would support Britain in the Middle East at a time of difficult negotiations with Egypt over the future of the Suez Canal base, to which Churchill felt Britain needed continued rights of access even if it withdrew its own garrison. This and other matters were discussed when he visited Eisenhower in January 1953 prior to his inauguration. The talks were amicable but, like Truman, the President-elect was privately sceptical about Churchill's rhetoric: 'He talks very animatedly about certain international problems, especially Egypt and its future. But so far as I can see, he has developed an almost childlike faith that all of the answers are to be found merely in British–American partnership.'[63]

Anthony Montague Brown, the last of Churchill's Private Secretaries, has written of the correspondence between him and Eisenhower as one-sided. Churchill's repeated emphasis upon the importance of British and American unity of purpose often, in his view, met with bland and negative replies from Eisenhower. This, however, did not seem to affect Churchill too much, Brown thought. 'In spite of all this,' he later wrote, 'the Prime Minister looked forward with almost childlike excitement to the arrival of the President's missives.'[64]

An early and striking proof of Churchill's concern to have the best possible working relationship with the new President was the way he vetted the final volume of his history of the war in order to delete anything from it that might focus on British-American tensions in the final months of the conflict. He wrote directly to Eisenhower about this: 'I am most anxious that nothing should be published which might seem to others to threaten our current relations in our public duties or impair the sympathy and understanding which exist between our countries.'[65] This was in March 1953, and with Stalin's death and ceasefire talks in Korea, Churchill was already hopeful of 'Big Three' summit talks with the new Soviet leadership. Increasingly, such talks and his role in them as a contribution to easing Cold War tension became a principal reason for him remaining in office.

Churchill's first official meeting with Eisenhower actually as President had to be postponed because of the stroke he suffered in late June 1953. By then, Churchill had already given out a series of signals that opportunities existed for a new approach to the Soviet Union's leaders, even as he became aware of Eisenhower's lukewarm reaction to the case for a revival of wartime summit diplomacy. On 11 May, in a major House of Commons speech, he made much of what he called the 'Supreme event' of recent months, 'the change of attitude and, as we all hope, of mood which has taken place in the Soviet domains and particularly in the Kremlin since the death of Stalin'.[66] Coming at the point when Western European leaders were in negotiations over a European Defence Community which would include a rearmed West Germany, this intervention upset both Eden, the Foreign Secretary, and the Foreign Office itself as well as confirming Washington in its unease over how Churchill was interpreting the international scene since Stalin's demise.

Once recovered from his stroke, Churchill returned, both in speeches and private conversation, to the urgency of meeting the Soviet leaders, but he also obtained Eisenhower's agreement to a meeting with him at Bermuda in December. The President, however, was careful to distance himself from the case for early talks with the Russians, something that became even clearer once the Bermuda Conference got under way. At the first plenary session, Churchill spoke not only of the importance both of the West's unity and military strength but also of the importance, in the aftermath of Stalin's death, of maximising every type of contact with the Soviet Union. Eisenhower replied in terms that seemed to Colville and others present to be crude and to give short shrift to Churchill: 'He said that as regards the P.M's belief that there was a "New Look" in Soviet policy, Russia was a woman of the streets and whether her dress was new or just the old one patched, it was the same whore underneath. America intended to drive her off her present "beat" into the back streets.'[67]

Other issues discussed were the proposed creation of a European Defence Community with West German membership on which Churchill and the President were at one. The still precarious ceasefire in Korea was also discussed, with Eisenhower insisting that if there was any breach of it America would be prepared to use atomic weapons for tactical purposes. Churchill, it seems, accepted this but Colville and others on his staff sensed his unease at Eisenhower's matter-of-fact language on weapons which filled others with foreboding. Colville, in fact, quoted Eisenhower saying to him that 'whereas Winston looked on the atomic weapon as something entirely new and terrible, he looked upon it as just the latest improvement in military weapons. He implied that there was in fact no distinction between "conventional weapons" and atomic weapons: all weapons in due course become conventional weapons.'[68] This, to his credit, was thinking that Churchill could not accept. Increasingly, too, he came to fear that a meeting by which he had set such store might do little to further the cause of direct talks with the Russians.

Eisenhower's attitude depressed Churchill, but he blamed it on the intransigence of his Secretary of State, John Foster Dulles. 'I cannot make it out. I am bewildered,' Churchill confided to Lord Moran: 'It seems that everything is left to Dulles. It appears that the President is no more than a ventriloquist's doll.'[69] Ten years earlier, he told Moran, he could have dealt with Dulles but he had lost the stamina for a confrontation with him. 'I have been humiliated by my own decay', he went on to say, as his mood grew bleaker. Once back in London, however, his morale recovered and it was soon clear that he had not given up hope of summit talks with the Russians.

In Cabinet on 18 January 1954, and again a week later, he made a strong case for increased trade with the Soviet bloc as a way of easing tension and preparing the way for talks. Eisenhower was not impressed, making it clear that he felt Churchill was in fact calling for a degree of trade liberalisation well beyond what both Congressional and public opinion in the United States would accept. He pointed out also, for Churchill's benefit, that trade controls should continue to apply 'to equipment and materials which were of high value to the Soviet war potential and that quantitative restrictions should be retained as part of the mechanism of control'.[70]

Such episodes discouraged neither Churchill's faith in the 'special relationship' nor his belief that talks with the Soviet leaders justified some risks. They were, he told R. A. Butler, his Chancellor of the Exchequer, over dinner on 12 March 1954, 'the only political interest he had left',[71] and he continued to speak eloquently in support of them in Parliament and outside. His eloquence was heightened by his fear of nuclear arms proliferation as the Americans pressed ahead with hydrogen bomb tests, yet loyalty to an old ally still inhibited him from accepting the case for pressure being brought to bear upon Washington to stop such tests. This made him vulnerable to Labour attacks in Parliament and the defence debate he led off there on 5 April 1954 quickly degenerated into a bitter shouting match between him and his opponents.

At that time, the most urgent issue for the Foreign Office was to persuade Washington to accept the decisions of the Geneva Conference on Indochina, especially the creation of a Communist state in North Vietnam which had followed France's defeat there by the Vietminh rebels. This sat uncomfortably with America's belief in containing the advance of Communism, and Eden led the British effort to reassure America at a time when there was still real fear of Indochina's potential to cause world war.

Churchill visited Eisenhower again in late June for wide-ranging discussions and used the opportunity to raise once more the issue of summit talks with the Russians. The communiqué which rounded off the series of meetings, however, made no reference to this and Dulles warned Churchill against embarking upon any exploratory missions of his own. None of this deterred Churchill on 4 July, on his voyage home, from sending a telegram to Molotov, the Soviet Foreign Minister, suggesting they should meet without American participation. This was done without reference to the Cabinet, Churchill invoking wartime precedents for unilateral initiatives of a similar kind. Selwyn Lloyd and Anthony Nutting, Foreign Office ministers, were so angry that they considered resignation, as did Lord Salisbury, the Lord President of the Council.[72]

Molotov's reply on 7 July was a discreet one, welcoming Churchill's proposal but expressing the hope that the meeting he suggested could be broadened to include the United States. This did not protect the Prime Minister from the anger of many ministers, though Eden supported him while in private making known his reservations about what had happened. Churchill defended his actions but also apologised to the Cabinet, telling it that 'in his anxiety to lose no opportunity of furthering the cause of world peace, he might have taken an exaggerated view of the urgency of the matter'.[73]

He also forwarded to Eisenhower on 8 July copies of his exchanges with Molotov, but prefaced them with contrite language, writing: 'I hope you are not vexed with me for not submitting to you the text of my telegrams to Molotov. I felt that as it was a private and personal enquiry which I had not brought officially before the Cabinet, I had better bear the burden myself and not involve you in any way.'[74] In response, Eisenhower insisted that he was not vexed: 'Personal trust based upon more than a dozen years of close association and valued friendship may occasionally permit room for amazement but never suspicion.'[75] Evelyn Shuckburgh, Assistant Under-Secretary at the Foreign Office, was deeply shaken by the whole business and confided to his diary that Eisenhower's reply was 'about as scathing and negative as it could be without actually being rude'.[76]

In the midst of this drama, Churchill put to the full Cabinet the case for a British nuclear weapon to be built and tested. He had made up his mind on the need for this the previous year, but in contrast to Attlee's handling of the acquisition of a British atomic bomb, he was fastidious about consulting his colleagues collectively. He may of course, as Paul Addison has pointed out,[77] have been more confident than his predecessor was of securing Cabinet support. Even as this decision was made, Churchill still pursued the hope of direct contacts with the Soviet Union's leaders which might halt the Cold War. Was he ahead of his time in working to bring about what finally happened after Gorbachev took power in 1985? Some historians consider this possible, and make the point that huge advantages would have accrued in economic terms to a Britain freed from the costs of becoming a nuclear power.[78]

Only Georghi Malenkov's fall from power and the need to give his successors time to establish their credentials with the West persuaded Churchill to give up what had become an increasingly personal search for agreement with the Soviet Union. His ultimately fruitless efforts created real problems for the Prime Minister during his final months in office, antagonising the Foreign Office and alarming Washington, but he seems genuinely to have hoped by this time to enter history as a peacemaker. Equally genuine was his horror at where an atomic and nuclear arms race could lead, even if he accepted the West's need to stay ahead while the race existed. Eden, while not challenging his leader openly, was becoming more frustrated at his long wait for the succession and was not averse to stressing in his contacts with Washington that personal initiatives like that of July 1954 could be linked to Churchill's growing senility.[79] Historians, however, must balance this possibility against an old man's belief that he could still help the cause of peace in a nuclear age. If this was an illusion, it was not a dishonourable one.

Before his resignation in May 1955, Churchill's last address to ministers was devoted to the importance of good relations with America. Lord Boyd-Carpenter recalls thinking of it afterwards as a departing leader's political testament.[80] Fifteen years earlier he had instituted a unique period in Britain's relationship with the United States without which victory over Hitler would have been impossible. If that victory meant yielding much, though by no means all, of British influence in the world to its ally, the price was one Churchill was prepared to pay, and his recent detractors have produced no sustainable alternative course he could have taken, or in which the British people would have followed him. He may have clung longer to this special relationship than was justified by the altered realities of a post-war world in which American priorities could diverge dramatically from Britain's. The 1956 Suez Crisis unleashed by Eden, his successor in office, was brutal proof of this. Yet Churchill was happy to continue visiting the United States and accepted honorary American citizenship in 1963. To the end, he talked and thought of himself as half-American and wrote of the United States' history as part of a shared English-speaking epic, even as the great federation he admired so much was overtaken by the politics of civil rights and ethnic pluralism, as well as by a war in Vietnam more destructive and savage by far than any which even his imperial vision had demanded of Britain.

4

CHURCHILL AND THE SOVIET UNION

'Churchill is the kind of man who will pick your pocket of a kopeck if you don't watch him. Yes, pick your pocket of a kopeck! By God, pick your pocket of a kopeck.'[1] This was Stalin's verdict on Churchill in 1944, delivered for the benefit of the Yugoslav Communist Milovan Djilas, who was in Moscow for meetings with the Soviet leadership. For those always sceptical of Britain's wartime alliance with the Soviet Union, this could only be read as a tribute to Churchill's readiness to try to drive at least some hard bargains with Stalin. His relationship with the Soviet dictator during the war, which at times was overlaid with more than a little conviviality and camaraderie, has an irony to it, for Churchill had been an implacable opponent of a regime which he made no secret of wanting to crush in the early years of its existence.

He was still unrepentant about this near the end of his political career, informing the Washington Press Club in 1954: 'If it had been properly supported in 1919, I think we might have strangled Bolshevism in its cradle, but everybody turned up their hands and said "how shocking."'[2] This may, of course, simply have been Churchill close to retirement and in mischievous mood, anxious to oversimplify a controversial episode in his career which did little to enhance the trust felt in him either by colleagues or the British public.

In 1918 and 1919, Churchill was not alone among British politicians in his aversion to Bolshevism, but he surpassed them all in the ferocious attacks he launched on Lenin and the other leaders of the new Soviet state. This was partly because he feared that Russia, unless purged of the ideology of its new rulers, could not take a creative part in building a new post-war Europe. He also blamed the Bolshevik leaders for their decision to make a separate peace with Germany.

'Every British and French soldier killed last year', he told an audience in April 1919, 'was really done to death by Lenin and Trotsky, not in fair war, but by the treacherous desertion of an ally without parallel in the history of the world.'[3]

Fundamentally, however, his aversion was to the ideology of Marxism, which he found both repellent and threatening. It was heightened by events at home, with the Cabinet of which he was a member sending tanks and 12 000 troops into Glasgow in January 1919, in response to an engineering workers' strike which the Secretary of State for Scotland called 'a Bolshevist uprising'.[4] His most urgent concern, however, was for the fate of Russia: 'Civilisation is being completely extinguished over gigantic areas while Bolsheviks hop and caper like troops of ferocious baboons amid the ruins of cities and the corpses of their victims.'[5]

One of Churchill's biographers, and a sympathetic one, has written: 'repugnant though it might be to make the analogy, Churchill's ferocious rhetoric and imagery bears comparison with Hitler's'.[6] He went on to compare their talk of Bolshevism as a plague virus threatening the world and sometimes, too, Churchill seemed to equate Bolshevism with Jewish influence and once denounced its leaders as 'Semitic conspirators'.[7] Four members of the first Politburo were Jews and this influenced Churchill, though he was never an anti-Semite. He was always proud of the way his father, Lord Randolph, had condemned the persecution of Russian Jews in 1881, and for most of his life was a strong supporter of the Zionist cause. Closer scrutiny of his reactions to events in Russia shows, in fact, that he argued that the role of Jews in power after 1917 could serve to expose their whole community to attack from counter-revolutionaries. 'This danger must be combated strongly',[8] he wrote in June 1919.

Lloyd George, as Prime Minister, felt the full force of Churchill's commitment to the overthrow of Soviet rule once he was able, after January 1919, to use his new position as Secretary of State for War to influence the way British troops in Russia were used. He had to answer his colleague's advocacy of the anti-Bolshevik cause in his government and later wrote of what he felt had been the blinkered nature of his thinking on the whole issue: 'Mr Churchill's morbid detestation of the Revolution that in 1919 baffled his most ingenious military dispositions in Russia, has rendered him incapable of weighing fairly the causes that led to the downfall of autocracy. The Revolution was the inevitable consequence of the failure of Czardom and not its cause.'[9]

British intervention in Russia was not in its original form influenced by Churchill, but when Cabinet decisions led to troop deployments to secure substantial allied military stores in the country's northern parts, his support was prompt and enthusiastic. He saw it as an opportunity to achieve strategic advantage against the Central Powers by reopening an Eastern Front and rallying and arming all available anti-Bolshevik forces. At the time of the Armistice in the West, this had not been achieved, yet significant British forces were still in both North and South Russia. Their role was unclear to many, but not to Churchill. Once appointed to the War Office, he threw his weight behind a policy of fighting withdrawal from vulnerable positions and restoration of the Romanovs.

At a Cabinet meeting on the last day of 1918, Lloyd George sought to outflank Churchill by formulating a policy that would preclude using British troops in any attempt to bring down Bolshevism or to force the warring parties in Russia to the conference table. The forthcoming Peace Conference, he argued, must work out a collective Allied policy, and the furthest he felt Britain could go was to help border territories on the Baltic and in the Caucasus which wanted independence from the Soviet state and which had clear non-Russian majorities. Lloyd George secured the positive support of ministers, so Churchill, on the eve of taking office as Secretary of State for War, must have been aware that his would be an isolated voice in support of intervention in an already bloody and destructive civil war.

This makes all the more striking the tenacity with which Churchill attempted to reverse agreed government policy by arguing his case in Cabinet, as well as making it to the Allied leaders in Paris for the Peace Conference. Philip Kerr, Lloyd George's private secretary, was warning him by February 1919 of Churchill's intentions: 'I cannot conceal from you that Mr. Churchill is bent on forcing a campaign against Bolshevik Russia . . . . He is perfectly logical in his policy because he declares that the Bolsheviks are the enemies of the human race and must be put down at any cost.'[10] Essentially, Churchill's view was that while he would not openly defy his Prime Minister and also President Wilson, who believed a military intervention in Russia would be impractical and politically divisive, he could keep open the case for action to help the anti-Bolsheviks if current peace talks among the warring parties failed.

'A united declaration in Paris would create a clear role for British troops',[11] he declared on 14 February, and three days later he was urging in writing upon Lloyd George the need to take the long view of what a Bolshevik victory could mean: 'There will be no peace in Europe until Russia is restored. There can be no League of Nations without Russia. If we abandon Russia, Germany and Japan will not. The new states which it is hoped to call into being in the East of Europe will be crushed between Russian Bolshevism and Germany.'[12] Lloyd George was unmoved and on 8 March, Churchill found himself in a minority when the Cabinet supported the Prime Minister's decision that British troops be withdrawn. He had to accept this, though a straw for him to clutch at was that General Denikin, the most effective leader of the White forces in South Russia, would at last be backed with war materials and a British mission, provided he made no threat to Georgia or any of the new republics in the Caucasus.

Denikin had always supported expansionist Russian policies in Asia and Lord Curzon, the Foreign Secretary, had to point this out to Churchill as a reason to be wary of giving him and his armies un-qualified support. This added to his growing appearance of isolation on the whole issue, even at the point when, in the late autumn of 1919, the White armies seemed for a time to be close to victory, with major offensives in the areas of both Petrograd and Moscow. The recovery of Trotsky's new armies undermined further Churchill's position and added to the impression of many observers that he was, in his passion for the anti-Bolshevik cause, acting alone, in defiance of his Prime Minister and without regard for increasing public hostility.

Proof that he had not given up hope of military action against the Bolsheviks became apparent the following year as war dragged on between them and the new Polish republic. Its leadership sanctioned a failed invasion of the Ukraine early in 1920 and the Red Army counter-attacked and seemed capable of reaching Warsaw. Although strike action in the London docks against munitions being shipped to Poland was widely supported by the formation of Councils of Action with accompanying talk of a general stoppage, Churchill pressed the case for military aid to the Poles as well as the creation of an independent Ukraine to be a counterweight to Bolshevik power. The Poles halted Trotsky's armies outside Warsaw by their own efforts but once again, Lloyd George had to make clear that there would be no British intervention.

The effective abandonment of intervention as a policy left Churchill bitter but also widely distrusted by the public as someone unabashed by failure at the Dardanelles and ready once more to put British troops at risk. At a time when the army's operational strength had been drastically reduced while its commitments were still large, deploying forces on any significant scale in Russia could have been a dangerous business. There was also the quality and reliability of the anti-Bolshevik leaders to consider. Sir Henry Wilson, Chief of the Imperial General Staff between 1918 and 1922 who was in much contact with Churchill at this time, had a poor opinion of them.

With the single exception of Denikin, I confess I see no use whatever in trying to bolster up the other Russian theatres. They have not got a leader in these other theatres who is worth a damn; they have not got a Corps of Officers who are either patriotic or knowledgeable; they have not got the slightest power of administration and, in short, to put the thing bluntly, with the single exception of Denikin there is no doubt that Lenin and Trotsky and those around them are far the abler men.[13]

Churchill's seeming disregard for considerations such as these alarmed Wilson, though his hatred of Bolshevism was no less, and his condemnation of interventionism as a policy was uncompromising. 'So ends in practical disaster another of Winston's military attempts', Wilson wrote in his diary on 29 March 1920. 'Antwerp, Dardanelles, Denikin. His judgement is always at fault and he is hopeless when in power.'[14] This may have been severe, but some soldiers agreed with Wilson, while others who observed Churchill at this time feared that over Russia he had lost contact with reality. Early in 1920, Frances Stevenson, secretary and mistress of Lloyd George, was present at a luncheon with Churchill when intervention in Russia was discussed. 'At times he became almost like a madman', [15] was her recollection of his behaviour.

Events in Russia appeared to allow for no compromise in Churchill's mind, even when the military resources for an interventionist policy were not there because of post-war manpower reductions which he had energetically driven ahead as Secretary of State for War. John Charmley claims that Churchill in fact wanted intervention on a scale larger than anything allowed for in Martin Gilbert's account, but does not substantiate his accusation that on this matter, Gilbert has been selective in his use of Cabinet records.[16] Both he and Robert Rhodes James[17] do, however, accept that Churchill was mindful of the limits to military action which might be imposed by unrest among serving soldiers. He had after all, in the winter of 1918–19, acted effectively to defuse the demobilisation mutinies in the army without serious reprisals against those involved.

Robert Rhodes James has also argued that alongside his often apocalyptic rhetoric about Bolshevism, Churchill was moved by compassion for those who had been encouraged by Britain's very limited intervention to identify themselves with the White cause. He writes:

> Throughout the saga of British intervention in Russia, Churchill's policies and attitudes may be fairly criticised. But at least he never averted his eyes from the human implications of supporting one side in a civil war, and the censure of history may indeed fall most heavily on those ministers – particularly Lloyd George – who had permitted that participation and then withdrew without remorse for the consequences that would fall upon those whom they had supported and encouraged.[18]

The end of intervention cleared the way for the recognition of the Soviet state and the resumption of commercial relations with it. This brought Churchill's rage back to the boil and in November 1920 he was considering resignation. The advice of his friend F. E. Smith, Lord Birkenhead, may have helped to deter him from this. At least after he and Lords Milner and Curzon had failed in their opposition in Cabinet to a trade agreement with Russia, Churchill received an affirmative answer to his question to Lloyd George about whether ministers were still free to make anti-Bolshevik speeches. That same evening, he declared to a meeting in London that 'the policy I will always advocate is the overthrow and destruction of that criminal regime'.[19]

Lloyd George and most of his ministers simply took the view that this was a goal beyond Britain's resources. They were, Paul Addison has written, 'determined to prevent Bolshevism in Britain. But Churchill was alone in his determination to suppress Bolshevism in Russia.'[20] If, however, the regime of Lenin and Trotsky was to be allowed to survive, then at least, Churchill argued, its complicity in sedition and subversion beyond Russia's borders could be confronted head-on. 'In every city', he told a London audience in November 1920, 'there are small bands of eager men and women watching with hungry eyes any chance to make a general overturn in the hopes of profiting themselves in the confusion and these miscreants are fed by Bolshevik money.'[21] The threat, he went on to declare, was a global one: 'Whether it is the Irish murder gang or the Egyptian Vengeance Society or the seditious extremists in India, or the arch-traitors we have at home, they will feel the weight of the British arm. It was strong enough to break the Hindenburg Line, it will be strong enough to defend the main interests of the British people.'[22]

There were Communists active within the British Labour movement at this time, though the greatest revolutionary of the post-war period, John MacLean, was not under any sort of control from Moscow. Churchill's virulent language was ungenerous to Labour's aspirations and his relentless association of these with Soviet intentions further alienated the Labour party from the coalition government while drawing him closer to the Conservatives. When they agreed to find him a seat in Parliament after his defeat in the 1922 General Election, the spectre of Bolshevism loomed just as large in his speeches and writings.

Even in the midst of his denunciations of Bolshevism and all its works, Churchill could, on occasions, see beyond his own rhetoric and accept that if the Soviet system remained intact it could change and represent a reality with which Britain and the other democracies would have to coexist. As early as February 1920, for example, he wrote:

> Great changes are taking place in the character and organisation of the Bolshevik Government. In spite of the hellish wickedness in which it was founded and has been developed, it nevertheless represents a force of order: the men at the head are no longer merely revolutionaries but persons who, having seized power are anxious to retain it and enjoy it for a time. They are believed earnestly to desire peace, fearing no doubt if war continues to be devoured later by their own armies. A period of peace coupled with commercial reorganisation may well prepare the way for the unity of Russia through a political evolution.[23]

Insofar as there was evolution, it was towards the brutal personality cult of Stalin, but even before he had consolidated his hold on power, Churchill kept up his attacks. He deplored the 1924 Labour Government's recognition of the Soviet Union and their moves to secure a commercial treaty with it and in 1925 and 1926, talked of the hand of Bolshevism behind industrial unrest in Britain. He continued to see Soviet foreign policy as a threat and in a Commons debate in June 1931, he spoke of the fear of Moscow felt by Europe's new small states. With Hitler's rise to power, however, Churchill's tone began to change.

In 1934, he gave a guarded welcome to Russia's admission to the League of Nations and began to speak of it, for all the regime's evils, as a counterweight to Nazi Germany. By 1936, he was openly supporting collective security through a League of which the Soviet Union had become an accepted member.

Two years later he was in regular and friendly contact with Ivan Maisky, the Russian Ambassador in London, and when, in April 1938, the Soviet government made proposals for a tripartite alliance with Britain and France, Churchill's response was enthusiastic even as Stalin's brutalities surpassed those of the regime in its early days. As always with Churchill, his vivid sense of history worked upon him. Russian participation in great coalitions had, in the eighteenth and early nineteenth centuries, helped to preserve the balance of power in Europe, but commending a Soviet alliance to the Chamberlain government was beyond even Churchill's eloquence in the foreign policy debates prior to the Second World War.

Stalin's August 1939 neutrality pact with Germany was a crushing blow to Churchill's hopes of having the Soviet Union's resources as a way to block the growing power of Hitler. 'Only totalitarian despotism in both countries could have faced the odium of such an unnatural act',[24] Churchill later wrote, but he went on to describe the consummation as the 'culminating failure of British and French foreign policy and diplomacy over several years'.[25] Even so, in the same passage he felt able to see the signing of the pact in terms of Soviet interests. 'If their policy was cold-blooded, it was also at the moment realistic in a high degree',[26] he also wrote in summary of Stalin's motives, though of course the Soviet leader signally failed to use such time as the pact had purchased to prepare his country for war.

After the outbreak of war Churchill, back in ministerial office, actually presented a memorandum to his colleagues welcoming the Soviet Union's military presence in Eastern Poland under the terms of the recent Moscow Pact. German forces would be tied down simply to guard against the movements of such a dubious ally, he argued.[27] In a broadcast on 1 October which is often quoted for his description of Russia as a 'riddle wrapped in a mystery inside an enigma'[28] he also took care to stress a community of interest between the Soviet state and Britain and France. Soon afterwards, in conversation with Maisky, he went further, predicting that Britain and Russia would soon be allies.[29]

Churchill took this conciliatory view of Soviet Policy a dramatic step
further when, on 16 October, he astonished ministers by making a case
for the Soviet Union's right to 'reclaim' territory lost as a result of the
First World War. This, he argued, could include the Baltic states and
Finland, because Soviet strength in the area could be a deterrent to
Germany. This was just four days after Stalin had presented demands
for naval bases on Finnish teritory and a major cession of land on the
Karelian isthmus. When the Finns refused these demands and the
Russians launched a full scale attack on 30 November, Churchill was
quick to change his tune, at least in public, and join the clamour for
support to be given a small victim state. 'All the resentment felt against
the Soviet Government for the Ribbentrop–Molotov Pact was fanned
into flame by this latest exhibition of brutal bullying and aggression',[30]
he later wrote in his history of the war. At the time, however, his
motives for identifying himself with the Finnish cause were more
complex.

Although Sir Edmund Ironside, Chief of the Imperial General Staff,
was shocked at the implications of it,[31] a substantial British and French
expeditionary force was formed for operations on Finland's behalf.
Churchill's intentions, however, went beyond aid to the Finns. Any
troops assigned to their support would, he reasoned, have to cross
Norway and Sweden and in doing so could seize the port of Narvik,
thus disrupting the flow of crucial iron-ore supplies for German industry. This was a course of action he had already been pressing for in
terms increasingly alarming to colleagues such as Lord Halifax, the
Foreign Secretary.[32]

Mercifully, given the inadequate preparation of this proposed operation, the Finns decided to accept Soviet terms on 12 March 1940. The
course of the soon-to-be-mounted Norwegian campaign gives some
hint of what fate might have overtaken allied troops committed to
the much more difficult task of operating in support of the Finns.
The "winter war" between the Red Army and its small but tenacious
neighbour was a brutal and bloody business in which Soviet forces
sustained heavy losses, but at least Churchill did not draw from it the
simplistic conclusions of some commentators that Russia could be dis-
counted as an ally. Yet, in the midst of this crisis, he could still support
the case for possible RAF action against Soviet oilfields in the Caucasus,
thought by British Intelligence to be supplying Germany under the
terms of the Moscow Pact, a scheme dropped well before the German
invasion of the West confirmed how impractical it was.

Soon after becoming Prime Minister, Churchill wrote to Stalin stressing the common danger from Hitler, and as early as October 1940, he was assuring sceptical military advisers that Hitler would attack the Soviet Union. He seems to have seen no special reason to woo Russia, feeling that any overtures for an alliance should come from Moscow. However, as more intelligence reports of German invasion plans came in, he saw the need to warn Stalin. On 3 April 1941, using a source, the Ultra decrypts, which he could not disclose to the Soviet leader, he reported a significant transfer of German armoured units into an area of southern Poland close to the Soviet border.[33] An uncertain situation in Yugoslavia raised doubts about the purpose of the movement and the British Ambassador in Moscow, Sir Stafford Cripps, was later blamed by Churchill for a delay in the transmission of the news to Stalin. He, however, had better warnings from other sources, had he wanted to listen to them, and as late as 12 June, Churchill's ministers, with his authorisation, were still trying to alert Maisky to the impending German onslaught.[34]

Churchill was at Chequers when Operation Barbarossa was launched and throughout the next day, 22 June, he worked on a broadcast which he completed to his satisfaction only twenty minutes before he delivered it. It can seem now perhaps an over-emotional and rhetorical performance, but its interest lies in the way he was able to square the content with his record of bitter opposition to the Soviet regime: 'No-one has been a more consistent opponent of Communism than I have for the last twenty-five years', he reminded his audience. 'I will unsay no word that I have spoken about it. But all this fades away before the spectacle which is now unfolding.'[35] What followed was a graphic evocation of timeless, peasant Russia girding itself for battle once more against a brutal invader.

Later that evening he told Colville that 'if Hitler invaded Hell he would at least make a favourable reference to the Devil'[36] and in a spirited after-dinner debate, he defended the tenor of his broadcast. In Colville's record of what was said, Eden and Lord Cranborne, later the Fifth Marquis of Salisbury, took the view that support for the Soviet Union should be put to Parliament and the country only in military terms, it being a regime no less evil than Hitler's. Churchill swept this argument aside. 'The P.M's view was that Russia was now at war; innocent peasants were being slaughtered; and we should forget about Soviet systems or the Comintern and extend our hand to fellow human beings in distress.'[37] His military advisers, however, inclined to the view that the Red Army would soon collapse and for General Ismay, Chief of Staff to Churchill, 'the prospect of being allies with the Bolsheviks was repugnant'.[38]

The huge drama of the Russian front did not for long, however, blind Churchill to the political implications of throwing British support behind the Soviet Union. This is neatly illustrated by his concern that the 'Internationale', the rousing Socialist hymn which was also the Soviet state anthem, should be excluded from a popular BBC Sunday evening broadcast which featured the anthems of all allied nations. It took the Ministry of Information six months to change Churchill's mind over this[39] but, only four months into the German invasion, he was in consultation with ministers and civil servants over 'what action was required to counter the present tendency of the British public to forget the dangers of Communism over the resistance of Russia'.[40]

These anxieties of Churchill's are ignored by his recent critics. One of these, John Charmley, whose case against Churchill's choice of allies is considered elsewhere in this book, argues that in his 'obsession',[41] as he calls it, with Germany's defeat, Churchill overlooked the implications of a Soviet alliance. In this view, Churchill is said to have hastened unheeding to Stalin's support because there was no guarantee of America joining the war and because he could not see beyond short-term advantage. Instead, he should have exploited Russia's need for his support and its fear that Britain might seek a compromise peace with Hitler. This is what Dr Charmley thinks Britain should have done anyhow, so it is logical for him to argue that 'Churchill's reassurances [that is, to Stalin] were to throw away a card which could have had some value.'[42] Just what value, and whether Churchill's government would have survived politically the opprobrium that such treatment of a heroic ally would have brought upon it, are not discussed.

Churchill's wartime dealings with the Soviet Union are too complex a subject to lend themselves to crude comparisons with Chamberlain's appeasement of Hitler. In this analogy favoured by John Charmley, Yalta logically becomes Churchill's Munich. In reality, however, Churchill, though often wrong in his judgement of Stalin, tried hard to put ideological antagonisms to one side for the greater good of victory, without mindlessly acceding to Stalin's demands. This is the view posited in a major article by Martin Kitchen in 1987,[43] which explores very fully the twists and turns of an always volatile relationship.

In response to Britain's first offer of all possible aid to Russia's war effort on 7 July 1941, Stalin was soon to make demands that Churchill felt were unreasonable. Two days later, in his reply, the Soviet leader was pressing the case for British landings in Europe, and on 13 September he called upon Churchill to send into the Soviet Union through Iran more divisions than were in combat-readiness in the whole of the British Isles. He also raised the question of a mutual assistance treaty as well as British–Soviet talks on a joint approach to any post-war European settlement. This, Churchill had to tell him, was impossible under the terms of the Atlantic Charter which he had signed and Stalin had commended, because it precluded either signatory power making bilateral agreements with other states.

Not until May 1942 was a British and Soviet treaty signed in London, Foreign Minister Molotov acting for the Soviet side. Churchill, although making no concessions to renewed demands from Molotov for a Second Front in Europe or on talks about post-war arrangements, agreed that neither side would seek a separate peace with Germany. Churchill felt that Britain's relations with the Soviet Union had been put on a firmer footing than before, but he took the opportunity to tell Molotov, in reply to a question from him, what Britain would do if the Red Army failed to hold out in 1942. His message was that the United Kingdom, with ever-increasing help from the United States, would fight on: 'ultimately the power of Britain and the United States would prevail'.[44] He made a point also of reminding his guest that during a full year of Russian neutrality, Britain had stood alone against a German-dominated Europe. Churchill's optimism about the Soviet alliance proved short-lived. New reverses in North Africa, the Far East and on the Atlantic made clear the need to spell out the fact that no European invasion was in prospect and Sir Archibald Clark Kerr, the British Amabassador in Moscow, urged upon Churchill the need to do this through a personal meeting with Stalin.

The Moscow conference, in August 1942, was the first of several meetings between Churchill and Stalin. Accounts of these by Churchill and others who took part still make dramatic and at times macabre reading. The initial meeting was a near-disaster, Churchill threatening to return home on the first day because of Stalin's denigration of Britain's conduct of the war. This set the pattern for later meetings, when angry exchanges could alternate with ponderous bonhomie. Churchill, despite his long aversion to the Soviet system, was consumed with curiosity about it and Stalin's role in it. During an interlude in the

1942 meeting, he asked his ally whether the stresses of war leadership had been worse than those of driving through farm collectivisation.

Stalin replied that collectivisation had been worse, 'a terrible struggle', but one he justified as his only option to raise food output. The ten million Kulaks who had stood in its way had been a necessary sacrifice: 'the great bulk were very unpopular and were wiped out by their own labourers'. Churchill's unease is apparent in his later account of this chilling conversation.

> I record as they come back to me these memories and the strong impression I sustained at the moment of millions of men and women being blotted out or displaced for ever. A generation would no doubt come to whom their miseries were unknown but it would be sure of having more to eat and bless Stalin's name. I did not repeat Burke's dictum, 'If I cannot have reform without injustice, I will not have reform.' With the World War going on all round us it seemed vain to moralise aloud.[45]

Fifteen months later at Teheran, Stalin joked about the merits of summary execution for 50 000 captured German officers once the war ended. Roosevelt entered into the spirit of the moment by proposing a figure of 49 000, but Churchill left the table in a rage, declaring he would rather be shot himself 'than sully my country's honour by such infamy'. He was persuaded by Stalin to rejoin the company, though still wondering whether it had been a joke.[46] Tensions eased at a subsequent conference dinner given to mark the Prime Minister's sixty-ninth birthday. Churchill told Stalin that he ranked with the great heroes of Russian history and drank a toast 'to the Proletarian masses'. Stalin's reply to this was: 'I drink to the Conservative Party.'[47]

The actual date of an invasion of Europe remained a crucial issue. Stalin had baited Churchill over it in August 1942 and there were times when Churchill did not seem to allow for how important the operation was to the Soviet Union, something which also took time for Russian historians to admit.[48] At their first Moscow meeting, Churchill told Stalin no Second Front was in prospect that year and in January 1943, after the Casablanca Conference, he wrote to Stalin that an invasion might be possible if enough troop- and tank-landing craft were available. Stalin, given what he knew of Churchill's belief in a Mediterranean strategy, correctly interpreted this as procrastination.[49] Only at the Teheran summit meeting in November was Stalin given the undertakings he wanted on European landings in 1944. By then, Churchill knew he was playing a weakened hand, with Roosevelt and his military advisers pressing for a decision and only limited progress to report to Stalin from Italy, the major front in the Mediterranean theatre.

Churchill's problem in an always testing relationship with Stalin was, in fact, deciding what Stalin really wanted and how far to believe his protestations of loyalty to the alliance with the Western democracies. From some of his meetings Churchill came away feeling he could trust Stalin, only for events quickly to disillusion and frustrate him. Kitchen describes him, in the summer of 1943, as being in 'a belligerently anti-Soviet mood'[50] and thinking seriously about the case for a strengthened post-war German state as a counterweight to Soviet power, and he upset Eden by putting this view to the Cabinet on 5 October. Three months later and after the Teheran Conference, however, he wrote to Eden in very different terms, stressing the effects of the Soviet war effort on 'the deep-seated changes which have taken place in the character of the Russian state and government, the new confidence which has grown in our hearts towards Stalin'.[51]

These swings of mood and of his assessment of Soviet intentions began to exasperate Churchill's advisers, especially those among them who had been assigned the responsibility for post-war policy formulation. In the summer of 1944, he made little effort to intervene in a debate prompted by a major speech given by Jan Smuts, the South African Prime Minister, in which he urged the need for a strong post-war bloc of European states, including Germany, to counterbalance American and Soviet power, yet a few months earlier he had talked to the Cabinet in broadly similar terms. At this point, Churchill had switched back to hopes of post-war co-operation with Stalin, only for them to be mocked by the Warsaw rising and Soviet reactions to it.

Policy towards Poland had always been a focus of tension between Churchill and Stalin. Sympathy for Poland's plight, horror at the German holocaust against Jews in captivity there and admiration for Polish heroism were all interwoven in Churchill's mind with deepening anxiety about how best to guarantee a post-war Polish state real political freedom. Given the certainty that the Red Army's 1944 offensive would go through Poland, there was the related issue of just what the country's post-war frontiers would be. The Free Polish government in exile, with whom Churchill found relationships increasingly difficult, stood four-square by the frontiers of 1 September 1939, but Churchill was certain Stalin would not yield up the territorial gains Russia had made under the Moscow Pact. Churchill and Roosevelt favoured the 'Curzon Line', agreed by the Allies at Paris in 1920 and 150 miles west of the point reached by Polish forces in their advance against the Bolsheviks that year. Acceptance of it for the Free Poles meant leaving four million compatriots on its Soviet side.

Churchill made it clear to the Free Polish leadership at the Teheran Conference that they had no choice, but could expect compensation on their country's western border at a defeated Germany's expense. This was of course what happened in 1945, but by then the Free Polish forces in Warsaw had taken their fatal decision to give battle to the Germans. The crushing of their rising by German forces broke the back of the non-Communist resistance and thus accorded entirely with Soviet interests. Churchill was never among those who believed that the Red Army had deliberately halted east of Warsaw to let the Home Army be destroyed, and the major work on the Eastern Front in 1944 bears him out.[52] Day by day, as the Warsaw battle ground on, he agonised over his inability to intervene without American support. Churchill urged Roosevelt to join him in making representations to Stalin over the need for allied aircrews to be given refuelling facilities on Soviet-held territory. Upon this depended any hope of supply drops to the Home Army in Warsaw.[53] American support, however, was not forthcoming.

Poland did not figure in the 'percentages agreement' on post-war spheres of influence agreed by Churchill and Stalin in October 1944, but it is arguable that its fate was sealed then anyhow. Stalin had already set up the Lublin Committee of pro-Soviet Poles to neutralise the influence of the London government in exile but their Prime Minister, Mikolajczyk, met the two leaders in order to tell them that his country's future was already the victim of a fait accompli. Churchill told him he must negotiate with the Lublin Committee and that Stalin had the right to a 'friendly' post-war Polish state, but without pressing the Soviet leader on whether 'friendliness' would mean in reality one-party pro-Soviet Communist control. 'All in all, it was not Mr. Churchill's finest hour, although he had little room to manoeuvre',[54] is the verdict of one American authority, Walter Kimball, and it is difficult to dispute.

The same verdict may well apply to the February 1945 Yalta Conference, at the end of which Churchill put his name to a hollow three-power declaration agreeing to a 'democratic' post-war Poland which would have as its frontier with the Soviet Union the 1920 Curzon Line. One of Churchill's biographers, Norman Rose, has argued that Churchill's position at the conference was a hopeless one: 'if Yalta was a sell-out, the main goods had been eyed, appraised and bought long before the Big Three met at the Crimean resort; only over the final packaging would there be some extra haggling'.[55] In the haggling process, the Western Allies had only a weak hand to play because a terminally ill President Roosevelt was desperate to ensure that Stalin would soon join the war against Japan. The price he was ready to pay for this was accepting meaningless promises about elections and multi-party democracy in Poland and other countries where the war's final campaigns guaranteed a Russian military presence.

'United States policy floundered in the hands of a mortally stricken President', Rose goes on to write: 'the British, hamstrung by their hopelessly gullible American partners, were powerless to foil the machinations of the Soviets'.[56] Important agreements were, however, reached with Stalin over co-ordinating the war's final operations and over the occupation of Germany. Churchill returned from the toasts and the banquets to defend Yalta in Parliament. 'I know of no Government which stands to its obligations more solidly than the Russian Soviet Government',[57] he told a House all too willing to be convinced, and only twenty-five members went into the division lobby against him.

He still seems to have believed, or wanted to believe, that Stalin would honour his main promises and told Colville, in an unfortunate comparison, that 'Chamberlain had trusted Hitler as he was now trusting Stalin.'[58] By the time of Germany's surrender, this optimism was wearing thin and his tone was becoming one of growing alarm at the Soviet Union's power and potential for expansion. This power, he told Eden on 4 May 1945,

constitutes an event in the history of Europe to which there has been no parallel and which has not been faced by the Allies in their long and hazardous struggle. The Russian demands in Germany for reparations alone will be such as to enable her to prolong the occupation almost indefinitely, at any rate for many years, during which time Poland will sink with many other states into the vast zone of Russian-controlled Europe.[59]

Three days later, in a telegram to Truman, Churchill made his first use of the 'iron curtain' metaphor to describe the divisions beginning to harden between the Western powers and Soviet-controlled Europe. 'I have always worked for friendship with Russia,' he told the new president, 'but, like you, I feel deep anxiety because of their misinterpretation of the Yalta decisions, their attitude towards Poland, their overwhelming influence in the Balkans, excepting Greece, the difficulties they make about Vienna, the combination of Russian power and the territories under their control or occupied.'[60] Nonetheless, his final meeting with Stalin at Potsdam in July, before his General Election defeat, was accompanied by much cameraderie, even though only a few Soviet concessions were secured over foreign troop withdrawals from Iran and a role for the Western powers in the occupation of Vienna. Much later, in 1956, Churchill could still write to another American President, Eisenhower, of how 'Stalin always kept his word with me.'[61] Churchill was not always a good judge of character and accorded more importance to his personal relationship with the Soviet leader than it ever justified. It grew out of the brutal imperatives for both countries of a war for survival and was never the basis for the long-term trust that Churchill and many others hoped would develop from it.

In his 'iron curtain' speech at Fulton, Missouri, in March 1946, Churchill took care to pay tribute to the Soviet Union's part in the war and to restate his belief in good relations with its leadership. 'We understand', he told his audience, 'the Russian need to be secure on her western frontiers by the removal of all possibility of German aggression. We welcome Russia to her rightful place among the leading nations of the world.'[62] The speech does not now seem to be the landmark in the West's response to the Cold War that was at one time claimed. Neither Truman's administration nor American opinion was ready to accept its full implications, though the eloquence of the speech may have influenced American policy towards Britain in ways considered elsewhere in this book.[63]

Arguably, Churchill never really departed from his Fulton analysis of what the West's posture towards the Soviet bloc should be. He accepted, although with ever-increasing alarm, the role that atomic and then nuclear weapons would have to play in the Western powers' defensive armoury, but never abandoned a faith in high-level contacts with Russia's leaders formed by his wartime experience. During the February 1950 General Election, he commended the case for such contacts to an Edinburgh audience: 'the idea appeals to me of a supreme effort to bridge the gulf between the two worlds...it is not easy to see how things could be worsened by a parley at the summit if such a thing were possible'.[64] This may have been the introduction of the word 'summit' to the language of diplomacy, and Churchill's belief in the approach it represented to lowering the temperature of the Cold War was genuine. This was why he resented so bitterly the *Daily Mirror*'s portrayal of him as a warmonger in the October 1951 General Election campaign.

Once back in power, his continuing faith in his own ability to lower tensions by personal contact with Stalin and his successors could exasperate those working with him. Evelyn Shuckburgh at the Foreign Office saw it as proof of an old man's hubris, 'a sentimental illusion'.[65] Anthony Montague Browne, his Private Secretary, found it hard to understand what seemed to be Churchill's abiding trust in Stalin: 'He profoundly wished for detente with the Soviet Union, but he was determined to maintain a stoutly defensive military posture against the Communist bloc. He said of Stalin: "He never broke his personal word to me", which seemed an almost incredible misreading of events by a great historian.'[66]

Both Shuckburgh and Browne marvelled at a Prime Minister approaching his eightieth birthday who remained tenacious in his belief in the virtues of personal diplomacy as a way of reaching and influencing the Soviet leaders who succeeded Stalin. They were also alarmed at the unease it injected into relations between Downing Street and the Eisenhower White House. The climactic example of Churchill's faith in what such contact could achieve was his personal telegram to Molotov in July 1954, sent without consultingeither Eisenhower or his own Cabinet colleagues.[67] It was an initiative that created nothing except embarrassment for him, as well as providing a firm reminder of where power now lay in Britain's special relationship with America. Even so, there was a generosity of spirit behind it and a hope for a future he would not see that shone strongly through his last speech to Parliament as Prime Minister.

In this, he spoke of how no superpower could hide from the awful might of nuclear weapons, a reality, he stressed, that was 'well understood by all persons on both sides – I repeat "on both sides" – who have the power to control events'. The urgency of creative personal diplomacy was thus greater than ever. 'Mercifully,' he told a hushed chamber, 'there is time and hope if we combine patience and courage', and he ended: 'The day may dawn when fair play, love for one's fellow men, respect for justice and freedom, will enable

5

CHURCHILL AND APPEASEMENT

The word 'appeasement' tends to be defined by dictionaries as meaning to pacify, propitiate or satisfy by concessions. In this sense, it is something which individuals and states have always done. Yet few political leaders today would happily use the word to describe or justify a policy, because it is trapped within a wholly pejorative historical context created by events in the 1930s. Then, appeasement became a term used to attack attempts by Britain and France to make territorial and other concessions to Hitler and Mussolini, even when treaty rights and the authority of the League of Nations were violated in the process. Appeasement in this form failed to save the peace and led on to a war infinitely worse than its predecessor. Yet earlier, in the 1920s and even in the debate over the Versailles Treaty, it was possible for politicians, including Churchill, to use the word 'appeasement' to support the aim of reconciliation with a democratic Germany and restoring it to the comity of European nations. It was Churchill, however, more than anyone, who became identified with what later seemed a real and necessary alternative to appeasement as a response to the European crisis brought on by Hitler's accession to power in 1933.

'It was a simple policy to keep Germany disarmed and the victors adequately armed for thirty years and in the meanwhile, even if reconciliation could not be made with Germany, to build ever more strongly a true League of Nations capable of making sure that Treaties were kept or changed only by discussion or agreement.'[1] So Churchill wrote in retrospect of what he judged to be the reasons why Europe had needlessly stumbled towards war in 1939. It was, of course, all a little less simple than that. As Robert Rhodes James later pointed out, Churchill's prescription would have meant giving a sovereign German state less than the sovereignty the victors had granted it in 1919, as well as an agreed readiness by them to take action to enforce long-term German inequality.[2]

Nonetheless, Churchill's critique, eloquently made in his hugely successful history of the war, loomed large for more than twenty years in debate on the war's origins. Its six volumes, completed between 1948 and 1954, were published in hardback in fifty countries and in eighteen languages. The first two volumes rapidly sold 250 000 copies each in Britain alone and the history was serialised worldwide in eighty newspapers and magazines. A television series based upon it followed in 1960 and achieved huge viewing figures.[3] Volume I, *The Gathering Storm*, is distinctive for being less cluttered by the minutes, telegrams and other documents which appear in profusion in the following five, and it remains a superbly graphic rendering by Churchill of his own role as a heroic Cassandra figure unhonoured for his lone prophecies of doom unless Britain rearmed adequately and stood up to Mussolini and Hitler.

During his lifetime, there were few challenges to Churchill's view of events set out in *The Gathering Storm*. In 1954, an American historian, Richard Powers, gave a short but critical view of Churchill's parliamentary record before the war, showing that he never cast a vote against the National Government until after the Munich Agreement.[4] Just over ten years later, Donald Cameron Watt, in a study of British foreign policy, accorded Churchill only a few references in four chapters on the interwar period. In Watt's account, Sir Warren Fisher, Permanent Secretary to the Treasury from 1919 to 1939, emerged as a figure more successful than Churchill in contributing any real urgency to British rearmament and defence planning, while Churchill's criticisms of government policy in these areas were blunted by his self-inflicted isolation over India (see Chapter 9) and his support for Edward VIII in the Abdication crisis. Churchill's role, Watt argued, 'was to act throughout this period as the quasi-leader of the Conservative opposition to the Liberal wing of the National Government'.[5]

Four years before Churchill's death, A. J. P. Taylor, in his 1961 book *The Origins of the Second World War*, famously and mischievously sought to equate Hitler's culpability for the war with that of politicians such as Baldwin and Chamberlain. The latter's signing of the Munich Agreement to dismember the democratic Czechoslovak state was described by Taylor as 'a triumph for all that was best and most enlightened in British life'.[6] This was Taylor's way of arguing that the policy of appeasement, of which Munich was and is still seen by many as the apotheosis, was in tune with public opinion and with a dissenting liberal–internationalist tradition in Britain's dealings with other countries rooted in a belief in equitable conflict resolution rather than war.

Taylor's book offered little in the way of a re-evaluation of Churchill's critique of appeasement, though he did mention in passing his reluctance to take sides in the crises in British foreign policy over Italy's invasion of Abyssinia in 1935 and the war in Spain the following year.[7] It did, however, provoke some bitter attacks on its author as well as starting a protracted debate about appeasement as a policy, in the course of which it has become important for historians to distance themselves both from Churchill's sometimes simplistic case against it in *The Gathering Storm* and his inevitably subjective view of his own part in opposing it.

Appeasement was already a pejorative word when Churchill began work on *The Gathering Storm* and continued to be so used for long afterwards, by Sir Anthony Eden in the 1956 Suez Crisis and by Margaret Thatcher in justification of her decision to go to war with Argentina over the Falkland Islands in 1982. Yet it had not always been so, nor had the thinking behind it. Paul Schroeder showed this in an important 1976 article in which he argued that after 1815, British policy towards Europe could be called appeasement in the sense that it involved siding with countries who wanted revisions of the Vienna settlement without risking war in the process.[8] It was not called appeasement at the time, but the word was readily used in debates on the Versailles settlement a century later.

Jan Smuts, the South African Prime Minister, used the word in March 1919, when writing to Lloyd George about the dangers of imposing a punitive peace upon a defeated Germany. 'Her appeasement now may have the effect of turning her into a bulwark against the oncoming Bolshevism of Eastern Europe', he declared, in a vain attempt to influence the direction of British policy.[9] Churchill himself used the word two years later when addressing the Dominion Prime Ministers' Conference in London. 'The aim', he told his audience, 'is to get an appeasment of the fearful hatreds and antagonisms which exist in Europe and to enable the world to settle down',[10] and his speech as a whole was devoted to the importance of reconciliation with Germany while taking proper account of the fears of France.

Between the November 1918 Armistice and June 1929, Churchill was out of senior office for only two years after the coalition broke up and he lost his Dundee seat in 1922. During this period, he gave general support to modifying the more punitive terms of the Versailles Treaty, bringing the new German republic back into association with its wartime enemies and into membership of the League of Nations. The Locarno Treaty of 1925 took this process of Germany's integration into the comity of European nations an important stage further. At this time, Churchill was a consistently active advocate of reductions in Britain's military expenditure. Throughout the 1920s, outlay on the armed forces dropped in each financial year and had Churchill been able to, he would almost certainly have reduced it further.

He often justified his case for these economies by invoking the Cabinet agreement of 1919 that the armed forces estimates should be based on the assumption that Britain and the Empire would not be engaged in a major war for the next ten years. He was ready to take on the service chiefs themselves and did so as Chancellor of the Exchequer in 1925, when he identified the Admiralty's cruiser-building programme as being too much in excess of the figure it had reached in the previous financial year. One naval historian has written of how close Churchill's case for reduction was to that of Lloyd George fifteen years earlier when he had challenged spending projections drawn up by Churchill as First Lord of the Admiralty.[11] Baldwin negotiated compromise figures which gave the navy more than Churchill would have done, though he got his way in other areas of service expenditure.

As always when in office, Churchill fought his corner tenaciously, arguing that economies were unavoidable if policies of social reform and tax reduction were to be implemented. Yet his position at this time can still seem perverse to historians of British defence policy in the inter-war period. 'Having spent five years at the Admiralty building up the Royal Navy [he] was now spending another five at the Treasury trying with equal zest to cut it down again',[12] one of them argued. Churchill was unapologetic and held to what he saw as the logic of the Ten Year rule, commending it to his colleagues as a standing assumption upon which policy should be based, though subject to annual review. All governments were under League of Nations pressure to reduce their armaments in the 1920s and Britain was represented at a major Geneva conference on naval limitation in July 1927. France and Italy declined to attend, so Britain was the only imperial power present and found itself faced with American demands for naval parity. Churchill, however, chose to fight this in Cabinet, supported by the Sea Lords, and was blamed for the eventual breakdown of the conference, especially by Lord Robert Cecil, who had led the British delegation.[13]

When Labour took power for a second time in 1929, Ramsay Mac-Donald attached enormous importance to a naval conference which he convened in London the next year. France and Italy stayed outside an agreement which was patiently negotiated, but Britain, the United States and Japan accepted a five-year 'holiday' in capital ship construction as well as a series of limits beyond which they would not seek to equip themselves with other types of vessel. MacDonald claimed much for the conference's work and his principal biographer has said of the 1930 Naval Treaty that 'it was a limited achievement no doubt, but it was a real one'.[14] Churchill, however, was on hand with the charge that 'never since the reign of Charles II has this country been so defenceless as this treaty will make it and never in the reign of Charles II was it so vulnerable'.[15] This was not as inconsistent as has sometimes been claimed. Churchill had held to the case for reduced defence expenditure as a domestic political requirement, but retained his reservations about it being demanded of Britain by the League of Nations or under initiatives taken by it.

Barely six months after the treaty was signed, Hitler and the Nazis won six and a half million votes in elections and 107 seats in the German Reichstag. Outside Germany this event, fraught with such danger as we now know it to have been, was overshadowed by the collapse of the American money markets and the onset of the Great Depression. Churchill, though consistent in his support for cost-cutting defence policies as well as the Weimar Republic's acceptance in the councils of Europe, had on occasions both spoken and written of darker currents at work in Germany. In September 1924, he had declared in an article that 'the soul of Germany smoulders with dreams of a war of Liberation or Revenge. These ideas are restrained at the present moment only by physical impotence',[16] and after 1930 he began to be critical of the Brüning government when it pressed for a scaling down of the newly adopted Young Plan's schedule for German reparation payments set after the Versailles Treaty, as well as for parity in armaments.

These moves were insufficent to save the Brüning government or to halt the rising tide of support for the Nazis. Even before they took power, he was warning Parliament against any approximation of military strength being conceded between France and Germany. In the summer of 1932, Churchill had in fact visited Germany to study

battlefields for his *Life of Marlborough* and had by chance made the
acquaintance in Munich of one of Hitler's confidants, Ernst Hanfstaengl, or 'Putzi', as he was nicknamed. Hanfstaengl offered to set
up a meeting between Churchill and his leader and Churchill agreed.
'I had no national prejudices against Hitler at this time', he later wrote.
'I knew little of his doctrine or record and nothing of his character. I
admire men who stand up for their country in defeat, even though I
am on the other side.'[17] He knew enough, however, to question Hanfstaengl about Hitler's anti-Semitism and the meeting was cancelled.
Churchill reacted philosophically. 'Thus Hitler lost his only chance of
meeting me. Later on, when he was all-powerful, I was to receive
several invitations from him. But by this time a lot had happened and
I excused myself.'[18]

The first real defiance of the authority of the League of Nations was
the work not of Germany but of Japan, whose forces invaded mainland
China in September 1931, the following year converting Manchuria
into the puppet state of Manchukuo. Japan had been lost to Britain as
an ally after the war with the non-renewal of the 1902 treaty between
them, but the new National Government showed little desire to challenge their aggression. Churchill accepted their reasons for this: 'His
Majesty's Government could hardly be blamed if in their grave financial, and growing European embarrassments, they did not seek a
prominent role at the side of the United States in the Far East without
any hope of corresponding American support in Europe', he wrote in
The Gathering Storm.[19] When in February 1933 the League of Nations
refused its recognition of Manchukuo, Churchill told Parliament that it
should avoid action against Japan and went on to declare to another
audience: 'I hope we shall try in England to understand a little the
position of Japan, an ancient state with the highest sense of national
honour.'[20]

He was, of course, influenced in these reactions by a real belief in
Japan's potential to be a barrier to Communism in East Asia. This
sympathy was diluted by the increasingly warlike nature of Japan's
rulers after 1933, but he showed only a very limited grasp of the
implications for Britain as both a European and imperial power if
their policy became even more aggressive. This is apparent in the
failure over the defence of Singapore for which he later accepted
responsibility. In fact, Japan had only a marginal place in Churchill's
speeches and writings on the dangers facing Britain in the 1930s and
his military assessment of its armed forces could be bizarre. Only a

week before Pearl Harbor, he was quoted as having told an American journalist, John Gunther, that 'The Japs will cave in – they are the Wops of the East.'[21] From January 1933, however, it was Germany which was uppermost in Churchill's concerns. It was never true that it was Hitler's intention to rearm which concerned him more than the nature of his regime. He acknowledged the demonic energy of the new Reich while detesting its brutality and anti-Semitism, and indeed, his condemnations of it became stronger as he reached out for Labour and Liberal support in his growing opposition to National Government policy. In an almost intuitive way, Churchill sensed that the Reich's nature was inseparable from predatory and aggressive intentions in Europe. 'He saw and felt', Robert Rhodes James has written, 'that the world was in the presence of a terrible personal and national phenomenon.'[22] How best to respond fell into the related areas of defence policy and diplomacy.

When Churchill talked of rearmament in the period after Hitler came to power, he really meant air power, something in which he had for long been interested. The debate over Britain's development of it in response to Hitler's rapid build-up of the new Luftwaffe was a complex one, involving concepts such as parity which were not always easy to define. The Air Staff itself disagreed over whether all operational aircraft should be included in calculations of British and German air strength, or only those actually ready for immediate service. Those who supported Churchill's warnings about Germany's growing air strength had sometimes to warn him against overstating his figures, and these were challenged with a degree of success by Baldwin in Parliament in November 1934, when Churchill moved an amendment to the Address calling for RAF expansion. The argument was not on the principle of rearmament, which the government accepted but, as John Charmley has put it, 'about the pace at which it should proceed and where the effort should be concentrated'.[23]

Among the questions which must be raised about Churchill's criticisms of defence policy is whether they suffered from being linked too closely to his own seemingly flagging fortunes in a period when he had few major political allies. Another has to be whether their impact was lessened by his desire to influence policy from within government itself. In March 1935 he very readily accepted a place on a new Air Defence Research Committee, where he could ask leading questions on policy while gaining privileged access to much important information, though he had other sources, as Chapter 1 points out. Baldwin made it clear that Churchill's membership of this Committee was not a move to muzzle him and Lord Swinton, who in June became Secretary of State for Air, valued the role which he believed he could play in adding urgency to air rearmament. Churchill paid a glowing tribute to Baldwin at that year's Conservative Party Conference and in 1936 it was no secret that he hoped Baldwin as Prime Minister would offer him the new position of Minister for Defence Co-ordination. This did not happen, but Churchill remained circumspect over directly attacking Baldwin or his successor, Neville Chamberlain. Churchill indeed was on hand in May 1937 to second his nomination as Conservative Party leader after Baldwin's retirement.

Prime Ministers such as MacDonald, Baldwin and especially Chamberlain all reacted to demands for increased defence expenditure in terms of the risks to the economy of new borrowing to fund it. Even when, partly at Churchill's urging, the Ten-Year Rule was finally abandoned in 1933, the government was strongly influenced by the Treasury view that rearmament, while necessary, had to be balanced against the capacity of the economy to sustain it.[24] For Churchill, a conviction once formed had to be fought for, and by September 1935 he was pressing for aircraft production to go on a war footing and the following April he was calling upon Chamberlain to bring the trade unions into full consultation on this over its implications for workers, advising him that 'you will not get the effective co-operation of the work people unless you can make sure that there are not a lot of greedy fingers having a rake-off'.[25]

Essentially Churchill's view had become that the national interest demanded rearmament regardless of either financial constraints or, indeed, the uncertainty of public opinion. On 12 November 1936, moving an amendment to the Address identical to the one he had proposed two years earlier, he confronted head-on the whole concept of government needing to justify defence expenditure on grounds either of finance or what the public might accept. 'Such a doctrine is wholly inadmissible', he told the House. 'The responsibility of Ministers for the public safety is absolute and requires no mandate. It is in fact the prime object for which Governments come into existence.'[26]

Between 1934 and 1936, many of Churchill's speeches were taken up with the need to rapidly build up a bomber force. In this he was influenced by the aerial warfare theorists of the time, who were writing of how a powerful knock-out blow by bombing aircraft could quickly destroy an enemy's command structure and reduce its cities to chaos and mass panic. Fighter defence systems were much less central to his questioning of government policy, which has led John Charmley to argue that 'Churchill owed his finest hour in 1940 to the fact that his advice had not been taken in 1934 and 1935.'[27] By mid-1937, much of the heat had gone out of the air rearmament debate and Churchill's interventions on the subject became less frequent. This was partly because of his continuing hopes of office but also because the Air Staff had arrived at conclusions similar to his own about the implications for Britain of German aircraft production. There was also a lull on the European scene with no dramatic new moves by Hitler. At the 1937 Conservative Conference, Churchill gave the appearance of being broadly in support of government policy and he actually told his Epping constituency party that he did not believe a major war to be imminent.

Where other areas of defence policy were concerned, Churchill's grasp of them sometimes seemed to suffer from his preoccupation with air power. He showed little conception of the implications for the Royal Navy of the expenditure cuts which he himself had driven through during his years at the Treasury between 1924 and 1929, nor was he alive to what fighter aircraft might be able to do to surface ships, especially in Far Eastern waters where the Japanese would soon use them to devastating effect. In June 1935, the National Government put its signature to a naval treaty with Germany which allowed the Reich to increase its fleet to one-third of the Royal Navy's total strength. France was given no prior notice, the League bypassed and Hitler's preference for bilateral agreements pandered to, but when the terms were debated in July, Churchill voted with the government. In a subsequent debate he adopted a critical tone: 'I regret that we are not dealing with this problem of the resuscitation of German naval power with the concert of Europe on our side', he told members, arguing that Britain had a common interest 'with many other nations whose fortunes are affected and whose fears are aroused equally with our own by the enormous development of German armaments'.[28] It must be said, however, that he was rather more censorious writing about the treaty twelve years later, when he called it a unilateral acceptance by Britain of treaty violations already made by Germany building warships to a size far greater than the Versailles terms permitted.

As to the army's role, he was slow to contribute anything important to debates about how to resolve manpower and logistic problems arising from Britain continuing to play a global imperial role while accepting an ultimate commitment to fight in Europe if all else failed. Chamberlain was consistently averse to the General Staff's regular demands for an expanded field army to support France if the time for it came, and he could enlist military analysts such as Sir Basil Liddell Hart, who was still arguing in 1939 that France could defend itself and Belgium without Britain's help. There were times when Churchill seemed to identify himself with that view. This was certainly the impression of Sir Edmund Ironside, General Officer Commanding Eastern Command and later Chief of the Imperial General Staff, who in December 1937 recorded in his diary how Churchill 'thought the French army an incomparable machine'.[29] Ironside tried to press him on the British army's development if war in Europe came but 'could get nothing out of him as to our need of sending an army to France'.[30]

On this occasion Churchill was more interested in extolling the strength of the Royal Navy and assured Ironside that 'a modern fleet was unassailable from the air' and that Singapore could be held if war came with Japan. 'The Far East he dealt with in a way that left me gasping,' Ironside continued in his diary, 'no mention was once made of the USA.' It was a different story in late August 1939 when they dined together on the eve of the war and Churchill informed Ironside 'that we must have a great Army in France, that we couldn't depend upon the French to do our effort for us. That we must get twenty divisions by Christmas. I told him that we had no such plans in being.'[31]

The extent to which, in this period, Churchill immersed himself in often very public controversy over what he claimed to be the short-comings of rearmament policy inevitably strengthened the hand of opponents, whose concern was to stress how limited Britain's options really were in response to each new act of treaty-breaking and aggression by Mussolini and Hitler. It has also given ammunition to historians who have contributed a revisionist view to an ongoing debate on the concept of appeasement. Some of them have argued that Churchill, had he been given the office he hoped for, might not in reality have been able to act very differently from those he was later to castigate with such eloquence in his writing on the war's origins. This chapter must therefore now turn to Churchill's role in the series of crises in Europe and beyond it which mark out the via dolorosa to renewed war in 1939.

Mussolini's invasion of Abyssinia in 1935 outraged a broad range of liberal and left-of-centre opinion in Britain which the League of

Nations Union had appealed to with some success in its Peace Ballot in October of the previous year. Some 11.5 million householders had responded to a questionnaire on their attitudes to the League of Nations and peacekeeping and the results were published just before Italy's action, revealing decisive support for collective security through the League by all means short of war, though a less dramatic majority did pledge support to military measures against aggressor states. The crisis aroused deep feelings over Italy's ruthless use of firepower and gas against an underarmed African people, and put the National Government under severe pressure to give a lead to the League. This it did, initially supporting sanctions against Italy and fighting a successful General Election in November on a policy of collective security.

Churchill's reaction was a muted one. He accepted the National Government's policy of support for the so-called Stresa Front under which Britain and France maintained an active relationship with Italy in order to keep it out of the German camp, so this was always going to inhibit his support for all-out League sanctions. He had also already spoken too indulgently on occasions of Mussolini's regime to condemn it outright for its attack on Abyssinia. In 1927 he had, for example, told journalists in Rome in answer to a question about his view of the Duce's rule: 'If I had been an Italian, I am sure I should have been wholeheartedly with you from start to finish in your triumphant struggle against the bestial appetites and passions of Leninism.'[32]

In the Commons debate of 24 October, he had in fact called the invasion 'a small matter'[33] in comparison to the growing threat from Germany, though he did argue that League of Nations decisions should be upheld. This was despite his reservations about Abyssinia's credentials for membership of it: 'No-one', he went on to say in his speech, 'can keep up the pretence that Abyssinia is a fit, worthy and equal member of a League of civilised nations.'[34] There was little in Churchill's response to commend itself to those who saw Mussolini's action as a moral issue and this was equally true when a fresh political storm broke in December 1935. This was over the revelation that the Foreign Secretary, Sir Samuel Hoare, had agreed with Pierre Laval, his French opposite number, on the principle of letting Mussolini annex a substantial and fertile area of Abyssinia for colonisation by Italy.

The reaction in Britain brought Hoare's resignation and united for a time the League of Nations Union, the churches, the opposition parties, *The Times* and a significant number of Conservatives. A. J. P. Taylor wrote of it as the greatest outcry over foreign affairs since the campaign against Turkish atrocities in Bulgaria in 1876.[35] Churchill, however, was on holiday in Spain when the storm broke and accepted the advice of his son, Randolph, amongst others, that he would achieve little by returning home. Later he wrote of how he regretted this: 'Looking back, I think I ought to have come home. I might have brought an element of decision and combination to the anti-Government gatherings which could have ended the Baldwin regime.'[36] Given his initial low-key response to the Abyssinia crisis, this seems unlikely.

Four months later Churchill, speaking in his constituency, even made a case for the Hoare–Laval deal, arguing that it would have at least allowed Haile Selassie, the ruler of Abyssinia, to retain his ancient throne, but he described Mussolini's victory over him and the League as a 'lamentable event'.[37] The government, he argued, should never have taken the lead in a policy of economic sanctions against Italy that had to be 'confined within limits which would not lead to war',[38] but the moment had passed for Churchill to make a real stand against a cave-in to blatant aggression by Mussolini against a League member. The criticisms, moreover, which Churchill was already making of Britain's rate of rearmament would have made it hard for him to sustain a case for going further than the National Government had been prepared to do.

Before Haile Selassie's flight from his country and the collapse of what remained of his army, Hitler, in flagrant and open breach of the Versailles and Locarno treaties, ordered German army units into the Rhineland on 7 March 1936. Churchill wrote a vivid account of this event and its repercussions in *The Gathering Storm*, asserting that if France had mobilised, 'there is no doubt that Hitler would have been compelled by his own General Staff to withdraw, and a check would have been given to his pretensions which might well have proved fatal to his rule'.[39] This was and must remain conjecture. Mobilisation would have had to be more than mere bluff but Hitler's gambling instincts might well have led him to treat it as such and risk a confrontation over the Rhineland.

Chamberlain, at the height of the Munich crisis two years later, raised this very question, arguing that the expectation of Hitler submitting to humiliation without a fight was 'not a reliable estimate of a mad dictator's reactions'.[40] Churchill's retrospective case for action over the Rhineland depended on Britain and France being ready to co-operate militarily in response to Hitler's fait accompli, but the French had written off the area unless they had a firm promise of British support.

This they never obtained, though the British Ambassador in Berlin had been warning the Foreign Office a year earlier that Hitler would reoccupy the Rhineland whenever the right moment came.

Churchill made no proposal for Britain to co-ordinate a military response with the French, certainly not when he referred to the Rhineland two days after its reoccupation in a general Commons debate on defence policy and on the appointment of the new Minister for Defence Co-ordination. Neville Chamberlain later wrote of Churchill's muted intervention in this debate and that he appeared to have 'suspended the attack he had intended and made a constructive and helpful speech'.[41] Churchill described it in *The Gathering Storm* as 'severe though friendly criticism of the Government',[42] but one of the most thorough treatments of Churchill's relationship to the National Government on foreign and defence policy has observed that 'the friendliness is more evident than the severity'.[43]

When a full debate on the Rhineland issue was held on 23 March, Churchill made a sombre speech contrasting the premonitions of 1936 with the optimism of five years before, but he did not dissociate himself from the National Government's response to Hitler's actions which the Führer had combined with the offer of long term non-aggression pacts to France and Belgium. Indeed, his words could only be interpreted as supportive of Eden, the new Foreign Secretary, who announced staff conversations with France and Belgium and reminded the House that the League's council had met and asked Hitler not to reinforce his troops already in the Rhineland pending further negotiations.

It was hardly a fighting reaction but it was one in keeping with the reaction of a press which mostly followed a *Times* leader entitled 'A Chance to Rebuild'. This, for all practical purposes, condoned what Hitler had done. Churchill did lay some stress on the strategic advantages to Germany of an occupied and refortified Rhineland, but offered little else that differed much from the government line. 'Shorn of its rhetoric, Churchill's proposals merged smoothly into the policy the government was actually pursuing',[44] one of Churchill's most sympathetic biographers has written, and a major study of Chamberlain's foreign policy has argued that only in retrospect did the remilitarisation begin to be seen as a self-evident moment for 'stopping Hitler'.[45] On the other hand, the Labour leader Attlee welcomed Churchill's call for all democratic states to act together to enforce the League's Covenant against aggression and congratulated him on coming over to 'our side'.[46] For all its limitations, his speech gave out a welcome

signal to bodies such as the League of Nations Union as well as to
Foreign Office dissidents such as Sir Robert Vansittart and Reginald
Leeper, who believed public opinion had to be mobilised against the
threat of Hitler.

Although Churchill's energies were diverted by his ill-judged decision to support Edward VIII in the Abdication crisis, he did speak at
the Albert Hall in December 1936 at the 'Arms and the Covenant' rally
sponsored by the League of Nations Union. His address was a powerful
one, on the need for the League to be given the fullest authority, but
his optimism about the likelihood of this happening has a hollow ring
to it. He avoided much reference to its recent humiliations over Abyssinia and the Rhineland and even argued that once the adequately
rearmed democracies were united under the League's Covenant, 'we
may reach a position where we can invite the German people to join
this organisation of world security; where we can invite them to take
their place freely in the circle of nations to preserve peace'.[47] Given the
Third Reich's recent adoption of a Four Year Plan drawn up by Hitler
to put the entire German economy on a war footing, this passage in
Churchill's speech has to be described as wishful thinking, even if its
overall emphasis was on the reality of a world heading towards 'calam-
ities and horrors the end of which no man can see'.[48]

Paradoxically, then, after the Abyssinia and Rhineland crises had
dealt severe blows to what authority the League still had, Churchill,
both in Parliament and at public meetings, began to speak in its support. In July 1936, he urged upon a Bristol University audience the
view that it was 'more urgent than ever to create in Europe a League of
Nations which will confront a potential aggressor with overwhelming
force, organised for use, capable of being used in support of a covenant
entered into between all nations on the basis that he who strikes at one
strikes at all'.[49] By then he was in contact with the all-party Focus
Group founded in the previous year by a German emigré, Eugen
Spier, in order to bring together politicians, academics and journalists
in what has been called 'a conspiracy to change the course of British
foreign policy through propaganda with Churchill as the chief public-
ist'.[50] The group operated secretively and receives no mention in
Churchill's history of the war, but it widened his contacts with people
he wanted to reach with his case for a real shift of British foreign policy
in response to the dangers he identified in Hitler's intentions.

Even as Churchill spoke at the Albert Hall, horror was a reality in
every news report from Spain as the Spanish Republic fought for its life

against the insurgent generals led by Francisco Franco and his allies. This was a brutal collision between the old Spain of Church and land-owners and a democratic new Spain struggling to be born. Hitler and Mussolini intervened on Franco's side from the outset, with Britain and France putting in place a non-intervention agreement which they sim-ply ignored. The generous indignation of the British labour movement was mobilised in a cause which took hundreds of mostly working-class volunteers to Spain in support of the young republic, whose victory they believed could halt the onward march of European Fascism.

They came from places and from a political culture of which Church-ill knew little or nothing, and their identification with the Spanish cause was beyond his understanding. From the start of the war his notion of it was an intellectually crude one. 'In this conflict I was neutral', he wrote later. 'Naturally I was not in favour of the Communists. How could I be when if I had been a Spaniard they would have murdered me and my family and friends.'[51] He took the unquestioning view that Britain also should be neutral, and was untroubled by the possibility of the National Government's non-intervention policy making the Popular Front Gov-ernment more dependent upon Soviet aid, thus strengthening the prestige of Spain's small Communist party.

He deplored the war's cruelty, but his language tended to be more highly coloured when it was the Republic's shortcomings that he was attacking rather than those of the insurgents. In essence he saw them as the lesser of two evils and it was not until the summer of 1938 that he accepted that a victory for them, enabling a client state of Hitler to threaten the Straits of Gibraltar, would have serious implications for Britain. He may have been influenced by the views of Duncan Sandys, a young Conservative backbencher, later to become his son-in-law, who visited Spain and talked to the Republican government,[52] and perhaps also by *Searchlight on Spain*, a best-selling Penguin Special by Katherine, Duchess of Atholl, the maverick Scottish Conservative MP for Kinross and West Pertshire, whose opposition to government policy was to cost her her seat before the year was out.

Another factor influencing Churchill's perception of the Spanish conflict was his continuing belief that Mussolini, even while giving direct aid to the insurgents, was still potentially a restraining influence on Hitler, perhaps even a counterweight to his ambitions. In 1934 there had indeed seemed to be some justification for such a belief when the Duce moved troops to his Austrian frontiers to warn off Nazis there from attempting a putsch against the Dollfüss regime, but by 1938 he was talking of the Austrian Republic's future as a purely German question. Any union or *anschluss* between it and Germany was of course still forbidden under the Versailles Treaty, but Hitler devoted the opening page of *Mein Kampf* to the case for it: 'German Austria must return to the great German mother country...one blood demands one Reich.'[53]

Hitler's moment came when the Schussnigg government in Vienna reacted to insults and intimidation from Berlin by announcing a plebiscite for 13 March to confirm Austria's independence. A German invasion began on the 11th, followed by a crudely manipulated vote for *anschluss* and a vicious round-up of Jews and active anti-Fascists. On 14 March the Commons debated Hitler's action, which Chamberlain condemned. He also announced a fresh and urgent review of Britain's defence expenditure and Churchill told members that 'Europe is confronted with a programme of aggression, nicely calculated and timed, unfolding stage by stage',[54] and talked of Austria as 'a small country, brutally struck down'.[55]

Chamberlain reserved his major statement on Austria until a debate scheduled for 24 March. Then, as Prime Minister, he set out what was in effect an elaborate case for continued inaction, opposing British undertakings being given either to support the Czechoslovak state against growing threats from Berlin over the position of its Sudeten German population, or to engage in talks with the Soviet Union about a co-ordinated response to a worsening European situation. He also claimed that Britain had stood by its obligations to the League and was still ready to work through it in the interests of peace. Then, as ten days earlier, Churchill spoke eloquently, calling for accelerated rearmament and dynamic collective security through the League, as well as a British initiative to launch a Grand Alliance with unnamed states including, his listeners assumed, the Soviet Union joining Britain and France in a solemn resolve to resist aggression. There was no chance of Chamberlain agreeing to such an alliance, yet once more Churchill voted with the government.

Early in May, Konrad Henlein, the Nazi leader in the German-speaking Sudetenland area of Czechoslovakia, visited London to press the case of his community against the authorities in Prague. Churchill agreed to meet him in secret and listened to his claims that he was acting without any orders from Berlin. He left the meeting reassured by Henlein's apparent willingness to settle for a measure of Sudeten autonomy but without prejudice to the territorial integrity of the

Czechoslovak state, and at once reported what had been said to Jan Masaryk, the Czechoslovak minister in London. Professor Lindemann was also present and, according to his notes, it had been put clearly to Henlein that if Germany marched against Czechoslovakia, 'France would come in and England would follow'.[56] Three days later, Churchill spoke at Bristol on the issue, declaring that he 'saw no reason why the Sudeten Deutsche should not become trusted and honoured partners in what was, after all, the most progressive and democratic of the new States of Europe'.[57]

The process by which the Chamberlain government came to acquiesce in what was in effect the dismemberment of Czechoslovakia has often been analysed. What decided this outcome was Chamberlain's conviction that the Czechs could be persuaded to give up the Sudeten territory while Hitler could be talked into agreeing to it without recourse to war. To these ends he resorted to the drama of highly personal diplomacy symbolised in his late September flights to Germany to speak directly with Hitler. Churchill's premonitions grew, as indeed they had done since Eden's resignation from the Foreign Office in February, though his successor, Lord Halifax, did briefly rebel against Chamberlain over the coercion of the Czechs.[58] Support for him in the Cabinet seemed to make war imminent by 27 September, only for Chamberlain to tell Parliament the next day that he was seeking a further personal meeting with Hitler.

According to Sir Henry 'Chips' Channon, the diarist and pro-Chamberlain MP, 'the House rose and in a scene of riotous delight, cheered, bellowed their approval. We stood on our benches, waved our order papers, shouted – until we were hoarse – a scene of indescribable enthusiasm – Peace must now be saved and with it the world.'[59] Some later accounts of the moment, as opposed to contemporary ones, claim that Churchill declined to join in and remained seated. Others have it that in fact he was among those who congratulatead the Prime Minister,[60] which in fact would not have been uncharacteristic of the relationship between them, whatever Churchill felt at the time about the likely outcome. This, on 1 October, was the transfer of the Sudetenland to Germany without a plebiscite, depriving at a stroke a democratic Czechoslovak state of a fortified frontier which it was well equipped to defend.

Two days later, Parliament began a four-day debate. Chamberlain, in defending the agreement in a sometimes emotional speech, put much emphasis on the need for rearmament to continue and responded to criticisms of his claims to a cheering crowd in Downing Street that he had brought them 'peace for our time'. He asked the House not to read more into these words than he had intended to convey. 'I do indeed believe', he went on, 'that we may yet secure peace for our time, but I have never meant to suggest that we should do that by disarmament until we can induce others to disarm too.'[61] When Churchill was called by the Speaker, he began by paying tribute to the Prime Minister's commitment to peace and acknowledged the strain he had been under, but went on, in one of his greatest speeches ever, to attack comprehensively the Munich Agreement and the thinking behind it. He was listened to with ill-concealed hostility by most occupants of the Conservative benches.

Chamberlain's policy, he declared at the outset, had inflicted upon Britain and France 'a total and unmitigated defeat... the utmost he has been able to gain for Czechoslovakia and in the matters which were in dispute has been that the German dictator, instead of snatching the victuals from the table, has been content to have them served to him course by course'.[62] Left to themselves, the Czechoslovak government, he argued, could have got better terms and could indeed hardly have got worse. He reminded the chamber of his own call after the Austrian *anschluss*, for military guarantees to the Czechs from Britain, France and all other willing states, and poured scorn on the notion that the Sudeten Germans were simply being offered self-determination given the brutal nature of the regime they were being united with. Correctly he predicted that possibly within months the Reich would seize the rest of Czechoslovakia, and hammered home his view that a major shift in the balance of European power had been brought about which threatened the safety and independence of Britain and France.[63]

That Churchill's case rested on a series of emotional over-simplifications is still argued by those who invoke American neutrality, the anxieties of the Dominions, the uncertainty of Soviet intentions, the global overstretch of Britain's still underfunded armed forces and the public's reluctance to face war, as all being reasons why the Chamberlain government could not act other than it did at Munich. It has also been argued that vital time was bought there for Britain to move closer to war-readiness but that was never part of Chamberlain's justification for treating directly with Hitler. Eleven months' borrowed time helped Germany to accelerate its rearmament and when they invaded the West in May 1940, they used a sizeable number of good-quality tanks acquired after the occupation of the rest of Czechoslovakia. Few

British survivors of Narvik and Dunkirk ever went on record with the view that time purchased at Munich had been used to good military effect, and such advances as there were in radar and fighter defence were due to plans nurtured well before September 1938.

As a sustained phillipic against the way the Czech crisis had been handled, Churchill's speech still reads superbly, but when the vote was called on the government's own motion, just twenty-nine Conservative members joined Churchill in abstaining. One of them was Alfred Duff Cooper, the First Lord of the Admiralty, who had announced his resignation early in the debate, the only minister to do so, but the government's majority was still over two hundred. Churchill's stand earned him little immediate support. He certainly did not receive the flood of congratulatory mail that reached Chamberlain after his return from Munich, 20 000 letters and telegrams having to be dealt with by Downing Street in late September and early October.[64] Nor did his speech secure him the leadership of Conservative dissidents over appeasement. The few opponents of Munich who had abstained with him still tended to see Eden as their leader and were dubious, to say the least, about Churchill's record on issues such as India and the Abdication.

In the weeks immediately after Munich, there were signs that Churchill felt his isolation, and some sensed a temporary loss of momentum in his criticisms of the government. There was a real chance both to challenge and damage Chamberlain at the Oxford by-election in November 1938 when A. D. Lindsay, the Master of Balliol College, stood as anti-government independent candidate against Quintin Hogg, the official Conservative. Hogg won the seat with a reduced majority but Churchill took no part in the contest and did not mention it in *The Gathering Storm*. This was partly because he had work to do in his own Epping constituency, where some activists were angered by his Munich speech in Parliament.[65] With a General Election due in 1940 at the latest, dissenters within the Conservative Party had to be wary if they wanted readoption by their constituencies and over the winter of 1938–39, the party's Central Office put strong pressure on the Epping party to deselect their Member.

Resignation of his seat to test opinion in a by-election was a course he certainly did not consider, unlike the Duchess of Atholl in the Kinross and West Perthshire constituency. Although supported by the Labour, Liberal and Communist parties, the 'Red Duchess' only just failed to hold the seat against a pro-appeasement official Conservative

candidate. Churchill advised her against resignation and did not campaign personally in her support, though the Duchess later recalled that
he had telephoned most evenings and also sent a message endorsing
her action and saying that victory could 'only have an invigorating
effect upon the whole impulse of Britain's policy and Britain's
defence'.[66]

Public opinion on appeasement and Munich is still pressed into
service by those concerned to defend Chamberlain's course as the
best of a series of bad choices for Britain. Opinion, however, can
change, sometimes quite quickly, while it is also true that in democracies political leaders can sometimes end up with the public opinion they
deserve. In 1947, Sir Horace Wilson, Chamberlain's chief foreign policy adviser, argued that appeasement had been unavoidable because
'there had been no education of the country...to support a more
robust stand against the dictators'. This is quoted in an illuminating
study of the British newspapers in the late 1930s which shows very
vividly that 'Chamberlain, helped by the press barons and certain
editors, did his utmost to ensure that there was no "education of the
country", thus allowing him to pursue his policy of appeasement as the
only available policy option.'[67]

It is, of course, not true that there was no debate on alternative
policies. Churchill helped to make it possible, even though it was not
until November 1938 that he cast his first vote against the government
and, prior to Munich, had moved cautiously in questioning its foreign
policy. Yet even in that same month Chamberlain accepted that victory
could not be taken for granted in a General Election fought on this
policy.[68] In early April 1939, after the National Government's guarantee of support against aggression to Poland, Churchill pressed the case
in Parliament for a 'Grand Alliance' against Hitler, which would include
the Soviet Union. 'No-one can say that there is not a solid identity of
interest between the Western democracies and Soviet Russia', he told
the House.[69] By June 1939, Gallup Polls were showing a clear majority
for a British military alliance with France and the Soviet Union, and
Chamberlain began to tell ministers to minimise the use of the word
'appeasement' in their speeches.[70] Opinion across Britain, through a
combination of guilt and unease, was starting to move away from
Chamberlain and towards Churchill.

Debate about appeasement continues to preoccupy historians. John
Charmley argues that Churchill unrealistically opposed a rational
policy for managing the decline of British power. In Europe, just as

in India, the National Government, in his view, simply sought to preserve what they could of it;[71] but Charmley's thesis, which is considered elsewhere in this book, has bigger implications, for he believes that going to war in 1939 and fighting on in the summer of 1940 destroyed what remained of British power and that a deal with Hitler was possible and preferable. Norman Rose[72] and Paul Kennedy[73] avoid going that far, while taking the view that Britain could not have fought any sooner than it did for reasons financial, military and diplomatic. What Churchill in office could have done to redirect policy or indeed to stop Hitler, they see as problematic; but Churchill, not just in office before September 1939 but as Prime Minister, might have been a different matter. Events after 10 May 1940 still seem to suggest that.

The problem for Churchill was that until war came, any ministerial office was beyond his grasp. He therefore had to deploy his case against the National Government's foreign policy within a party, which was suspicious of him and within which, it has been said, opposition to appeasement was a matter 'of sporadic and discontinuous dissent, of individual critics and small cliques but no cohesive group'.[74]

6

CHURCHILL AND EUROPE

'Where is my frog speech?' Churchill demanded of his staff in October 1940, shortly before he was due to broadcast in French for the BBC's European service. A French translator present at the time was described as 'looking pained'.[1] He had reason to be, but Churchill was capable of thoughtless remarks about Germans as well. His declaration that 'A Hun alive is a war in prospect' at a lunch party earlier that month was recalled by a fellow-diner as his only noteworthy remark.[2] Asian and African people were also the subjects of insensitive and sometimes outrightly crude language from him, yet his thinking about a multiracial world and Britain's place in it went deeper than these lapses might suggest.

Similarly with Europe, Churchill's vision of its history and its potential as a continent was more complex and rooted in far more respect than occasionally hostile or dismissive aphorisms about particular nationalities might suggest. It was a vision also profoundly influenced by the history he had both been taught as a boy and had later read voraciously. He told a London audience in 1947,

> At school, we learned from maps hung on the walls, and the advice of our teachers, that there is a continent called Europe. I remember quite well being taught this as a child and after living a long time still believe it true. However professional geographers now tell us that the Continent of Europe is really only the peninsula of the Asiatic land mass. I must tell you in all faith that this would be an arid and uninspiring conclusion, and for myself, I distinctly prefer what I was taught when I was a boy.[3]

This speech was made at a time when Churchill seemed to many to be an enthusiast for the post-war movement towards a united Western Europe. His view of this process and how it developed and changed will be explored in this chapter, which will, however, begin by looking at his relationship with the two nation-states to whom a turbulent half century drew him closest, France and Germany. For nearly all his life, this relationship was deeply affected both by aversion to the dark forces within it which twice made Germany an aggressor ready to drag Europe and the world into war and a real and even romantic love of France. Yet after both wars he would work patiently for the cause of Franco-German reconciliation.

Prior to the 1945 Potsdam summit conference, Churchill had paid only three brief visits to Germany, two before 1914 and the third in 1932. His grasp of the German language was minimal and he had little grounding in the country's history and culture, although while on an official visit in 1909 he recorded his admiration for German achievements in social welfare legislation. He was also impressed by the power of the Kaiser's army, which he watched on manoeuvres, though it took time for him to see the imperial regime as a threat to Britain. Once in office as First Lord of the Admiralty in 1911 his views changed. German policy in the Balkans and elsewhere began to alarm him and by 1912 he was arguing that Britain's fleet was a necessity while Germany's was only a luxury. He came increasingly to see Germany as a threat to the European balance of power and well before the war came, was clear in his own mind that Britain must support France if Germany attacked her.

After August 1914 he remained unshaken in his belief that Germany must be defeated and that the cause of the Allies was a just one. He opposed all talk of a negotiated peace although without succumbing to the virulent Germanophobia that grew in Britain as the war dragged on. By November 1918, he was talking of collective German war guilt and the need for all its colonies to be taken from it as well as Alsace-Lorraine to be restored to France.[4] This was an election speech and despite the mood of his audience, he argued against the notion that Germany could ever be made to meet the full expenses of the war. Churchill had no direct role in the peace conference which followed, but made the case against a punitive settlement which would simply stoke the fires of vengeance in a people already undergoing acute privation from both the war and their defeat in it.

On the very evening of the Armistice, he lectured his fellow-diners 'on the great qualities of the German people, on the tremendous fight that they had made against three quarters of the world, on the impossibility of re-building Europe without their help',[5] and urged the need for food ships to be sent at once to Hamburg. So when Churchill wrote later in his history of the Second World War of how 'The economic clauses of the Treaty were malignant and silly to an extent that made them obviously futile',[6] he was not simply laying claim to the wisdom of hindsight. As early as March 1920, he was pressing upon Lloyd George the case for treaty revision in full consultation with 'a new Germany, invited as an equal partner in rebuilding Europe'.

Belief in a humane peace settlement that would not store up problems which Britain lacked the military resources to meet never blinded Churchill to the real fears of France that a hostile Germany would seek its revenge on her. At the July 1921 conference of Dominion prime ministers in London, he put a strong case for a British treaty of guarantee which would ensure that France would never face an aggressor alone. This, he argued, was not incompatible with the larger goal of peace in Europe. The conference was not supportive on this issue, but in arguing for such a treaty he used a word which could still serve in a non-pejorative context. A pledge to France, he declared to the conference, 'is not connected with the militaristic triumph of one set of nations over another, but aims entirely, in my opinion, at the *appeasement* and consolidation of the European family'.[7]

While alert to the long-term dangers of treating Germany like a pariah, Churchill could also see that its resentments, once effectively politicised, could be a dire threat to peace. 'The enormous contingents of German youth growing to military manhood year by year', he wrote in 1924, 'are inspired by the fiercest sentiments and the soul of Germany smoulders with dreams of a War of Liberation or Revenge. These ideas are restrained at the present only by physical impotence.'[8] This was part of a powerful article he contributed to *Nash's Pall Mall Magazine*, under the title 'Shall We All Commit Suicide?' In it, he reverted to France's still unassuaged fears but also stressed that 'Germany is a far stronger entity than France and cannot be kept in permanent subjugation.'[9]

The danger of Germany being allowed to rearm and to achieve military parity with France was something Churchill warned against even before the Nazis took power. Once they did, he could invoke traditional balance-of-power concepts while also arguing that democratic Europe should be wary of taking on trust any promises from a regime led by Hitler. Churchill's response to the new situation after January 1933 and his views on how Britain should confront it were not quite as consistent as he later claimed. He understood Hitler better than most of his contemporaries, certainly better than those among them who thought rational compromises with him were possible.

Perhaps this was because of some of the similarities in their early lives, such as childhood unhappiness and failure to enter higher education. This view has been argued by John Lukacs, an author who also stresses what, in his view, set them apart and enabled Churchill to get the measure of Hitler: 'One of the essential differences between Hitler and Churchill was this: the former was a nationalist, the latter a patriot.'[10] Churchill, Lukacs goes on to argue, saw Hitler as 'a reincarnation of some very ancient evil; at the same time he stood for something that was thoroughly untraditional and terribly modern'.[11] Hitler, above all, 'was moved by resentments and hate. Churchill was not.'[12] In this powerful analysis, Churchill, a man of true principles although often capable of changing his mind, would always have seen through and outfaced an amoral and paranoid antagonist driven by demonnic and brutal beliefs.

Even Goebbels came to have a grudging respect for Churchill, but only late in the war after years in which his state propaganda apparatus had vilified him as a glutton, voluptuary, alcoholic, military incompetent and self-serving opportunist in the pay of Jewish financiers, and also a dupe of Stalin. Not until 1944 did personal attacks on Churchill ease off, with the emphasis shifting to the apocalyptic consequences of a German defeat and to Churchill's responsibility for the hegemony of Asiatic Bolshevism that Goebbels insisted would follow from it.[13]

The imperatives of survival and victory are sometimes claimed as reasons for a full Cabinet debate on Germany's post-war future never taking place during Churchill's time as Prime Minister. This became a matter of increasing concern for Eden once he became Foreign Secretary, although Churchill did quite often allude to the 'German question' in conversation. Despite the remark quoted at the start of this chapter, he rejected the case for another draconian peace and as early as January 1941, in response to a fiercely anti-German booklet by Sir Robert Vansittart,[14] Chief Diplomatic Adviser to the Foreign Office, he declared privately: 'I contemplate a reunited European family in which Germany will have a great place.'[15]

There were, however, times when Churchill let himself be diverted from this anxiety not to repeat the errors of 1919. At the September 1944 Quebec Conference he accepted a plan drawn up by Henry Morgenthau, the American Secretary for Trade, for the virtual post-war dismantling of Germany's industrial capacity. Morgenthau's strongly pro-British views and Roosevelt's apparent support for him made outright rejection difficult, although Churchill later claimed in his history of the war that he had been given insufficient time to study the plan's implications.[16] Other accounts attribute his initial agreement to the influence of Lord Cherwell, as Professor Lindemann had become, who was with him at Quebec and appears to have argued the dubious case for the economic advantages to Britain of a deindustrialised Germany.[17] Cordell Hull, Roosevelt's Secretary of State, intervened decisively against the Morgenthau plan and by the end of the year, Cherwell was sending memoranda to Churchill about how a revived post-war German economy would benefit Britain as well as providing a counterweight to Soviet power.[18]

At Yalta and Potsdam Churchill could do little to avert what soon became the effective partition of Germany and its loss of territory and population in the East. Yet he was always clear in his own mind that Germany, or at least its Western Zone, should be part of any movement towards closer relations politically and economically among Europe's democracies. In August 1949, speaking at Strasbourg to the new Council of Europe formed the previous year, he asked his audience rhetorically: 'Where are the Germans?', and argued against any delay over their admission. 'Given how much of his life had been dedicated to mortal combat against them,' it has been said, 'Churchill's determination to bring the Germans back into the fold so soon was an imposing monument to his magnanimity',[19] though of course the worsening Cold War was another and practical reason for him to want Germany to be accepted into the community of European democracies.

Konrad Adenauer, the wily old Rhenish patriarch who dominated post-war West German politics and was the architect of the Christian Democratic party's long ascendancy, first met Churchill at the 1948 Hague Congress of the United Europe movement. He admired him and was already encouraged by the pro-European speeches he had made but three years later, when Churchill was back in office, Adenauer already had doubts as to whether he really understood the full complexity of European politics. Churchill, he felt, was still preoccupied with a Europe of Great Powers when what was needed were more co-operative and integrated relationships. After the two elderly leaders met at Downing Street in late October 1951, Adenauer left with the impression that Churchill saw Europeans as no more than good neighbours: 'With Europe, but not in it',[20] was how he had put Britain's position. Adenauer, however, was a pragmatist, who accepted this as he did whatever mechanisms of integration were on offer, such as the Coal and Steel Community and the Council of Europe, West German membership of which Churchill, like the 1945–51 Labour Government, had at least supported.

When in 1950 René Pleven and others launched a French initiative to set up an integrated multinational European army responsible to a European Council, Adenauer was not enthusiastic, even with West German membership on offer and the support of the United States and Britain. He would have preferred some form of European coalition army including Britain, rather than the highly integrated and functionalist structure of what became known as the European Defence Community (EDC). Churchill also had his doubts, though he could understand France's reasons for wanting to control any German rearmament so soon after the war within the framework of some military equivalent to the Coal and Steel Community.

Worsening relations between the West and the Soviet Union and the outbreak of war in Korea seemed to strengthen the case for the creation of the EDC, especially in the minds both of President Truman and his advisers and the Republican administration under Eisenhower who replaced them at the start of 1953. This influenced Churchill's continued support for the Defence Community, but when it collapsed after the French National Assembly rejected it in August 1954, he tried hard to be equally fair to France and to West Germany. He had already referred in private to the EDC as a 'sludgy amalgam',[21] but in September, he set out his reactions more fully in a letter to Eisenhower:

> When I came to power again I swallowed my prejudices because I was led to believe that it was the only way in which the French could be persuaded to accept a limited German army which was my desire. I do not blame the French for rejecting the EDC but only for inventing it. Their harshness to Adenauer in wasting three years of his life and much of his power is a tragedy.[22]

The 'agonising reappraisal' of America's military commitment to Europe through NATO which Eisenhower's Secretary of State Dulles had hinted at, was averted by the patient shuttle diplomacy of Eden. With Churchill's support, he secured French agreement to West German membership of NATO provided it incorporated its forces into it fully and renounced any right to nuclear weapons. Crucial to these Paris agreements signed in May 1955 was Britain's acceptance of a permanent military role in West Germany, where it already had substantial forces.

Although West German rearmament within NATO on terms acceptable to France was very much Eden's achievement, Churchill made one very important contribution to it. This was in the form of a telegram he sent to Adenauer on 3 September 1954. He had already discussed with Eden and Cabinet colleagues how best to put to Adenauer that he must recognise that any German contribution to the West's defence 'must remain subject to limits acceptable to her partners'.[23] Eden favoured the point being put only in a very general way but Churchill went ahead with a message, urging that under any new European defence arrangements, West Germany should not seek a larger military force than that allowed for under the now defunct EDC scheme. His telegram continued:

> This might well be expressed in terms in no way derogating from the equal and honourable status of the German Federal Republic and would indeed open a new chapter, by the very fact that the decision was taken on the initiative of Germany herself. I beg you to think this over as coming from one who after so many years of strife has few stronger wishes than to see the German nation take her true place in the worldwide family of free nations.[24]

The tone and substance of Churchill's intervention over the German rearmament issue reassured Adenauer about British policy towards his country after a period which had tried his patience and caused him much alarm. The West German Chancellor had always been fearful of the major powers using German as a bargaining counter in the search for agreement to defuse the Cold War. On his October 1951 visit to London, Churchill had given him firm assurances that Britain would never negotiate about West Germany behind its back. Churchill honoured this pledge and in April 1953 in correspondence with Eisenhower, he declared: 'I am entirely with you on not letting Adenauer down. He seems to me the best German we have had for a long time.'[25]

On 11 May however, Churchill responded to the recent death of Stalin with a major speech to Parliament on the case for an early summit with the new Soviet leadership. He also stressed the need to guarantee Russian security against Germany while his government's obligations to West Germany remained.[26] Adenauer reacted with concern to the prospect of any summit without a fixed agenda and at which an ageing and ailing Churchill might be outmanoeuvred at West Germany's expense. The opposition Social Democrats, with an eye on approaching elections, used Churchill's speech as proof that any permanent West German association with the West should go on hold until there had been four power talks and real initiatives to bring about unification. Adenauer was due to visit London just days after Churchill's speech and, after talks at Downing Street, returned to Bonn with his fears allayed.[27] On 16 May, almost at the same time as Adenauer was holding a reassuring press conference with West German newspapers, a senior Foreign Office official reported to colleagues with alarm that Churchill had made it clear in conversation that he still 'had not closed his mind to the possibility of a unified and neutralised Germany'.[28]

A three-page memorandum written by Frank Roberts, who had served in the British Embassy in wartime Moscow, set out the arguments against a shift in Churchill's thinking which, he maintained, would deeply damage NATO's forward defensive strategy and undermine Adenauer and his policy of aligning his country firmly with the West.[29] The scare subsided, thanks in part to the brutal repression by the Soviet authorities of the East Berlin strikes in June 1953. In correspondence with Adenauer shortly after this, Churchill reaffirmed his support for the West's common German policy and the proposed summit meeting with the Soviet leaders did not take place.

Adenauer never held any of this against Churchill, attributing it to a decline in judgement induced by age and failing health, but he clearly felt the Eisenhower administration had been more sensitive to West Germany's position, telling his party executive in July: 'It is impossible for our relationship with the USA to be too close.'[30] When Churchill finally resigned as Prime Minister, he accepted the Charlemagne Peace Prize and flew to Aachen in May 1956 to make his acceptance speech. He delivered this on the 10th, sixteen years to the very day that he had entered Downing Street to assume overall direction of Britain's fight against Hitler. He urged Germans to be alert to any new Soviet initiatives which might ease Cold War tensions, as well as warning them against the impetuous pursuit of unification.[31] Adenauer subsequently received him in Bonn with all the ceremonial which would have been observed if he had still been Prime Minister, and nine years later, paid generous tribute to him after his death.

It thus took two brutal conflicts and the onset of the Cold War before Churchill could really conceive of German politicians and people as partners in a common cause. With France, a country he knew infinitely better, whose language he spoke with a celebrated style all his own and which he frequently visited, both as a public figure and privately, his relationship in contrast was one of lasting affection. This was deeply rooted in admiration for its culture and history, even though it had been more often at war with Britain than had Germany. It was an affinity to be sorely tested by his often turbulent dealings with Charles de Gaulle.

Churchill's first official visit to France was in 1907 when he was Under-Secretary at the Colonial Office. He was invited to attend French army exercises and, nearly forty years later, recalled his emotions as he listened to the 'Marseillaise' and watched regiments moving to their positions: 'I felt that by those valiant bayonets the rights of man had been gained and that by them these rights and also the liberties of Europe would be faithfully guarded.'[32] Heightening tensions and German truculence drew him to France's side and the years of war after 1914, it has been said, 'anchored Churchill to France's heart'[33] as he saw at first hand the bravery of its soldiers and the passion of a leader such as Clemenceau.

In the inter-war period Churchill always argued the need for Britain to understand France's fears and to co-operate with it but in the Conservative government under Baldwin, which he joined at the end of 1924, he clashed more than once with Austen Chamberlain, a Foreign Secretary who saw an alliance with France as a 'cardinal object of our policy'.[34] Churchill upset Chamberlain by moving beyond his remit as Chancellor of the Exchequer to express strong views on foreign policy as well as maintaining his own political contacts in France.[35] He opposed any unilateral British commitments to France until the major Versailles Treaty revisions could be achieved in order to reduce Franco-German tensions. 'France will come to us if we do not offer ourselves to her',[36] he told Cabinet colleague Arthur Balfour in February 1925 and in what was intended as a conciliatory memorandum to Chamberlain, he affirmed that when France had made a real peace with Germany, Britain should 'seal the bond with all her strength'.[37]

Even after Hitler came to power, Churchill did not immediately abandon his view that Britain should stay clear of treaty commitments to France but he continued to visit the country regularly, talking to French politicians and military men, and he wrote regular articles for the British press in which he explained French fears. He was not averse to exploiting a privileged relationship in order to seek to influence events in France, as when, at the height of the Czechoslovak crisis in September 1938, he urged Georges Mandel and Paul Reynaud to reconsider their resignations from the Daladier Cabinet in order to impede further appeaasement of Hitler by France.[38] By then, Churchill was arguing 'for an immediate and close military alliance with France',[39] and any suggestion to him that the strength of the French army should not be taken for granted 'nearly made him froth with rage', in Desmond Morton's recollection.[40]

The seeds of doubt about this, however, began to be planted in Churchill's mind by several visits he made to France during the first winter of the Second World War. Within the army he sensed that 'the disintegrating influences of both Communism and Fascism were at work',[41] while civilian apathy about the war and inactivity at the front had a corrosive effect on the morale of units which, in his view, would have fought far better in autumn 1939 than eight months later.[42] Not all of the French army collapsed under the Wehrmacht's 1940 onslaught and its troops, it should also be remembered, made a crucial contribution to the British Expeditionary Force's escape from Dunkirk. That was why Churchill acted decisively during the evacuation to make certain that full equality was accorded to French soldiers where places on the rescue ships were concerned.[43]

In the awful weeks of May and June 1940, Churchill's goodwill to France survived his encounters with military leaders either infirm of purpose or 'mockingly incredulous',[44] such as the aged Marshal Pétain in response to his appeals to France to fight on at the Briare meeting on 11 June 1940. This goodwill made some of those close to Churchill doubt whether he would have the heart to tell the French that no more RAF fighter squadrons would be committed to the air battle over France. They need not have done. When the moment came, he put it to the French political and military leaders that 'if we can keep command of the air over our own island – that is all I ask – we will win it all back for you'.[45] Terrible though the moment was for him, it was his way of telling an ally on the verge of collapse that Britain would fight on regardless.

Churchill's grief and indeed guilt over France's travail in May and June of that year, as well as his anxiety to keep her in the war, have been given as reasons for the extraordinary offer of a permamanent union with Britain which he made to the Reynaud Cabinet on 16 June. Charles de Gaulle, by then Under-Secretary of State for Defence, had lunch in London with Churchill that same day and it was then that Churchill made the offer known to him and authorised him to phone its content to Reynaud, who was in special session with his ministers in Bordeaux where they had taken refuge from the relentless German advance across their country. Contact was made with Reynaud at around 5 p.m. and we have a vivid account of his reaction from Major-General Sir Edward Spears, who was Churchill's liaison officer and personal representative to the French.

Spears was present when de Gaulle came on the telephone to inform Reynaud of Churchill's offer and that the British Prime Minister was waiting to speak to him. They talked for some time, then Spears recalled:

> Reynaud put the receiver down. He was transfigured with joy and my old friendship for him surged out in a wave of appreciation at his response, for he was happy with a great happiness in the belief that France would now remain in the war. This was his thought as it was ours, and in those first few moments this was all that mattered. The sense of the generosity of the offer was overwhelming, the sincerity of the gesture completely convincing.[46]

In London, the Cabinet agreed that Churchill should travel at once to Bordeaux to confer with Reynaud about how best the draft declaration of union might be implemented. A Royal Navy vessel at Southampton made ready to take the Prime Minister, but this was a journey he never made. Reynaud resigned later on the evening of 16 June, handing over power to the defeatist Marshal Pétain.

Churchill, a realist as well as a Francophile, had not been the instigator of this declaration and, as his own account makes clear, was indeed initially sceptical about it.[47] Support for it came strongly from Desmond Morton and Vansittart and on the French side from Jean Monnet and René Pleven, but Churchill was quick to see that some dramatic initiative might be needed to save Reynaud, though how real and practical substance could have been given to the 16 June declaration must remain hypothetical. Churchill's readiness to support it was, however, of a piece with his generosity of spirit to a France in dire straits and sense of Britain's share of the 1940 disaster being only a limited one. As he wrote later, 'nine tenths of the slaughter and ninety nine hundredths of the suffering had fallen upon France and upon France alone'.[48]

That after the 23 June armistice British forces might have to turn their guns on the French was a prospect that appalled Churchill once the terms agreed by Pétain became clear. The eighth article stating that all French naval vessels should come under German and Italian control forced his hand and at the War Cabinet on 3 July it was agreed that if there was no alternative, the Royal Navy would indeed attack and destroy French ships. This was done the following day after French naval commanders at Oran and Mers el Kebir had declined other options. Churchill's speech in Parliament justifying the action despite the loss of French lives it had exacted was acclaimed, but as he left the chamber he turned to Leslie Hore-Belisha, former Secretary of State for War under Chamberlain, and said simply: 'This is heartbreaking for me.'[49]

All the same it was a decision as crucial for Britain as his refusal two weeks earlier to commit any further RAF fighter squadrons to the defence of France. It has also been claimed as a vital signal to Roosevelt that, despite the defeatist reports reaching him from Joseph Kennedy, his ambassador in London, Britain would fight on.[50] De Gaulle had not been consulted and was at first shaken and angry at Churchill's action. One of its more immediate results was to reduce to a trickle recruitment to his government in exile of those French soldiers and sailors still in Britain after Dunkirk. The General changed his mind, however, and on 8 July broadcast to his compatriots in support of the British Prime Minister.[51]

By then Churchill had recognised de Gaulle as leader of the Free French in London, though their following was still minimal. This, along with the scale of France's collapse and the status which the General soon demanded as an ally, as well as a strong element of hauteur in his character, quickly contributed to a tension in his relations with Churchill which worsened as the war continued. Exacerbating this process was Roosevelt's aversion to de Gaulle as a self-promoting French imperialist, a view which Churchill had to take increasing if reluctant account of, especially once the United States joined the war.

It seems unlikely that Churchill ever said the greatest cross he had to carry in the war was the Cross of Lorraine (the Free French emblem), but he had some angry confrontations with de Gaulle. Eden, once he became Foreign Secretary in December 1940, was strongly pro-French, perhaps more so than Churchill, and believed in the importance of a liberated and rejuvenated France as an ally with whom Britain could work as a counterweight to what he feared would be the dangerous power of the Soviet Union in a post-war Europe. He worked hard to maintain and sometimes restore relations between his Prime Minister and de Gaulle, especially as Roosevelt's intransigence towards the Free French leader deepened.[52]

One early manifestation of Churchill's desire to accord de Gaulle respect as an ally was his decision in September 1940, against the advice of his service chiefs, to commit British forces in support of a Free French attempt to capture the port of Dakar in Senegal. The hope was to encourage French colonies in equatorial Africa to rally to de Gaulle but the expedition was an ill-planned fiasco. Even so, Churchill still tried to persuade his Chiefs of Staff of the merits of a further attempt to land troops at Casablanca in Morocco, where a Free French administration could be set up as a means of mobilising anti-Vichy forces. This time he let himself be warned off on military grounds, though he regretted it and wrote to Lord Halifax that he still saw the operation as being essential if he was to pursue the policy 'of aiding General de Gaulle to which we are publicly and earnestly committed'.[53]

It was, however, the territories in the Middle East mandated to France by the League of Nations which became an early cause of acute tension in Churchill's relations with de Gaulle. Pro-Vichy loyalties were particularly strong in Syria and as Britain's fortunes in the North African campaign worsened, control of airfields there became a vital issue. Churchill ordered a British campaign to prevent them being made available to the Germans by Vichyite elements in Syria. This decision was made without reference to de Gaulle who had already refused to compromise on what he perceived as French rights. The General was also excluded from any negotiations with the Vichyites after their defeat and repudiated the terms agreed with them by British commanders on the ground.

This led to a tense confrontation between Churchill and de Gaulle in September of the same year. Churchill's aides were fearful of the outcome but his approach was emollient enough to defuse the situation. He impressed upon his guest that Britain intended to respect French interests in Syria while the General denied that Free French policy was driven by suspicion of British intentions in the area. Some confidence was restored and mutual respect was already there but the encounter was a foretaste of more serious collisions.

One of these was over Madagascar in May of the following year when, again without consulting de Gaulle, a British force landed in order to remove a pro-Vichy regime. Churchill saw this as a necessary way to exclude Free French participation, which he feared might stiffen the resistance of a garrison which included many who felt hatred for compatriots they deemed disloyal to the patriarchal figure of Marshal Pétain. Frosty meetings between the two leaders followed, with Churchill once more having to assure de Gaulle that Britain had no designs on the French empire and in fact wanted to see a great and strong France emerging from the war.[54]

The new and urgent factor in the relationship by this time was the entry into the war of the United States. Roosevelt had been suspicious of de Gaulle ever since he became Free French leader and his administration was careful to maintain its diplomatic relations with Vichy. Late in 1941, for example, it assured them that the two French islands of St Pierre and Miquelon, off Newfoundland, should remain under Vichy control, only for Free French forces to seize them barely two weeks after Pearl Harbor.

Roosevelt was determined that de Gaulle's aims would have no part in the North African landings planned for November 1942. What really outraged the General, however, was Roosevelt's decision to deal directly with the pro-Vichy Admiral Darlan and to accord him wide-ranging executive powers once the Allied forces landed. Churchill was appalled, also, when American intentions became clear, but his position was weak, as he had appealed over Eisenhower's head to Roosevelt in order to secure agreement to any landings at all in North Africa. De Gaulle put his premonitions to Churchill at lunch at 10 Downing Street on 16 November: 'Imagine the incalculable consequences if France came to the conclusion that for her allies, liberation meant Darlan. You might perhaps win the war militarily but you would lose it morally and there would be only one victor in the end, Stalin.'[55]

Churchill had done his best to defend American policy in a Commons debate in secret session but was more than halfway to agreement with de Gaulle's views. The best he could do was to urge patience and caution his ally against a head-on collision with the Americans which could only damage Free French interests. Much of this tension was relieved by Darlan's timely assassination, almost certainly a British undercover operation. It has been said that Churchill 'no more needed to order the killing of Darlan than did Henry II that of Thomas à Becket'.[56]

Darlan's removal from the scene should in theory have made for easier relations, but in fact Churchill's impatience grew as de Gaulle proved unco-operative over the policy of building bridges between the Free French and the former supporters of Vichy in North Africa who had now joined the Allies. Only Eden's tact persuaded de Gaulle to go to Algeria to support the formation of a French National Committee, although he soon took effective control of it. Churchill resented this and as 1943 wore on, it took all Eden's resources to keep in being any sort of relationship with de Gaulle, 'this vain and malignant man',[57] as Churchill called him in a May telegram from Washington to Eden and Attlee. Tensions resurfaced over Gaullist intentions in Syria and Lebanon, where repressive measures were the response to nationalist parties gaining ground in new elections, but what made matters worse was the imminence of major allied landings in occupied France.

Again, de Gaulle was not made privy to the strategic planning of this operation, but Eden advised Churchill that he should at least be fully briefed before its actual launch. This led to near-disaster, with de Gaulle taking angry exception to the content of Eisenhower's invasion proclamation to occupied France because it had no reference either to him or to the Free French.[58] Churchill backed Eisenhower, taking the view that Operation Overlord's prime purpose was not to provide de Gaulle with the 'title deeds of France'.[59] By the afternoon of the actual landings, Churchill was so angry that he was talking of preventing de Gaulle landing in France, even of expelling him from Britain, yet when he heard the General's own broadcast to France to mark the landings, he was deeply affected, especially by its emotional expression of gratitude to the allied forces.

De Gaulle's fear was, of course, that the Allies, and especially the Americans, planned an occupation of his country on Italian lines, so almost as soon as he himself landed on French soil he proclaimed himself the leader of a provisional government. Roosevelt refused to recognise it and Churchill aquiesced in this until October. By then it had become an untenable policy, but even when it was finally abandoned later that month, tension between Churchill and de Gaulle remained high over what the General considered other deliberate snubs to him, such as his exclusion both from the September confer-

ence of Western leaders in Quebec and from the British Prime Minister's October visit to Moscow to meet Stalin.

Eden as always worked to redress the damage done, as did Alfred
Duff Cooper, who reopened Britain's Paris embassy after the liberation
and then prepared the ground for a 11 November visit to the city by
Churchill. This was a great public success and a highly emotional
occasion as Churchill later recalled it, but a failure from de Gaulle's
point of view. He wanted firm pledges of support for the rapid
build-up of French forces, a specific offer of a French zone of occupation of a defeated Germany and the assurance of full British respect for
French interest in the Middle East and Indo-China. 'It was evident', de
Gaulle later wrote of Churchill and Eden, 'that they considered themselves players of a game to which we ourselves were not admitted.'[60]

This was not wholly fair to Churchill and certainly unfair to the
always pro-French Eden. Churchill, in his reports to Roosevelt of that
Paris visit, was much more favourable to France's case than he ever was
to de Gaulle in person, for example urging upon him the need for a
strong post-war French army to reduce American commitments in
Europe and to ensure an effective occupation of Germany. Churchill's
position was not an easy one and his problem has been described as
'that of maintaining his own privileged position among the Allies, whilst
clearly realising that Britain would be dependent on the help of a
restored France if she were to have any hope of meeting her European
security commitments'.[61]

At bottom, the unease in Churchill's dealings with de Gaulle was a
product of exasperation compounded by real admiration for a fellow
patriot who had risked all in his country's cause, and in the last great
military crisis of the war in the West he rendered him one final service.
At the height of Von Rundstedt's Christmas offensive in the Ardennes,
Eisenhower let it be known that to contain it the Allied line might have
to be shortened, even if this meant abandoning the recently liberated
and symbolic city of Strasbourg in Alsace. De Gaulle was enraged and
predicted brutal German reprisals against a population who had
already acclaimed Free French forces.[62] Churchill arrived at Eisenhower's headquarters in time to tell of his support for de Gaulle, and
the Allanbrooke diaries credit him with persuading Eisenhower to
reverse his decision.[63] Churchill claimed in his history of the war that
de Gaulle expressed his gratitude[64] to him, but the French General
Juin, who was at de Gaulle's side in this drama, has been quoted as
denying this.[65]

Tensions between Churchill and de Gaulle continued even after both had retired from office. This was because of the former's rhetorical enthusiasm in the early post-war period for the idea of a united Europe. In September 1945, Churchill urged upon a Zurich audience the need for 'a kind of united states of Europe', citing Switzerland's success over the years in federating its culturally and linguistically diverse cantons. De Gaulle reacted by arguing that any form of European union needed Britain and France as founder members, though Churchill's speech had made no reference to this. The Frenchman's fear was, of course, that a rejuvenated Germany would dominate any sort of federal European structure. He put it to Churchill that it was premature to talk of it without real prior agreement on the long-term occupation of Germany, as well as control of its industrial resources.

Ironically, de Gaulle was later to use his power as President of France to block British attempts to join the European Common Market created by the 1957 Treaty of Rome. Churchill had retired by then and his enthusiasm for Europe, while eloquently expressed in some of his early post-war speeches, did not convert itself into any substantial policy initiatives either as his party's leader in opposition or as Prime Minister again after October 1951.

He did, however, support the post-war United Europe Movement and attended the Hague Congress in 1948 which led to the formation of the Council of Europe. He was, naturally, a guest of honour and in a major speech he alluded to European co-operation being dependent upon 'some sacrifice or merger of national sovereignty'[66] by those who supported it. When the new Council met the following year, Churchill dominated its proceedings, yet close colleagues, such as the strongly pro-European Harold Macmillan, felt that they had to press him to seize important initiatives, as with the publication of the Schuman plan in 1950 for a European Coal and Steel Community.

Macmillan saw this as a unique chance for Britain to take a leading European role and urged Churchill to give his full backing to the plan. He seemed to move towards doing this in a speech to Parliament in June 1950. This encouraged Macmillan, yet only a few weeks later and just a day after he had given more public support to the Schuman plan, Churchill told the Council of Europe how the British people would never accept that a supranational European body could have the power to close down its pits and steelworks.[67]

Macmillan was frustrated by these declarations of support for European co-operation which seemed at once to be followed by equivocations and even retreat from real British commitment. At least he was not humiliated in the way that David Maxwell-Fyfe was at the 1951 Council of Europe. This ambitious and able Scottish lawyer was appointed Home Secretary when Churchill formed his new government in October 1951 and went to the Council of Europe's Consultative Assembly the following month in order to make known to its delegates Britain's willingness in principle to join a European army. He had cleared his prepared statement with the Cabinet and duly delivered it to much acclaim, only for Eden to inform a press conference in Rome a few hours later that Churchill's government would take no part in such a project.

Maxwell-Fyfe and the Conservative delegation telegrammed Churchill begging him to act in order to save British prestige. It was to no avail, yet three years later Eden found himself having to accept the broad implications of a policy brusquely abandoned in 1951. Maxwell-Fyfe, or the Earl of Kilmuir, as he became in 1954, felt that this was behaviour calculated to close the door on any British role in the co-operative development of post-war Europe and in a bitter passage in his memoirs wrote of the later failure of attempts by the Macmillan and Wilson governments to join the Common Market as the 'payoff for our faint-heartedness and apparent duplicity in 1951–52'.[68]

It is unlikely that it was simply the process of ageing which diminished Churchill's enthusiasm for the European idea. His age did not deter him from working hard to renew the 'special relationship' with the United States or from seeking personal dialogue with the Soviet leadership. It was his priorities which had changed when he formed his second government in 1951, or perhaps they reverted to what they had always been. Eden, whom he appointed as Foreign Secretary, was lukewarm on closer ties with Europe. His two most pro-European ministers were Maxwell-Fyfe and Macmillan, but both were quickly drawn into departmental duties not directly related to Europe. Macmillan became depressed by the belief that Churchill 'had now abandoned or postponed any effort to realise his European conception',[69] and at the fact that Europe was barely discussed at Cabinet level between 1951 and 1955.

Within the Foreign Office there was no effective European lobby to influence debate among ministers. That came only a decade later, and over the crucial three years after 1953 its Permanent Secretary Sir Ivone Kirkpatrick took a pessimistic view of European initiatives, believing them to be doomed by a Franco-German enmity which he

had seen at close quarters in his pre-war career. France's rejection of
the EDC in 1954 seemed to bear out his pessimism yet within three
years of that crisis, French and German ministers had put their signatures to the Rome Treaty. Anthony Montague Browne, who was close to
Churchill as his personal secretary in his final years, believed that he
could have made a priority of the creation of a new Europe but only
with Britain as a founder and leader rather than the aspirant memebr
seeking acceptance in the 1960s and early 1970s.[70] Perhaps his conception of Europe was in reality close to that of de Gaulle's. Both
believed passionately in the nation-state but on returning to power in
1958, de Gaulle had to wed his mystical faith in France with the reality
of its membership of the Common Market.

Churchill's disinclination to lead Britain into Europe after 1951 was a
vital factor in the country's post-war history, deferring important decisions on the modernisation of both industry and industrial relations.
His commitment to active partnership with the United States as well as
with an emerging Commonwealth of Nations was always going to vie
with Europe as a policy priority. Near the end of his life, Churchill did
seem to support the need for Britain seeking entry into what had by
then become the European Economic Community, provided the best
terms were available. These terms, he made clear in a letter to his
constituency party in 1961, would, however, have to be compatible
with her wider interests outside Europe.[71] Yet the very fact that a
democratic Western Europe re-emerged in 1945 to forge new institutions and relationships to bring former enemies together, owed everything to Churchill's decision that in 1940, Britain should fight on
against Hitler whatever the risks or the cost.

7

CHURCHILL, PARTY POLITICS AND SOCIAL POLICY

In April 1908 Churchill, as the law then required, had to offer himself for re-election in his north-west Manchester constituency because he had joined the Liberal Cabinet as President of the Board of Trade. The seat had been a marginal one until the Liberal landslide two years earlier and Churchill experienced the indignity of losing it. An embarrassing absence from Parliament was averted by the prompt action of the Liberal Association in Dundee who offered to adopt him as its candidate in a forthcoming by-election. The city was a Liberal stronghold and Churchill was easily elected. His less than happy relationship with Dundee was to last for fourteen years.

As a biographer of Churchill put it in 1992, Scotland at this point in his career was 'terra incognita'[1] for him and so it was to remain, even when he embarked upon the task of writing the history of our islands and their dealings with Europe and the world beyond it. In the third volume of his *History of the English Speaking Peoples*, the 1707 Treaty of Union was accorded just one trite and simplistic paragraph; while of the Scottish highlands before the 1745 Jacobite rising, he could write: 'Living in their mountain villages like hill tribesmen, a law unto themselves, the immemorial zest for plunder and forays was still unslaked among the clans.'[2] He might have been writing of Pathans along the Khyber Pass. The only other appearance of Gaelic Scotland in this volume is after its metamorphosis into loyal and kilted cannon fodder for the Anglo-British state.

This loyalty was a theme he would return to, for example in a speech to his Dundee constituents in July 1917, when he urged them to ignore talk of a negotiated peace: 'Do not let it be said that in a struggle of this kind the Germans are able to endure hardship from which the Scottish race recoils.'[3] He had by then himself commanded a Scottish battalion on the Western Front for a short period, and when Prime Minister in June 1940, was much affected by the loss of the 51st Highland Division, survivors of which were cut off after heavy fighting at St Valéry in northern France and entered long years of captivity in German hands. 'The fate of the Highland Division was hard,' he wrote in his history of the war, 'but in after years not unavenged by those Scots who filled their places.'[4] Accusations that Churchill handpicked the division for its fate to convince a collapsing French ally and a watching America that Britain had the will to fight on in 1940 have caused anger, but have not been fully substantiated.[5]

Images of Scotland such as these could be comfortably enough accommodated within Churchill's concept of Britishness. Its aspirations to any radical recasting of its role within the Union or even to independence were another matter, yet early in his political career Churchill was receptive to the case for decentralisation of power away from London. While Home Secretary in 1911 he came out in support of the devolution of legislative authority throughout the British Isles, subject, however, to the continuation of an 'imperial' Parliament in London. Liberal Unionists such as Joseph Chamberlain had supported this formula as a way of neutralising Irish separatism, and for many Liberals it commended itself as a solution to a major anomaly in party policy, that of offering Ireland continued Westminister representation while entrusting sole responsibility for domestic Irish affairs to a Dublin Parliament.

Churchill could not see an imperial Parliament coexisting easily with an English one, and in March 1911 he submitted a paper to the Cabinet calling for the conversion of the United Kingdom into ten legislative areas to be represented in a fully federal Parliament. This was more ambitious and complex than existing Liberal policy and would have restored some real self-government to Scotland, but it was dropped in favour of the older Gladstonian formula of an Irish Home Rule Parliament in Dublin. Churchill's transfer to the Admiralty later that year drew him away from this debate in the Cabinet and in 1912 he was speaking strongly in favour of the government's bitterly contested Irish Home Rule Bill. In his Dundee constituency in September, however, he still made a case for the Bill on the grounds that it could be the basis for a British form of federalism within which Scotland and Wales could achieve their own Home Rule,[6] and he returned to this argument in speeches there during the December 1918 General Election.[7]

Liberals in Scotland had long favoured Home Rule so he was telling them what many already wanted to hear. The collapse of the Liberal vote in Scotland, exemplified by Churchill's loss of his Dundee seat in 1922, removed any pressing need for him to speak on the Scottish constitutional question and the new Scottish National Party, formed in 1934, made slow electoral headway. It did, however, win a famous by-election victory at Motherwell in April 1945 and its successful candidate, Dr Robert McIntyre, made immediate news on entering Parliament. This was because his defiance of the convention of the House by refusing sponsors from other parties to witness him taking his oath delayed Churchill's tribute to Roosevelt, who had just died.

This 'absurd incident',[8] as the diarist and socialite Harold Nicolson described it, probably did little to commend the nationalist cause to Churchill. Paul Addison, however, has written of how, five years later, he 'flirted outrageously with nationalist sentiment'[9] by telling a Scottish audience that they would be right to resist the authority of Westminster if the alternative was assimilation within a British Socialist state. By then, Conservative policy was to promise Scotland a Minister of State who would act as deputy to the Secretary of State, as well as a Royal Commission on the country's constitutional position.

Christopher Harvie may have exaggerated just a little in claiming that, to an Edinburgh audience in 1950, Churchill sounded like his father 'playing the Orange card' in Belfast in 1886.[10] His declaration on this occasion that he would 'never adopt the view that Scotland should be forced into the serdom of Socialism as a result of a vote in the House of Commons'[11] was populist rhetoric. It was rooted in no real grasp of the measured case for the restoration of a national Parliament made by the recently constituted Scottish Convention, a campaigning body which went on in 1949 and 1950 to raise nearly two million signatures in support of its stated aim.[12]

Churchill's patriotism, expressed so eloquently in some of his greatest wartime speeches and broadcasts, owed little to any real sense of Britishness as the sum of its variegated cultural parts. 'For the first but also the last time,' John Charmley has written of 1940, 'Churchill and the English people were at one. The Welsh and the Scots, not to mention the Irish, seem to have been less susceptible to his appeal which was after all to an imperial race.'[13] This, however, disregards the reality that the Empire was always called British, never simply English, and that Scots played an active part in its creation and maintenance. Churchill's unexamined sense of Anglo-Saxon Britishness did not allow sufficiently for this or for the dual and, over time, increasingly divided identity of which many Scots began to feel conscious. Political nationalism in modern Scotland was rooted in this, but Churchill had no grasp of it. As with the working class, so with Scotland: he could take a benign view of both so long as they kept to their place and were not rebellious or intemperate in their demands.

After his return to office in October 1951, Churchill made little further contribution to debate on Scottish Home Rule and any real political connection he had with Scotland had been severed in 1922 when he lost his Dundee seat. He was seriously ill with appendicits when that year's General Election campaign started and his defeat earned him the sympathy of Buckingham Palace. 'His Majesty', the King's secretary, Lord Stamfordham wrote to him, 'is very sorry about the Dundee election but of course realises how heavily handicapped you were after your severe operation. But the Scotch electorate is rather an incomprehensible body.'[14] Then, as now, London and the home counties knew little of Scottish politics. There were, in fact, good reasons for the Dundee result, and Churchill had lost what rapport he had ever had with a working-class constituency where the voters' roll was hugely enlarged by the 1918 Representation of the People Act.

Dundee was a city with stark social problems in 1922, as indeed it was when Churchill was elected to one of its two seats fourteen years earlier. Over a third of its labour force, many of them women and children of Irish descent, worked in jute mills in appalling conditions. Relations between the mill companies and increasingly unionised workers were bitter, overcrowding in tenement housing was acute and child mortality levels were among the highest in Scotland.[15] Labour already held one of the city's seats in Parliament when Churchill arrived there in 1908. As a reforming Liberal and declared friend of Ireland, his election was no more of a problem than his adoption had been. This led him for too long to assume the constituency's loyalty to him would continue but in Dundee, as in working-class localities elsewhere, political allegiances and expectations began to undergo seismic changes during and after the First World War.

The enlarged electorate created by the 1918 franchise extension did not stop Churchill holding the seat with more than 60 per cent of the vote, but the patriotic and anti-German hysteria of the 'Khaki Election' passed quickly. An increasingly militant Jute and Flax Workers' Union blamed Churchill for not using his ministerial influence to bring their working conditions and wages under the protection of the Trade

Boards he himself had created before the war, and he was criticised for not doing enough about post-war job losses in the industry. Traditionally Liberal United Irish League branches began to ask damaging questions about his membership of a government they held to be guilty of ruthless military measures in Ireland between 1919 and 1921. With the signing of the Irish Treaty in December 1921, Labour became the obvious political home for an Irish immigrant electorate who no longer had to vote Liberal. As a major authority on Dundee's history put it, by then the local Irish community was 'able to merge Labour and Irish sympathies with a fervour made pronounced for having been so long frustrated and to an effect which was bound to spell danger for Churchill'.[16]

Attacks on Churchill became ferocious as the 1922 election got under way. 'The correct thing for all Taysiders', the *Dundee Catholic Herald* advised its readers, 'is to see that this dangerous, double-dealing, oily-tongued adventurer is not given the power to do further harm.'[17] The decisive role in his defeat, however, was played by Edwin Scrymgeour, a radical prohibitionist who knew the city better than Churchill had ever tried to do. His long campaign against the drink trade reached many working-class voters as powerfully as his more general message of moral and social regeneration. Also working for him was the reality that whether or not he could admit it, Churchill was no longer the radical Liberal he had appeared to be in 1908.

For much of the campaign Churchill was a sick man and in its initial stage his wife Clementine, who had given birth only a few weeks earlier to their fourth child Mary, faced bitterly hostile audiences on his behalf. Outside one meeting a crowd spat on her, but she wrote to her husband: 'My darling, the misery here is appalling. Some of the people look absolutely starving.'[18] When Churchill's strength was sufficiently restored for him to address some meetings, he too was taken aback by the ferocity of his reception, recalling later that if he had not had to be carried to the platform, he might well have been physically attacked.

He bore the victor Scrymgeour no malice for the loss of his seat but Churchill never set foot in Dundee again. Twenty-one years later, he curtly refused the freedom of the city which the council had decided by just one vote to offer him, after an acrimonious debate. Much more recently, the question of whether Dundee should commemorate its association with him in any way at all again proved divisive. A Labour councillor gave her verdict on this to a national newspaper: 'Churchill was not popular in Dundee because of the poverty and unemployment he presided over. If he himself did not want to be honoured by Dundee in 1943, why should we do so now?'[19]

Nonetheless, the early years of Churchill's period as Member for Dundee can be set apart from the rest of his career because as a Liberal President of the Board of Trade, then Home Secretary, social policy, indeed social reform, was his greatest priority. This, then, is the time to attempt an assessment of what he achieved in that field. The cynical view will always be that as a social reformer Churchill had an eye to the main chance and that his real relish was for confrontational class politics in which he could call the bluff of militant labour as in 1926. An opposing view, voiced by Martin Gilbert, remains that, whether as Liberal or Conservative, Churchill was always a radical on social questions, 'a believer in the need for the state to take an active part, both by legislation and finance, in ensuring minimum standards of life, labour and social wellbeing for its citizens'.[20]

In the 1899 Oldham by-election which took him fresh from his exploits in South Africa into Parliament as a Conservative and Unionist, Churchill lost no time in declaring himself for social reform. He may have known little of urban problems or of Oldham's textile workers, but he had no hesitation in linking his case for it to the needs of an expansionist Britain. 'To keep our Empire we must have a free people and an educated and a well-fed people',[21] he told one election meeting, and he began to devour reports on urban poverty and degradation such as that compiled by Seebohm Rowntree. Balanced budgets and reduced public expenditure were urged by him as the best hope for the poor because they alone could gurantee an expanding economy. Even when, in 1903, he crossed the floor of the House once the Conservative commitment to Free Trade was called into question by Joseph Chamberlain, his speeches from the Liberal benches on social questions differed little in content or in their negative view of the state's role.

Beatrice Webb was dismissive of his grasp of social questions and of the role of an interventionist state in tackling them when she met him in 1904. 'I tried the "national minimum" on him but he was evidently unaware of the most elementary objections to unrestricted competition and was still in the stage of infant school economics',[22] she wrote in her diary. Yet barely two years later, as a junior minister in the new Liberal government, he was putting her case for state-funded cover against the hardships caused by sickness, unemployment and old age to be available to the whole population. This was in a Glasgow speech during which he argued that humanity would always share both individual and collective needs and that 'the whole tendency of civilisation is toward the multiplication of the collective functions of society'.[23]

Powerful intellectual currents in Edwardian Britain were putting heavy pressure on laissez-faire concepts of state power, and Churchill was adept at identifying himself with them while not yielding up his credentials as a Free-Trader. He read and listened to thinkers like Beatrice and Sydney Webb, also J. A. Hobson, whose analysis of the problem of underconsumption in mature capitalist economies and of the need for surplus capital to be redistributed by fiscal measures was beginning to influence the emergence of a 'New Liberalism' well to the left of the party leadership and intellectually more flexible than Labour. 'It was Churchill', the historian of this trend has written, 'who voiced the intellectuals' concerns most effectively and this because he had evidently taken the trouble to understand their arguments.'[24]

Churchill's speeches on these themes, spanning the period before and after he took Cabinet office in 1908 as President of the Board of Trade, came out the following year as the book *Liberalism and the Social Problem*. Hobson, in a review for the *Nation*, acclaimed it as 'the clearest, most eloquent, and most convincing exposition of the new Liberalism'.[25] The Webbs had already started to have high hopes of him, especially when he turned down the Local Government Board in favour of the Board of Trade, where there would be a more interventionist ethos among officials interested in tackling unemployment. Beatrice Webb now saw Churchill as endowed, thanks to his father's choice of a wife, perhaps, with 'the American's capacity for the quick appreciation and rapid execution of new ideas while hardly comprehending the philosophy beneath them'.[26]

Once in office, Churchill impressed the Webbs, especially Beatrice, by the energy with which he drove through the legislation needed to create Trade Boards for the protection of wages in designated 'sweated trades', as well as Labour Exchanges to help the unemployed find work. Churchill never had a universalist conception of social welfare, seeing rather the state's necessary role as being the provider of a safety net to help working-class families escape the worst effects of joblessness and low pay. Beatrice's optimism about him grew. 'He is brilliantly able', she wrote in her diary in October 1908, and went on to call him 'more than a phrasemonger I think – and he is definitely casting in his lot with [the] constructive state action.'[27]

Like others involved at this time in social policy debates, Churchill was interested in developments in Germany, and in December 1908, in

a letter to Asquith, he made what he called a 'Bismarckian' case for
National Insurance legislation, greatly extended compulsory education, a modernised Poor Law and an active state role in industry.
'Germany', he argued, 'is organised not only for war, but for peace.
We are organised for nothing except party politics.'[28] He saw his own
department as having a strategic intelligence-gathering role on movements within the labour market and protecting Britain from world
trends which could adversely affect employment.[29] This ambitious
conception of the state's part in controlling the trade cycle came to
little, but there were other issues on which he could make his presence
felt in the Cabinet.

One was the funding of increasingly interventionist social policies,
and in 1908 and 1909 he supported Lloyd George in a Cabinet battle
for reductions in army and naval expenditure in order to free funds for
other purposes. Charles Hobhouse, the Financial Secretary to the
Treasury, recorded in his diary the divisive impact Churchill was having. His introduction to the Cabinet, he wrote, 'has been followed by
the disappearance of that harmony which its members all tell me has
been its marked feature. He and Lloyd George have embarked upon a
crusade against expenditure and are fighting Asquith, Grey and Hal-
dane.'[30] Hobhouse was dubious about Churchill's motives, adding: 'I
cannot help thinking Churchill is deliberately urging Lloyd George to
ride for a fall.'[31]

Events soon belied his scepticism, for Churchill was to the fore in
support of Lloyd George when he introduced his 'People's Budget' in
1909. One of its purposes was to fund expenditure on new ships for the
Royal Navy agreed to in the Cabinet controversy of the previous year,
and it called for a tax of 20 per cent on unearned increment from land
values, increased death duties and income tax and a supertax on
exceptionally high incomes. The Conservative reaction was close to
hysteria, but few thought they would resort to the disastrous strategy
of using their Lords' majority to defeat the Budget. In the ensuing
constitutional drama, Churchill was Lloyd George's most loyal lieute-
nant. He accepted the chairmanship of the Budget League and threw
himself into the fight as if the legislation were his own, drawing upon
himself the venom of his own class as he poured scorn on the Tory
peers and what he represented in a succession of combative speeches as
their short-sighted greed and stupidity.

Amid Churchill's ridicule of the Budget's opponents there was a
more complex theme. Lloyd George's proposed new taxes, he told a

Leicester audience in September 1909, signified 'a new attitude of the state towards wealth',[32] and, he went on, the basis for taxation must be not 'How much have you got?' but 'How did you get it?'[33] Liberal policy was to differentiate clearly between profit from productive enterprise and investment and profit from the merely passive and inherited ownership of land. Legitimate profit and property rights had nothing to fear from the government, he stressed in several of his speeches, but they might not survive if a level of poverty was permitted to exist which could only lead to 'savage strife between class and class'[34] and sow 'the seeds of Imperial ruin and national decay'.[35]

The intransigence of the Lords made inevitable a General Election which, in January 1910, left the government in office though dependent upon Labour and Irish Nationalist votes in Parliament. The Lords passed the Finance Bill in late April but notice had already been served of the government's intention to reform the powers of the upper house. Churchill, as Home Secretary, was present at inter-party talks in June. These failed to reach any agreement on the constitutional question but they also overlapped with remarkable and highly secret talks in which Lloyd George took soundings from the Conservatives on their views on a coalition. This, it has been said, was Lloyd George 'seeking to leapfrog over the constitutional obstacle by making an overtly political deal, via a national government which would roll up social reform and Tariff Reform and Home Rule into one constructive package of measures'.[36] Home Rule for Ireland was the sticking point for the Conservatives who, of course, knew that House of Lords reform could only clear the way for it, and the talks foundered.

Churchill supported Lloyd George in this coalition initiative but his motives were never altogether clear. Lucy Masterman, wife of the Liberal politician Charles Masterman, confided to her diary the thought that Churchill took the view that he did in the mistaken belief that Lloyd George would offer him a position in any coalition cabinet.[37] He may, however, have been looking for some kind of compromise on the issue of the second chamber's powers, despite his fiery election rhetoric on the subject. The Prime Minister's daughter was probably closer to the mark, when she wrote many years later of Churchill's inability to commit himself totally to a party: 'Though a natural partisan he was never a party politician. In order to extend himself he needed a national, or, better still, an international setting.'[38] He was, she argued, never a natural Tory because on issues such as social reform his views could transcend his class origins but, also, 'never quite a Liberal'.[39]

She identified something that would be one of Churchill's great strengths, especially as Prime Minister after 1940, but it was also part of his political vulnerability before 1914 when Conservatives hated him as a renegade, while many Liberals could never fully accept him despite his reformist energy in office. This continued to be evident when he was for a limited period Home Secretary in 1910 and 1911. His remit was a wide one and he was active over a range of issues, reviewing many court sentences, especially those passed upon the young and the poor, and recommending reprieves of nearly half the death sentences referred to him. He lost, however, the major legislative battle upon which he embarked as Home Secretary. This was his Shops Bill, a humanely conceived attempt to regulate the crippling hours which the retail trade demanded of its workers. The most important clause, providing for a maximum sixty-hour week, was destroyed in committee, many Liberal MPs with business interests voting against it, and the Bill was in tatters when, in October 1911, Churchill left the Home Office for the Admiralty.

Much emphasis in some recent work has been given to what is represented as Churchill's preoccupation while Home Secretary with near-racist policy debates about sterilising unfit elements of the population in the longer-term interests of controlled breeding and national efficiency. One biography has gone so far as to claim that 'Churchill was one of the few politicians to take a serious interest in the subject and his views were extreme even among the small group of people interested in social eugenics.'[40] In reality, a wide body of opinion was interested in eugenics at this time and Churchill's readiness to listen to them did not make him an extremist on the subject. As Home Secretary he had to consider a response to a Royal Commission, set up by the previous government, to inquire into the 'feeble-minded'. Its report in 1908 called for designated categories of the mentally subnormal to be detained in institutions.

It was at this point that Churchill received a paper based on the American state of Indiana's already adopted policy of sterilising 'degenerates'. He read it and took part in a debate with senior Home Office officials. Insofar as Churchill showed himself sympathetic to the idea, it was on the libertarian ground that sterilisation might be preferable to the long-term incarceration of the unfit. Nothing was decided and debate continued long after he left the Home Office. Fabian Socialists such as the Webbs took a harder line than Churchill on the matter, as indeed did the birth-control campaigner Marie Stopes, whose advocacy of sterilising the unfit and subnormal is described by a biographer as being 'inspired by the simplistic notion of human perfectibility'.[41]

Another matter which has exposed Churchill to attack from biographers is his response as Home Secretary to the demands and tactics of militant Suffragettes. In the Asquith Cabinet, Churchill did initially support votes for women but in the knowledge that it was unlikely to be given much legislative priority. His support was always of a very qualified kind and needs to be seen as part of his more general reservations about mass democracy itself which, on occasions in the inter-war period, he would criticise for the opportunities it could give to demagogues intent upon becoming dictators. In 1911, in fact, he came out against an abortive bill which would have given women votes on the same basis as the existing household suffrage, but by then he had already incurred the bitter enmity of both the Women's Social and Political Union and of more moderate and constitutional campaigners. This was because he often dismissed militant tactics as irrational and hysterical and because he defended the forcible feeding of Suffragette prisoners on hunger strike, although he also used his ministerial position to ease greatly prison rules for them. Furthermore, he did himself no favours by defending what seemed to many eye-witnesses to be outrageously aggressive police methods against women who attempted a march on Parliament in November 1910.

Much more serious in the longer term for Churchill were accusations dating from this time that he had a predilection for using military force against strikes. The period before the First World War was one of mounting unrest in British industry, with some union activists influenced by syndicalist doctrine and seeking to give rank-and-file workers greater confidence in what strikes could achieve. This alarmed Churchill, as it did many others in the Liberal and Conservative parties, but not to the point where he came to see himself as an enemy of the working class itself or the Labour movement, whose 'moderate' majority he was always careful to differentiate from the militants.

It was his appointment as Home Secretary, with law enforcement responsibilities, which made him a very public target for trade union attacks. This began with the strikes in the South Wales coalfield which became widespread in the winter of 1910. Two years earlier Churchill, as a strong supporter of his government's legislation for a maximum eight-hour day in the industry, had been warmly received there when he spoke of industrial democracy and justice for miners. The Eight-Hour Act, however, was used by some coal companies as an excuse for resisting new wage demands to make up for reduced output. Strikes spread rapidly, with the Cambrian Company in the Rhondda their major target. When the local Chief Constable requested troops to support his men, Churchill was directly involved once the Home Office was informed, although William Abraham, president of the South Wales Miners' Federation and a good Liberal, begged Churchill to veto the use of soldiers.

As Home Secretary, his first preference was to hold the troops back, but as rioting accompanied the strikes he felt compelled to authorise troop movements into the Rhondda, and in particular the village of Tonypandy, where there had been a brief outbreak of looting. No fatalities resulted from this military presence. Churchill's son Randolph later wrote an account of the incident which makes no reference to soldiers actually being sent there.[42] This was part of an attempt to dismantle a version of events in which the very name 'Tonypandy' had been used by sections of the Labour movement to demonise Churchill.

Troops, in fact, remained in the area for many months, indeed, until after Churchill's departure from the Home Office, and their presence ensured the miners' defeat as well as destroying Abraham's influence in their union. In the midst of all this, the Cabinet had to decide its position on the right of unions to raise political funds from their membership, which had been declared illegal by a court in the Osborne case in 1909. Ministers had to decide whether to let unions establish such funds if members voted in favour, while letting objectors 'contract out' from paying. Churchill opposed this but lost the argument. It fell to him to introduce the resulting Bill to Parliament in late May 1911, and whatever his private reservations, he stated in his speech: 'I consider that every workman is well advised to join a trade union',[43] and much of what he said was a general defence of union rights.

Events in and near Tonypandy produced an important shift in the balance of civil and military power over the policing of strikes, with Churchill appointing an army general, Sir Neville Macready, to command both soldiers and police. This has rightly been called 'an extraordinary constitutional innovation',[44] and is clear proof of how seriously Churchill viewed the industrial unrest of this period, which continued over the following months, with him sending troops to support the police during dock and railway workers' strikes.

In doing this he cast aside the legal convention under which troops were deployed during industrial disputes only when the civil authorities asked for them. Once railway workers answered their union's call for strike action with massive support in 1911, he ordered army units to numerous strategic points, and in August soldiers shot dead two strikers near Llanelli, in South Wales, after they had tried to block the passage of a train driven by non-union workers. Prior to that, another man was killed by soldiers during strike action by dock workers in Liverpool. Labour attacked Churchill bitterly over his role and Ramsay MacDonald issued a sombre warning of where coercive force against strikers could lead: 'If capital is to command the military as the railway directors did, workmen must shoot as well as be shot. Let Mr. Churchill sow his tares; then do not let him suppose he is only to reap wheat.'[45]

Churchill was unrepentant over his actions, arguing in Parliament that the alternative was economic paralysis and, far worse, loss of life from the dislocation of essential food supplies to working-class areas. The railway strike was ended by Lloyd George's direct intervention but, according to Lucy Masterman in her biography of her husband, Churchill had telephoned his colleague to express his regret and to declare that: 'It would have been better to have gone on and given these men a good thrashing.'[46] This was Churchill at his crudest and most unthinking, reacting, as he saw it, to an insubordinate challenge by workers to his own view of a benign state ready to dispense reform in its own good time. Deciding the content and pace of reform was central to his conception of party politics before 1914, but his deepest fear was, and continued to be, of party politics becoming class politics.

The thought that his own actions could have contributed to this was not one he could have easily come to terms with, any more than he could have accepted the loss of his credibility as a patrician reformer genuinely concerned with social issues. That was gone by the end of 1911, thanks to the strikes of that year and his confrontational and often intemperate response to them. Labour could vilify him as a truculent enemy of the working class and the legend of Tonypandy assumed a political life of its own that would dog him for years to come.

When the miners went on strike again in February 1912 and then during a bitter dock strike a few months later, Asquith was careful to exclude Churchill from the Cabinet's negotiating team. By then he was at the Admiralty. He had, it is claimed in one account of his career at this time, 'jumped out of social reform as quickly as he had jumped into it'.[47] This is true in the sense that the enthusiasm with which he immersed himself in the Royal Navy's affairs diverted him away from social reform, as did the war itself after August 1914. Increasingly, too, his public speeches were taken up with a virulent anti-Socialism that overshadowed other concerns.

Nonetheless, something remained of the Churchill who had chaired the Budget League in 1909 and taken pride in his legislative work for the unemployed. Only ten days after the Armistice he wrote to Lloyd George to put the question: 'Why *should* anybody make a great fortune out of the war?'[48] and he fought hard in Cabinet for action to combat post-war unemployment and to build houses. In April 1919 he fought and lost battles for both a minimum wage and a national tax on war profits. He still had it in him to do this, even though his remit as a minister lay elsewhere. In July 1921, when he was Secretary of State for the Colonies, he gave strong support to Christopher Addison, Britain's first-ever minister to have joint responsibility for health and housing, who resigned in protest at what he perceived as Lloyd George's lack of support for his plans.[49] This was a different Churchill from the one more readily recognised by many of his Dundee constituents, but the onset of the class politics he dreaded was already eating into his support there as into the Liberal vote more widely.

The November 1922 General Election which unseated Churchill gave the Conservatives a majority of eighty-eight seats over all other parties. A year later Baldwin, who had taken over as Prime Minister from the terminally ill Andrew Bonar Law, decided to ask for a dissolution of Parliament in order to fight an election on the issue of protective import duties as the only practical answer to growing unemployment. His decision, which brought Labour to office for the first time as a minority government, allowed Churchill to return to the political arena. He stood for the last time as a Liberal in West Leicester on a programme of Free Trade and anti-Socialism but lost again to Labour.

Three months into the lifetime of the new government another opportunity came when the seat for the Abbey Division of Westminster fell vacant. With the support of the 'press lords' Beaverbrook and Rothermere, Churchill stood as an independent, hoping to mobilise Liberal and Conservative votes against the spectre of advancing Socialism. He lost by only forty-three votes to an official Conservative party candidate. Fenner Brockway, the Independent Labour Party candidate who came third, later recalled Churchill turning to him after the count to assert: 'This election has been too short. In ten days the machine has defeated ideas. Had it lasted three days longer, ideas would have triumphed and either you or I would have been elected.'[50]

The Liberal vote in this contest collapsed, but some of those close to Churchill urged him to hold back from a premature attempt to rejoin the Conservatives. By May, however, he was in Liverpool enthusing the first of a series of their party rallies with impassioned anti-Socialist rhetoric, and in September he was adopted by the safely Conservative Epping constituency as a 'Constitutionalist' candidate. The Labour government fell the next month and in the ensuing General Election, dominated by the Zinoviev letter and claims of Soviet-backed subversion in Britain, Churchill was in his element and returned to Parliament with a majority of almost 10 000. After this victory he was readmitted to membership of the Conservative party and also asked to join Baldwin's Cabinet.

The Prime Minister's decision to bring in Churchill was influenced by premonitions as to the trouble he might cause from outside the Cabinet. 'If you leave him out he will be leading a Tory rump in six months' time',[51] Austen Chamberlain had warned, but many, including Churchill, were surprised at Baldwin's offer of the Chancellorship of the Exchequer. Joy and excitement followed upon surprise when he realised he was being given the chance to make his mark in a great office of state which his father had held under Lord Salisbury.

Churchill's term of almost five years as Chancellor is still best remembered for his decision in April 1925 to take Britain back on to the Gold Standard and his role in the General Strike thirteen months later. The 'return to Gold' was not in fact an impetuous move by Churchill, but had been under consideration for some time. The world's money markets had been severely shaken by the war and legislation soon after it had suspended the Gold Standard – the fixed price at which gold traded in major currencies – for a six-year period. So the question of whether or not to end the suspension would have had to be faced by any government. Churchill listened to a wide range of opinion before accepting the traditional view of the Gold Standard as essential to stable money markets and expanding trade. This view may have been 'imbued with the rectitude of hairshirt economics',[52] but it was generally seen at the time as a way of upholding the value of Britain's currency and averting deflation.

The decision was in keeping with all the economic orthodoxies Churchill had grown up with, even though he feared that a return to gold might force up the Bank Rate, thus adversely affecting investment and exports. This was indeed what happened. He later told Lord Moran that it was his worst-ever mistake,[53] and even hostile biographers such as Clive Ponting accept that he had grave doubts about it.[54] He overcame them, however, acting upon a Bank of England and Treasury view which had far more supporters than critics at the time, with the obvious exception of Keynes.

One effect of Britain's return to Gold was to deepen the existing crisis in the coal industry. This culminated in the General Strike of May 1926, when the General Council of the Trades Union Congress called on the major unions to support the miners in a strike against wage cuts and an extension of hours demanded by the coal companies. A. J. P. Taylor would later compare the mobilisation of Kitchener's citizen army in 1914 with the way workers answered the strike call. Both, he declared, close to the time of Churchill's death,

> were acts of spontaneous generosity, without parallel in any other country. The first was whipped on by almost every organ of public opinion; the second was undertaken despite their disapproval. Such nobility deserves more than a passing tribute. The strikers asked nothing for themselves. They did not seek to challenge the government, still less to overthrow the constitution. They merely wanted the miners to have a living wage.[55]

Never in a lifetime could Churchill have ever warmed to, let alone even understood, such a justification of working-class solidarity. His role in the events of that time served simply to reinforce an image he had acquired from his response, as Home Secretary, to the strikes before 1914. Some accounts suggest he even played a Machiavellian part in drawing the TUC into a General Strike by influencing the *Daily Mail's* famous 'King and Country' editorial.[56] At a critical stage in negotiations between the Baldwin government and the TUC General Council, the wording of this editorial provoked the *Mail's* printers into strike action, which in turn led Baldwin to call off further talks. Churchill knew Thomas Marlowe, the newspaper's editor, and had been with him prior to the editorial's preparation, but it may be as likely that Churchill's constant talk of class war and imminent revolution simply steeled Baldwin's resolve to confront any challenge from the TUC well ahead of the *Mail* printers' action.

This, of course, cannot be substantiated and those close to Baldwin were never in doubt about his determination. J. C. C. Davidson, Conservative Party Chairman in 1926 and Deputy to the Chief Civil Commissioner appointed by Baldwin once the strike was called, put it very clearly in his memoirs, stressing how the Prime Minister 'took an extremely simple but very stubborn line that the General Strike was an attempt at political revolution – the destruction of the Constitution – and the perpetrators must surrender before conversations were possible'.[57] This was little different from Churchill's view and he was well suited to the task given him by Baldwin of bringing out the *British Gazette* to put the government's case, given the closure of most of the press by strike action. He applied himself to his duties with extrovert and sometimes vainglorious energy, driving the paper's hastily recruited staff relentlessly and further enraging the unions by what they saw as the one-sided hostility of its coverage.

He also made a lifelong enemy in the person of John Reith, Managing Director of the new British Broadcasting Company. For him, the General Strike came at the worst possible time, threatening his timetable for converting it into a public corporation with a Royal charter. Churchill was quick to see radio's information and propaganda potential and enraged Reith by saying of the company at a Cabinet committee on the strike that 'it was monstrous not to use such an instrument to the best advantage'.[58] Reith interpreted this as meaning a threatened takeover of radio. The General Strike was called off before this could have happened, but Reith still circulated a private memorandum to all his managers justifying the way the strike had been handled to prevent any commandeering of radio.

Right from the outset of the strike, Churchill's position was that two disputes were at issue. One was an unconstitutional challenge to the state itself, over which Baldwin could entertain no compromise. The other was the coal strike, which dragged on for many months after the TUC called off the General Strike. Where this was concerned, Churchill's view was much more flexible and even conciliatory, though at times he reverted to the language of threat and coercion. Baldwin put him in charge of negotiations with the miners' leaders and before long a colleague, Sir Archibald Steel-Maitland, the Minister of Labour, was complaining of his sympathy for the miners. 'Churchill', he told

Baldwin in a letter, 'had worked himself into the false position of supporting the miners against the owners.'[59]

This hardly accords with the Left's preferred view of Churchill's role in 1926 but in fact, when the coal companies had continued to press their case for a cut in miners' wages, Churchill's answer was that a parallel cut in their profits should be applied simultaneously. He went on to argue for a statutory minimum wage throughout the industry but by November, his frustration at not being able to bring the two sides together was palpable. He resented the Cabinet's reluctance to force the coal owners to accept a minimum wage but he blamed the Miners' Federation of Great Britain for not calling for a return to work on the basis of an interim agreement which he would underwrite. He even began to talk of ending Poor Law relief for the families of miners who rejected a settlement. This was truculent talk which he quickly retracted, but by this time hardship was driving most miners back to work.

Any version of 1926 based on the notion of Baldwin as the moderate and Churchill the uncompromising class warrior is clearly misleading. It was, after all, Baldwin who was primarily responsible for presenting to Parliament the draconian Trades Disputes Bill, with its provisions for banning sympathy strikes and replacing the process of union members 'contracting out' of the political levy to the Labour Party with 'contracting in'. Churchill supported this, yet only three years earlier he had argued for state funding of parties and written of the need 'not to hinder by want of funds the less wealthy classes in the nation from using to the full their constitutional rights and so being continuously assimilated into the British Parliamentary system'.[60]

Fiercely critical writing based on the selective use of all Churchill's most visceral and uncompromising responses to the General Strike and its aftermath, as in Ponting's biography,[61] must be weighed against other accounts. In some of these, notably Martin Gilbert's, a wholly different Churchill emerges, ready to isolate himself in Cabinet through his advocacy of an agreement covering the entire coal industry in which the owners would be compelled to make substantial concessions.[62] This was Churchill, the one-nation paternalist, talking but also the same Churchill who still saw the hand of Soviet Bolshevism behind most industrial unrest. Yet the British Communist Party was, and remained, small. The government, moreover, of which Churchill was a member, had taken care to have twelve of its leading militants arrested and imprisoned well ahead of the General Strike, thus neutralising their influence on events.

As Chancellor, Churchill supported Neville Chamberlain's increased funding for old-age and widows' pensions and his legislation to dismantle what remained of the nineteenth-century Poor Law. As unemployment grew after the return to the Gold Standard, he cast around for ways to reduce it while remaining wary of schemes such as Lloyd George's for loan-financed public works. His decision in his 1928 Budget to remove rates from agriculture and reduce them on industry by 75 per cent was one he had defended tenaciously in Cabinet as a badly needed initiative to stimulate employment. Despite his pledge of a new profits tax to recoup some of the cost and a restructuring of central government grants to local authorities, the opposition parties attacked the scheme and there was, in fact, little time for any of its benefits to work through before Baldwin's defeat in the 1929 election. Beyond that point, Churchill's priorities moved away from domestic policy though a residual pride in social reform remained with him. 'He regarded it', Paul Addison has written, 'like the Empire, as a great British achievement in which he was proud to have played a part.'[63]

This essentially retrospective and complacent view of social policy made him increasingly vulnerable to criticism as the financial crash of 1929 drove up unemployment in Britain to disastrous levels. The acute hardship and near-despair this inflicted upon working-class communities evoked the compassion and anger of writers such as George Orwell, J. B. Priestley and Edwin Muir, as well as prompting cross-party groupings of those who felt solutions had to be found. Arthur Marwick has written of how bodies such as Political and Economic Planning (PEP) and the Next Five Years Group created 'a movement towards a "middle opinion" based on public investment to create jobs, co-ordination of social services to achieve a National Minimum, location of industry in depressed areas and a major expansion of education'.[64] Harold Macmillan, who was to serve as a minister under Churchill in the Second World War and again in the 1950s, was strongly drawn to this embryonic concensus politics but Churchill, with his Indian and European preoccupations consuming all his energies, remained aloof.

The coming of war and Churchill's attainment of power at the head of an all-party coalition dramatically altered the political landscape. Full employment and a managed economy, along with the rhetoric and the reality of shared danger and sacrifice mirrored in the popular culture of wartime Britain, made it hard to ignore a growing debate on post-war social policy. Churchill, in fact, made some attempt to stay in control of this debate without involving himself in its detail, as Cabinet Office papers began to flow on every aspect of post-war policy and in 1941, his government set up an interdepartmental committee to examine social insurance and allied services. Its chairman, Sir William Beveridge, a prickly and egocentric civil servant, had wanted a major job in Ernest Bevin's empire, the Ministry of Labour, but Bevin disliked him and thought the chairmanship of the new committee would marginalise his influence. This was one of the great political miscalculations of the war, for within two years Beveridge's committee had produced a report that laid down the entire basis of Britain's Welfare State.

The Beveridge Report and the huge popular acclaim it received caught Churchill badly off balance. His own earlier credentials as a social reformer, on which he laid much store, made it impossible to reject a document which appeared to map out a comprehensive strategy for slaying the 'five giants' of want, disease, ignorance, squalor and idleness, the last Beveridge's preferred word to unemployment. His report called for the financing of social services by contributory funding rather than by Labour's formula of redistributive taxation. It made no claims that the trade cycle could be controlled to eliminate unemployment for good, and it took a patriarchal view of women's role in the labour market. Even so, by calling for practical measures of social justice such as a health service and family allowances, it seemed to many people to convert rhetoric into attainable reality and to give a fuller meaning to the concept of democracy, which they were constantly being told the war was being fought to uphold.

Churchill, in his history of the war, made little reference to the Beveridge Report, but he did quote a memorandum he circulated to the Cabinet in January 1943, warning ministers of a 'dangerous optimism'[65] which he felt might build up over the type of social legislation which could be afforded in uncertain post-war conditions. Churchill kept to this position even as a huge groundswell of opinion in support of Beveridge developed. His alarm at the likely cost of implementing Beveridge's plan was reinforced by the opinions of his Chancellor of the Exchequer, Sir Kingsley Wood, but he also had some very fundamental reservations about the principles involved. The plan aimed at a minimum standard of support for all classes, while Churchill's conception of welfare had always been a more selective one, rooted in a 'safety-net' role for the state in protecting society's casualties.

Analysis of Churchill's response to Beveridge has become part of a more general debate among historians about how far a wartime consensus on social reform took shape after 1942 or even before. Churchill's reservations about Beveridge, as Paul Addison has argued, were not inconsistent with his own record on social legislation,[66] but in public, he followed the Treasury line about the rashness of over-ambitious post-war commitments. So, too, did the new Cabinet Reconstruction Priorities Committee he set up in January 1943. The coalition Conservative vote began to suffer, however, in contested by-elections and George Orwell wrote at this time of how 'no one believes that Beveridge's plan will actually be adopted. The usual opinion is that "they" [the Government] will make a pretence of accepting the Beveridge Report and then simply let it drop.'[67]

This cynicism about the Coalition's intentions lay behind a major backbench Labour revolt when Beveridge's plan was debated in Parliament in February 1943. A total of 119 members, nearly all Labour, went into the 'no' lobby on the issue of implementation. Churchill began to take a more conciliatory tone which was reflected in a radio broadcast four weeks later. In this, he held to the case against a binding commitment to Beveridge but he did talk of a 'Four Years Plan' for social legislation after Hitler's defeat, which he made clear should incorporate extended social insurance, educational reform and a National Health Service. He has had his defenders in recent writing on the period. One of them, who was a civil servant in Churchill's Cabinet Office,[68] has argued that while still entitled to think of himself as a social reformer, he was right to insist that all likely claims upon scarce funds should be costed before major legislative commitments were adopted.

This view, of course, leaves to one side what turned out to be the fatal political implications of Churchill's caution, given the way in which the war was sharpening many people's expectation of the social justice which victory could bring with it. The May 1944 White Paper on Employment Policy went some way to match this mood, even if the instruments it proposed for maintaining a high long-term level of post-war employment were weaker than Keynesians would have wished. By then, Churchill's consuming preoccupation was with the invasion of Europe, and he only read the White Paper in summary form.

Even without the demands which running the war made upon him, Churchill would have had problems in keeping his party behind an increasingly interventionist legislative agenda. A protracted and acrimonious Whitehall debate about the best way to control post-war development of urban and rural land had gone on since 1941, with Conservatives taking an increasingly intransigent position on the right of owners to profit from their land without the state exacting a share or abridging their development rights. As far back as February 1942 Churchill had placated them by dismissing his old enemy Reith from his position as Minister of Planning. Two years later, the matter remained unresolved because property rights were at issue.

Another instance of Conservatives digging in on what they defined as private rights was in February 1943, over Ernest Bevin's Catering Wages legislation. This sought to create mechanisms to enforce minimum standards for the protection of a notoriously exploited labour force. Conservatives in Parliament treated this as unwarranted interference in an area of employment not directly related to the war effort, and Churchill was powerless to prevent over 100 of them going into the division lobbies against the Bill, which had to be carried with ministerial and Labour votes.

As the tide of war began to turn in favour of Britain and her allies, the limits of consensus over the direction of post-war social policy were beginning to show. Churchill may still have believed in the case for carefully managed post-war reform, yet he could lapse into impatient attacks on developments which disturbed his preconceptions on how far political debate should be allowed to go in wartime. In May 1942, he seriously considered using his powers to close down the *Daily Mirror* because of a cartoon which had offended him[69] and he reacted absurdly to the Army Bureau for Current Affairs promoting debate among serving soldiers on topical issues such as the Beveridge Report.[70] Although in both instances Churchill had prudent second thoughts, he had revealed his growing unease at an embattled Britain becoming an increasingly vocal and radical democracy.

It was the verdict of this democracy which Churchill knew he had to face once it was clear to him in May 1945 that Labour was not prepared to let the coalition government continue. The magnitude of the Conservative defeat in the July election, it has often been said, was as great a surprise to Churchill as it was to Labour's leadership, yet his conduct of the campaign was vigorous. He was received with popular acclamation wherever he went and put much of the emphasis of his speeches and broadcasts on how voters could safely entrust major post-war social legislation to him and his party. In coalition, he pointed out, they had already delivered Family Allowances and an ambitious Education

Act, and he offered them his vision of an enterprise-based economy and a benignly interventionist state guiding Britain into a new era of peace.

His mistake was to allow this message to be drowned by his increasingly virulent attacks on Labour and its leaders, the very men who, like Attlee, had been valued colleagues in government only a few weeks earlier. For many voters this was Churchill reverting to type and his 4 June broadcast, during which he predicted a Labour Gestapo in Britain, confirmed their fears. It was made against the advice of his wife[71] and might not have been made at all if his daughter Sarah, serving with the WAAF, had written earlier the letter she sent to him the day after the broadcast. In it, she told him of the ordinary people alongside whom she had carried out her war service and of their modest hopes for a better world. 'Socialism as practised in the war, did no-one any harm and quite a lot of people good', she stated, putting to him the question, 'cannot this common sharing and feeling of sacrifice be made to work as effectively in peace?'[72] Her fellow servicemen and women, she warned him, while rejecting any form of totalitarianism, would still vote Labour in sizeable numbers.

With the election result due to be made public on 25 July, Churchill retired to bed the night before as serenely as he had done after first taking office in 1940. Later he would recall how his confidence in the victory predicted by his party managers had ebbed away during the night and that he had awakened before dawn with real premonitions of defeat.[73] The decisive swing against the Conservatives had begun long before this. It can be measured from by-elections and early exercises in opinion polling. Tom Harrison, the founder of Mass Observation, predicted Churchill's defeat in any peacetime election as early as January 1944. Labour, without really realising it, was in a position to place itself at the head of a tide of generous progressive thinking which it had helped to shape and to which the common hopes and sacrifices of a people's war had given a decisive moral ascendancy.

It is easy to argue now that Churchill should have read the danger signals sooner, but his role as a national leader in a global conflict had made relentless demands on his stamina. If he failed to read them it was in part because he often had to delegate responsibility for Home Front policy to colleagues, often Labour ones, while he grappled with awesome decisions and struggled to maintain an equal relationship with two emerging superpowers. Perhaps too, as Paul Addison suggests, his reading of Professor Van Hayek's 1944 philippic, *The Road to*

Serfdom, with its warning of how state planning led inexorably to totalitarian rule, had led him at least for a time to believe his ill-judged Gestapo broadcast during the election.[74] The same author is almost certainly right to say that Churchill had lost touch with the political scene at home and to describe him as a leader around whom the movement for post-war reform had flowed 'like a tide cutting off an island from the shore'.[75]

The result was, of course, a bitter blow for Churchill but he never resorted to the language of some Conservatives such as Sir Henry Channon, who wrote in his diary for 28 July of how he was 'stunned and shocked by the country's treachery'.[76] For a rather late convert to Churchill's cause in 1940 these were perhaps extravagant sentiments. Two days earlier, Churchill himself had shown rather more magnanimity to the voters than he had done to some of his former Labour colleagues during the election campaign. After conceding defeat he had gone on to say, 'it only remains for me to express to the British people, for whom I have acted in these perilous years, my profound gratitude for the unflinching, unswerving support which they have given me during my task, and for the many expressions of kindness which they have shown towards their servant'.[77]

In the six opposition years which followed, Churchill's role in the gradual revival of Conservative fortunes was at best an intermittent one, certainly where the re-examination of policy was concerned. Despite growing demands for a clear party programme, he told an Edinburgh audience in 1946 that Conservative policy could be defined as: 'Liberty with security; stability combined with progress; the maintenance of religion, the Crown, and Parliamentary Government'.[78] He failed to be much more specific than this at the party conference that year and took no great interest in R. A. Butler's Industrial Charter. This document was a serious attempt to answer Labour accusations that the party was still essentially driven by uncaring laissez-faire attitudes. It committed them to full employment and the need to humanise industry rather than to nationalise it, though in fact the only pledges in the document to denationalise those industries Labour had brought into public ownership involved steel and road haulage. Churchill's preoccupations were with the international scene, but he could still land telling blows on Labour ministers, and by 1950 and 1951 his attacks on continued austerity and state bureaucracy were beginning to register with a new disaffected middle-class element of the electorate who had voted Labour five years before.

Demands from within the party persuaded Churchill to modernise its organisation and fundraising. He preferred to delegate this work to others such as Lord Woolton and Sir David Maxwell-Fyfe, but the results paid off in the closely fought General Election of February 1950 and again in October 1951, when the Conservatives returned to office, although with a smaller share of the total vote than Labour. Much has been made in some accounts of the period that followed of Churchill's physical decline and unfitness for office. It is true that he suffered and recovered from a stroke in June 1953, but for his three and a half years as Prime Minister he was well able to pace himself, delegating matters of detail while using his Parliamentary Private Secretary Christopher Soames and the Cabinet Office to keep a clear overview of policy. Hugh Massingham, the *Observer*'s political correspondent, wrote in June 1954 that: 'Sir Winston [as he had become shortly before the Coronation] seems to have acquired an ascendancy over his Cabinet that he certainly did not have during the early days of the administration.'[79]

The October 1951 election had been a bitter one, with the *Daily Mirror* vilifying Churchill as a warmonger and Labour arguing that its welfare legislation would be at risk under a change of government. Yet once in office, Churchill held spending on the National Health Service at a level similar to what it had been since its inception in 1948. In December 1951, plans to introduce charges for hospital treatment and dental care for children were rejected by the Cabinet's Economy Committee.[80] Harry Crookshank and then Iain Macleod, as Health Ministers, worked hard to show that the new Health Service was safe in their hands and Churchill supported them, though he took a more active interest in housing, seeing it as an area in which his government could outdo Labour's performance.

'Set the people free' had been an election slogan enthusiastically supported by Churchill, and a bonfire of wartime controls and regulations was carried out by his ministers. This was, however, only an acceleration of a process already started by Labour. The iron and steel industries were denationalised but a central board still exercised considerable control over the industry and road haulage was only partially transferred back to private ownership. Within a year of Churchill's return to power the press was commenting on the absence of extremist Tory policies and of how this was serving to strengthen his government's position.[81] After October 1951, he led as a moderate and demanded moderation from his colleagues.

Nowhere was this more apparent than in Churchill's handling of his government's relations with the trade unions. Unsurprisingly, given the image of intransigence towards the unions with which he was still saddled, Churchill accorded the highest priority to industrial peace. In this he succeeded. Not until 1955 did the incidence of strikes even begin to edge above the level for any single year between 1946 and 1951.[82] Those who justify the 1980s strategy of the Thatcher government, of trying to break the power of organised labour in Britain by a combination of high unemployment and punitive legislation, write of 1951–55 as a time in which trade unions were appeased regardless of the cost.

Andrew Roberts[83] and Anthony Montague Brown[84] have both taken this line, representing the emollient skills of Sir Walter Monckton, Churchill's Minister of Labour, as being central to securing short-term advantage from strikes averted and wage claims met, especially in the new public sector. Roberts has argued that the long-term needs of the economy were sacrificed and demands from Conservative constituency activists for tougher legislation on industrial relations ignored.[85] His description of a 1960s and 1970s doomsday in which shopfloor militants wrecked production as in some way a direct result of Churchill's concern to work with rather than against trade union bureaucrats in the 1950s does not hold up well to examination. For a series of complex reasons, power within trade unions did start to become localised in ways that could work to the advantage of shop stewards. In the motor industry, engineering and shipbuilding they were for a time able to apply some real pressure on both employers and unions and, indeed, to win some victories. British industry's problems of under-investment and defective management, however, pre-date all this by a long way. Churchill, after October 1951, thought he was applying the right lessons from his political lifetime when he sought accommodation with trade union leaders, whom he saw as 'a patriotic estate of the realm'.[86]

Kenneth Morgan, writing on post-war Britain, referred to the second half of the 1950s as the 'Conservative compromise'.[87] Churchill in his autumnal years would have accepted this description, for in some ways this period has a symmetrical relationship to how he began his ministerial career as a moderate reformer who feared class conflict but believed that it could be averted. Even so, there were limits to the blurring of Conservative and Labour policy differences which was soon to be incorporated in the concept of

'Butskellism' and real and harsh inequalities continued to exist in British society. Churchill's most important contribution to attacking these had been as a Liberal before 1914, and how comfortable he really felt within the Conservative Party is a question still worth posing. Part of the answer may be that he could still, until 1955, live with and lead a party that at least gave no obeisance to market forces as the panacea for all human needs and had some residue of compassion for society's losers. Margaret Thatcher, on the basis of no known acquaintanceship, liked on occasions to invoke the memory of 'Winston', but his priorities in domestic politics, whether as a Liberal or maverick Conservative, bore little relationship to hers and the regime over which she presided in the 1980s.

8

CHURCHILL AND IRELAND

Ireland featured in Churchill's very earliest recollections because his father, Lord Randolph, went there in 1876 as secretary to his own father, the Duke of Marlborough, who had been appointed Viceroy by Disraeli. His nurse, Mrs Everest, was much afraid of the Irish Republican Brotherhood, or the Fenians, as they were better known. On one occasion when the infant Churchill was having a donkey ride in the Viceregal estate in Phoenix Park, Dublin, Mrs Everest became convinced that Fenians were in the area. Her alarm must have affected the donkey because Churchill was thrown from it and suffered concussion. 'This', he wrote later, 'was my first introduction to Irish politics.'[1]

Six years later the Liberal Chief Secretary for Ireland and the Under-Secretary T. F. Burke, who had once given the young Churchill a toy drum as a present, were savagely murdered in Phoenix Park by Irish terrorists. Churchill, as a young man and throughout his political life, was well aware of how far some Irish rebels would go in their fight against British rule and for some time he adhered to the strict Union-ism of his grandfather and father. The latter, of course, became a hero of Irish Unionism and of Protestant Ulster through the fervour of his opposition to Gladstone's Home Rule legislation of 1886, only to destroy his political career by an ill-judged quarrel with Lord Salisbury, whom he served briefly as Chancellor of the Exchequer that some year. Churchill supported his father passionately and blamed the Conservat-ive leaders for his treatment.

'There are no lengths to which I would not go in opposing them if I were in the House of Commons', he wrote to his mother from India in 1897. 'I am a Liberal in all but name .... Were it not for Home Rule –

to which I will never consent – I would enter Parliament as a Liberal.'[2] Seven years later he had crossed the floor of Parliament to join the Liberals, though at a point when Home Rule as an issue was on hold. The party leadership was only too mindful of the split caused by Gladstone's conversion to Home Rule and left it well alone until 1910. Churchill was, however, beginning to distance himself from his father's position, even in the biography of him which he completed around this time. In it he actually made a tentative case for an Irish 'colonial Parliament'[3] being compatible with the country's continuing allegiance to the Crown.

Not until early 1911, however, did Churchill have to take a ministerial role in the Irish question. By then the reckless Conservative strategy of trying to block Lloyd George's radical 1909 Budget by recourse to the Lords' veto power had failed. The government survived two elections in 1910 and emerged with its Budget intact and a clear readiness to deal with the Lords' powers over legislation from the elected chamber. Asquith had already made it known that an Irish Home Rule Bill would follow once this had been done and his dependence upon Irish nationalist as well as Labour votes in the Commons made it certain that he would seek to force it through Parliament.

There was no surprise in Churchill coming out strongly for Home Rule once a Bill was presented to Parliament in 1912. He had already circulated discussion papers around the Cabinet on constitutional reform and the devolution of power away from Westminster, and as Colonial Under-Secretary between 1905 and 1908 he had supported the restoration of self-government to the defeated Boer republics in South Africa. The two constituencies he represented as a Liberal between 1906 and 1914, Manchester North-West and Dundee, had well-organised Irish nationalist communities whom he would have been foolish to antagonise. Churchill's position was that a Home Rule Parliament could be acceptable to British interests, or English interests, as Mary Bromage prefers to put it in her study of Churchill and Ireland: 'The principle from which he never wavered in his approach to the Irish question was simply what was good for England.'[4]

Privately Churchill would have preferred an Irish constitutional settlement which the Conservatives could live with, and had hopes of a federal legislative structure both to achieve that and to accommodate Irish aspirations. In the event he was unable to carry his own colleagues with him on this, and after 1911 there was little chance of compromise with a Conservative leadership ready to outbid the Ulster

Unionists in its intransigence on the Home Rule issue. Andrew Bonar Law, the new Conservative leader, deeply disliked Churchill and enraged him by attacks on the government which appeared to legitimise all-out resistance and even defiance of Parliament by Ulster Loyalists. Law's Ulster–Scottish family connections lay behind this but Churchill was quick to reply with bellicose warnings to the opposition.

Typically he resolved to take his case to Belfast itself and in February 1912 would even have spoken in the city's Ulster Hall, where his father had roused Loyalist audiences to fever pitch twenty-five years before. He accepted police advice against doing this and settled for the relative safety of the Belfast Celtic football stadium in a nationalist area off the Falls Road. Only his wife Clementine's presence saved him from having his car overturned by furious Loyalists and his effigy was publicly burnt during his visit. His Belfast speech was an eloquent one, but with a strong emphasis on how the Home Rule Bill could help reconciliation in Ireland and contribute to the unity and consolidation of the British Empire.

That same month however, Churchill also put to the Cabinet the need to consider offering Ulster's Protestant counties at least some temporary exclusion from Home Rule. In August he put this possibility in a private letter to John Redmond, the Irish Nationalist leader,[5] and in September he raised the matter in an open letter to the chairman of the Dundee Liberal Association.[6] He arrived at this position ahead of his colleagues and for different reasons from his father, for whom in 1886 the cause of Protestant Ulster was a rallying cry with which to abort any measure of Irish Home Rule. His commitment to it as a way of defusing a worsening crisis made him the key figure in 1913 and 1914 in a complex series of clandestine initiatives to bring the parties together behind a compromise.

These involved him in talks with Bonar Law at Balmoral in September 1913 and with Austen Chamberlain in November. Chamberlain was impressed by Churchill's fear of what the Ulster issue might do to the army and navy if military force was decided on and came out of their talks feeling that neither Churchill nor the government would rule out the permanent exclusion of Protestant Ulster from the jurisdiction of a Dublin Parliament.[7] Churchill's best efforts were only to be frustrated when Asquith and Bonar Law failed to come to any terms while Redmond felt unable to compromise on the principle of a fully united Ireland, but Churchill's close friend on the opposition front bench, F. E. Smith, took his championship of the Ulster cause to the point where he began to agree with the case for the exclusion of designated counties.

Eventually and belatedly, Asquith did announce in Parliament on 9 March 1914 that any Ulster county could, by a majority vote of its electors, opt out of Home Rule for a six-year period. This looked dangerously like appeasement of the open defiance of the 1912 Ulster Covenant and of a paramilitary Loyalist movement, and a calculated risk was certainly involved. Sir Edward Carson, the Unionist leader, with the full support of his Conservative allies, rejected it as a 'sentence of death with a stay of execution for six years',[8] and Bonar Law followed with threats of blocking the annual army act in the House of Lords in order to undermine the government's authority over serving soldiers.

Churchill's reaction was that this intransigence justified draconian measures: 'We now felt that we could go forward with a clear conscience and enforce the law against all who challenged it', he wrote later. 'My personal view had always been that I would never coerce Ulster to make her come under a Dublin Parliament, but I would do all that was necessary to prevent her stopping the rest of Ireland having the Parliament they desired.'[9] His immediate answer to the rejection of Asquith's 9 March compromise over Ulster was to give a stern warning at Bradford to those who would wreck Home Rule. 'There are worse things than bloodshed,'[10] he told his audience, making it clear that by this he meant any surrender to Carson and his political allies and he ended his speech with the words: 'let us go forward together and put these grave matters to the proof.'[11]

The government had no clear plans to coerce Protestant Ulster but police reports of the intentions of an increasingly formidable Ulster Volunteer force alarmed Asquith sufficiently to ask Churchill to chair a special Cabinet committee with responsibility for preparatory troop movements in Ireland. This, along with Churchill's position as First Lord of the Admiralty, gave him a critical role as rumour grew about the Ulster Loyalists' intentions. He authorised new military dispositions and ordered the navy's Fifth Battle Squadron to take station off Lamlash in Arran, no great sailing distance from Belfast Lough. Conservative and Unionist fears of an imminent operation to coerce Ulster were heightened by the disastrously handled episode known as the 'Curragh mutiny'.

Responsibility for this lay not with Churchill but with Colonel John Seely, the Secretary of State for War, who on 18 March called to the

War Office General Paget, commander at the Curragh, the army's biggest base in Ireland. Seely gave Paget an alarmist briefing on the situation and the possible role of the army but then weakly gave a promise that officers with objections to any coercion of Loyalists would be excused from carrying out any orders relating to this. A significant number of officers and serving soldiers did have such objections,[12] but Seely's action created the impression that their moment of decision was imminent. Ulster could indeed have been a crisis for army discipline and Paget made the situation worse by rashly warning his officers that operations were about to start, advising them to 'disappear' or resign their commissions if they felt unable to obey orders.

The Conservative press was quick to pounce, blaming Churchill as much as Seely. *The Times*, in a leader called 'The Plot that Failed',[13] and the *Pall Mall Gazette* accused them both of responsibility for 'a fiasco unparalleled in the history of this country'.[14] Seely's offer of resignation was refused by Asquith despite demands for it from the opposition, and Churchill angrily rejected in Parliament what he called the 'hellish insinuation'[15] that the intention had been to provoke the Ulster Volunteer Force into making the first move.

The government survived but Churchill's bellicose language, in public and in private, fed the belief of many that he saw armed action as the way to resolve the crisis. H. A. Gwynne, the editor of the *Morning Post*, quoted Sir John French, the Chief of the General Staff, reporting to him Churchill's promise that if Belfast should fight, 'his fleet would have the town in ruins in twenty-four hours'.[16] That this was never an option was clear in Asquith's response to the Curragh 'mutiny' and it was clearer still just four weeks later when on 25 April 1914 the Ulster Volunteer Force was able to unload formidable quantities of German weapons and amunition at two Ulster ports without military intervention.

Churchill's position, even in the midst of such a crisis, was not impregnable. In the winter of 1913 he had clashed bitterly with Lloyd George over his demand for increased naval estimates but found himself isolated. Asquith resented the way Churchill had dramatised the issue by taking it beyond the Cabinet. In fact Churchill misjudged the support for his position and many colleagues thought he would resign. 'Ever since our last Cabinet Ll-G [Lloyd George] has been hardening to the view that he and Churchill must part and that W. S. C. is only waiting to choose between Home Rule and the Navy before he quits a sinking ship.'[17] This was the opinion of a Cabinet diarist and junior minister, Charles Hobhouse. He also claimed that nearly all the Cabinet shared his assessment of Churchill's position.

There was now little alternative to compromise over the position of Protestant Ulster but Churchill's continuing capacity for excoriating attacks on opponents of Home Rule who made light of illegality and talked of insurrection became an impediment to it. In a tense Commons debate on 28–29 April 1914 he mocked the opposition motion on Ireland as 'a vote of censure by the criminal classes on the police'[18] and reminded them that an audience much larger than that in the chamber, comprising a restless working class at home and a disaffected element of India's population, might well draw its own conclusions from the behaviour of the 'party of law and order'. Violet Bonham Carter thought it 'one of the greatest fighting speeches of his life',[19] but Churchill ended it with the message for Carson and the Irish Unionists listening to him: 'there will be neither rebellion nor civil war unless it is of your making'. His final words were a call for compromise. He urged Carson to take 'some risk for peace'[20] and for a settlement that would 'safeguard the dignity and interest of Protestant Ulster', yet leave 'Ireland an integral unit in a federal system'.[21]

This olive branch from Churchill to ultras of the Unionist cause such as Carson did him no favours. Many Liberals and Redmond's Irish Nationalists smelt betrayal and surrender, yet his call for an eleventh-hour compromise, as well as his continued secret contacts with F. E. Smith, kept alive hopes of a settlement. In July 1914 a conference of party leaders met at Buckingham Palace in a last attempt to achieve agreement before the Home Rule Bill became law, but they had not succeeded when the European war broke out the following month. The Ulster crisis confirmed Churchill's enemies in their belief in his opportunism and reckless urge to confrontation, while Ulster Loyalists gave him little credit for his ultimate attempt to exempt them from Home Rule. They and their supporters nursed long memories. On the day of Churchill's funeral, when a minute's silence in tribute to him was observed at football grounds around Britain, it was interrupted at Easter Road Park in Edinburgh prior to a league game in which Hibernian beat Rangers. The Glasgow club's famously Protestant support included one man who called out that Churchill would have 'given Ulster to the Fenians'.[22]

War, the 1916 Easter rebellion and Britain's abortive attempt to impose conscription transformed the politics of nationalism in Ireland. When in January 1919 Churchill, as Secretary of State for War, found

himself responsible for troop deployments in Ireland, the constitutionalist Home Rule party had been swept away at elections by Sinn Fein
and the IRA was ready for a guerrilla war against British rule. It took
him a little time to grasp the full seriousness of the situation, but once
he did he was characteristically confident that the enemy could be
crushed without a full commitment of the army.

Their role, as he saw it, was to back up the Royal Irish Constabulary
(RIC), who had already been reinforced with several thousand hardened ex-soldiers who became known as the Black and Tans because,
along with army-issue khaki, they wore the black and dark green caps
and belts of the RIC. Churchill welcomed the stiffening of the police
which they represented, as indeed he did later in 1920 when a fresh
intake of former officers was added to them. They were designated
Auxiliaries and were soon vying with the Black and Tans' reputation
for brutality. For a time Churchill was ready to excuse the behaviour of
these irregular forces and was certainly doing so when in June of that
year he took the chair of the Cabinet Committee on Ireland.

Police units were in theory accountable directly to the civil power and
under the authority of the Irish Secretary in the Cabinet but as violence
increased controversy over their role began to have implications for the
army. Senior officers such as Sir Henry Wilson, Chief of the Imperial
General Staff, began to have doubts about what he called 'a semi-
military semi-police operation',[23] but it took time for Churchill to see
the political dangers of increasingly ruthless tactics against the IRA and
its real or suspected supporters. This was despite his wife's appeals to
put himself in the place of Irish people and to think again about where
draconian security measures might lead: 'It always makes me sad and
disappointed', she wrote to him in February 1920, 'when I see you
inclined to take for granted that the rough, iron-fisted "Hunnish" way
will prevail.'[24]

Churchill's view of police and military methods was not quite as
crude as she implied, but for most of 1920 he inclined to the belief
that over an extended period the Irish Republican Army could be
contained and worn down. Yet this year was a particularly bloody
one, and Wilson grew anxious over random reprisals by the crown's
forces in Ireland for which he felt the government in London must be
prepared to shoulder the full responsibility. Churchill came round
to this view and in December 1920 fully supported Lloyd George's
decision to apply martial law to a total of eight designated Irish
counties.

This was followed by the Government of Ireland Act, setting up a Parliament and administration in the North; similar provision for the rest of Ireland was ignored by Sinn Fein and the IRA leadership. Partition had become a reality and the new mini-state governed from Belfast had to struggle to keep control as mounting IRA attacks were met by brutal Loyalist reprisals against the nationalist minority. Yet as the violence worsened prior to the elections scheduled for the new Dublin and Belfast Parliaments, Churchill, who moved to the Colonial Office in February 1921, came out in support of Lloyd George's view that a truce in Ireland might be possible. This was premature and a majority of ministers on 12 May voted against it. Churchill's belief was and remained that since the crown's forces now had the upper hand in the war against the IRA there would be no weakness involved in talking to its leaders.

By July the Cabinet decided in favour of a truce and fighting in Ireland ended at noon on 11 July 1921 and nine days later a formal offer of Dominion status was made by Lloyd George and his government. Churchill played a key role in the complex manoeuvres which preceded the Anglo-Irish Conference on 11 October and was selected by Lloyd George to join him on the British delegation. For Michael Collins and the Irish negotiators the critical issue was not partition but the nature of the constitutional relationship between any Irish state and the British Empire. On this, Churchill's position was a clear one. He envisaged an honourable settlement based on Dominion status and continued Irish allegiance to the Crown, and it was his and Lloyd George's insistence on this that ultimately compelled Collins and his colleagues to sign the treaty as a necessary compromise on the longer road to full Irish freedom.

Collins understood better than Churchill ever could have done what the implications of his signature might be. Famously, and almost as soon as he had given it, he called the treaty his death warrant. Yet Churchill, who had worked closely with Collins during the negotiations, sensed something of his agony. 'In all my life,' he later wrote, 'I have never seen so much passion and suffering in restraint.'[25] Churchill's major contribution to the negotiating process had been to secure agreement with Collins on Articles Six and Seven of the treaty which allowed the Royal Navy's right to maintain strategic naval bases at Queenstown and Berehaven in the south and Lough Swilly in Donegal. For Churchill this involved no infringement of Irish sovereignty and sixteen years later his reaction was one of incomprehension and fury when a Dublin government led by men who had fought Collins over the treaty abrogated Articles Six and Seven.

The treaty had still to be steered through Parliament and Churchill took a leading part in this, facing down opposition with eloquence and tenacity and seeking to reassure Ulster Unionists who feared the Boundary Commission promised Dublin by Lloyd George would lead to unsustainable loss of territory to their fledgling state. It was during one of these debates that Churchill made his gloomy and often quoted observation about how, after the cataclysm of world war and 'as the deluge subsides and the waters fall short we see the dreary steeples of Fermanagh and Tyrone emerging once again'.[26]

Tributes from colleagues did not blind Churchill to the horror which accompanied the treaty's passage through Parliament. IRA attacks along the new border continued and spread to Belfast, where sectarian carnage reached new depths. In early March 1922 he appealed to Collins and Arthur Griffith, President of the Irish Dáil, to try to use their influence along with Ulster Unionist leaders to bring the killing under control. Collins met James Craig, the new Ulster Unionist leader, at the end of the month and they agreed on an end to IRA operations in the North as well as tougher security measures to protect the Catholic population. Even so, another 150 lives were lost in Belfast alone before the year's end. Appalled though he became by this rage to kill in the North, Churchill strove in correspondence to convince Collins of the need to coexist with Ulster Unionists: 'They are your countrymen,' he wrote to him in April, 'and require from you at least as careful and disciplined handling as you bestow on the extremists who defy you in the South.'[27]

Churchill could hardly say otherwise to Collins, for throughout the previous year's treaty negotiations he had held firm for separate treatment for Protestant Ulster. This, as has been pointed out, was implicit though perhaps not explicit in the position his father had taken against Home Rule in 1886, and 'Ulster, after years of resisting Home Rule was now owed something by Britain, as Churchill saw it, for its acceptance of a compromise.'[28] Yet he never concealed his belief that at some future point partition would become redundant and that Ireland's 'natural' unity under the Crown could be achieved.

In the immediate situation created by partition, however, Churchill's instincts were to support Northern Ireland and on 3 June 1922 he moved 1000 British troops with heavy artillery into the Pettigo-Belleek area on the County Fermanagh border. This was in response to Free

State troop movements on their side of the border and some limited IRA activity. The narrow triangle of disputed territory was precisely the sort of area that Dublin hoped might be ceded to it if the Boundary Commission began its adjudications, but Churchill's response inflamed the situation and has been described as 'disproportionate, even faintly ludicrous'.[29] Collins protested at Churchill's action and Lloyd George took a hand by warning him sternly of the risks of headlong measures. These, he stressed, could easily jeopardise the very treaty which Churchill had worked to secure. The crisis was resolved by the withdrawal of Free State forces, but Churchill's fairly typical intervention did no harm to his relations with the Ulster Unionists.

Even as this slightly melodramatic border crisis ran its course Collins, despite his concern at Churchill's handling of it, found himself drawn closer to him as the Free State and its Provisional Government came under increasing threat from the anti-Treaty IRA. Churchill consistently defended in Parliament the actions of Collins and Griffith and after the elections of June 1922 gave the pro-Treaty party a clear majority of Dáil seats, he argued that they must assert their authority, with British help if need be, against the rebels who had already seized the Four Courts building in Dublin. By the time Collins did this, shelling anti-Treaty forces into surrender, Churchill was sleeping with a loaded revolver beside him for safety, since an IRA offensive in London was rumoured and Sir Henry Wilson, former Chief of the General Staff who had become an Ulster Unionist MP, had been assassinated.

As the battle raged for the Four Courts, the Ulster Unionists were finalising plans to phase out proportional representation in local council elections in Northern Ireland. This was a clear signal to the nationalist community that state policy was to keep to a minimum their presence in local administrations. Collins was angered and alarmed when this intention became public but it was to Churchill that he turned for help. He wrote to him at some length on 9 August urging the need for the Unionist government to be overruled.[30] The power to do this was written into Article 75 of the 1920 Act creating the northern state, but Churchill did not feel able to make the case in Cabinet for what would have been a dramatic confrontation with the Unionists. Even so, the last message Collins left for Churchill before his own assassination two weeks later read: 'Tell Winston we could never have done anything without him.'[31] Churchill, in his turn, was generous in tribute to a man he came to see as a patriot with a major part to play in his country's transition to statehood.

Churchill's place in these events is difficult to disentangle from an Irish nationalist historiography which found it hard to move far from the viewpoint that the treaty and partition were integral to some Machiavellian British strategy designed to abort the dream of uniting the 'four green fields'. In reality there was as little basis for a workable and non-violent unification of Ireland after 1918 as there was for the continued existence of Yugoslavia after 1990. Yet Churchill could accommodate the view that partition would not necessarily be permanent. He said as much in public speeches, though the future for Ireland he envisaged lay in some form of association with the Crown, but in the shorter term he was ready to support an increasingly intransigent Unionist administration in Belfast with little thought for the consequences.

What also seems clear is that over the issue of the border itself Lloyd George was devious in the way he behaved to the Irish delegation in 1921. Article 12 of the treaty did state a boundary commission would have the right to alter the border and that all parties concerned would have to accept its rulings. Collins certainly left the treaty negotiations under the impression that substantial territorial concessions would in due course be made to the Free State. Churchill denied that he had ever led the Irish to believe in such an outcome[32] and four years after the treaty, in November 1925, a *Morning Post* report revealed that no more would be on offer from the Commission than a minor two-way transfer of territory intended merely to rectify the existing border. The Fine Gael government led by W. T. Cosgrave reacted with a fury born in part from fear for its own survival of the consequent crisis.

Cosgrave received no sympathy from the Baldwin government in London and was rebuffed by the Ulster Unionist leaders when he pressed for some concessions on the rights of the Catholic minority in return for abandoning Article 12. When on 1 December 1925 Churchill agreed to chair an emergency session of the Boundary Commission, whose full recommendations were not published until 1969, it was merely to lay to rest any remaining Dublin hopes of real changes to the border demarcation set out in the treaty. A sop to the Free State, though Churchill as Chancellor of the Exchequer had some initial doubts over it,[33] was British acceptance that repayment of its already agreed share of the British National Debt could be phased over a sixty-year period: Irish resentment remained and could also focus on continued land annuity payments to Britain as well as an imposed share of the costs of the post-1918 'troubles'.

The following year Churchill visited Belfast to accept an honorary degree from Queen's University and he also addressed Unionists in the Ulster Hall. He made no allusions either to his father or his own role in recent events but strongly defended Northern Ireland's constitutional status under the 1920 Act. Irish unity, if it ever came, he told his audience, could only be unity within the Empire.[34] This had been, as it remained, integral to his view of the Irish question. It lay also behind his reaction to the 1931 Statute of Westminster which enacted into law the autonomy of the British Dominions. Under it, each of them would be free to determine the nature of its constitutional association with the Crown. Churchill pointed out that this could let a republican Dáil majority unpick or repeal the 1921 treaty. 'His attitude on Ireland and his attitude on India were cut from the same cloth',[35] Mary Bromage wrote, but Churchill could influence neither the Labour Government nor the Conservative leadership with his warnings of where he believed the statute might lead.

Eamon de Valera's victory in the Dáil elections the following year shocked Churchill because of the threat it posed to what for him was the 1921 treaty's legal inviolability. The Westminster Parliament, he told Daily Mail readers, had accepted the treaty because it believed an Irishman's word was his bond. 'Michael Collins gave his life to prove that this was true',[36] he went on to argue, and in later articles and speeches he reiterated what he saw as Britain's obligations: 'We would no more allow hostile hands to be laid upon the liberties of the Protestant North than we would allow the Isle of Wight or the castles of Edinburgh or Caernarvon to fall into the hands of the Germans or the French.'[37] This, of course, was rhetoric which bore little relationship to de Valera's political skills or his aversion to giving hostages to fortune on the border question.

The relationship of the Irish Free State, or Eire as it became under de Valera's 1937 constitution, and British strategic concerns, preoccupied Churchill prior to the outbreak of war in 1939. Moreover, his appointment to the Admiralty by Chamberlain gave him every chance to keep up attacks on Irish policy which he had already been making in speeches and press articles. These were almost without exception rooted in his belief that the Irish 'treaty ports' made available to the Royal Navy under the 1921 agreement with Britain should not have been placed under Dublin's control by the Chamberlain government in

1938. Central to this view was his conviction that Irish neutrality, proclaimed by de Valera almost as soon as war was declared, had little real basis in legality.

Only days into the war he was putting it to the Cabinet that it 'should take stock of the weapons of coercion' in order to secure use of the treaty ports and urging that the Crown's law officers report on the legality of Eire's refusal to join the war. If their opinion was that Irish neutrality was illegal then Churchill argued Britain could seize the treaty ports. Chamberlain was unconvinced and little that Churchill said on the issue was grounded in any real understanding of de Valera's priorities. In fact, Chamberlain and Baldwin also took a more flexible and even benign view of de Valera than Churchill ever felt able to at this time. This owed much to the work done by Malcolm MacDonald as Dominions Secretary between 1936 and 1938. He strove patiently to interpret for the Cabinet every nuance of what de Valera said, as well as explaining the fraught political context in which his every utterance on questions like the treaty ports or partition had to be made.

MacDonald's message had been that de Valera was at heart a grad-ualist on the issue of ending Irish partition and that he genuinely believed that the real political sovereignty of his country was compat-ible with British interests in time of war. De Valera had said this in a series of speeches and articles supporting the Baldwin government's policy, later abandoned, of economic sanctions against Italy over its invasion of Abyssinia, and he had stressed that if war came his govern-ment 'would not allow their country to be made the base of attack on Great Britain'.[38] A little later, in an interview in October 1938, he talked of the possibility of an Irish alliance with Britain. Always, however, the theme of shared strategic interests was, and had to be, linked to the need for an agreed end to what de Valera saw as the historic injustice of partition.

Once in power in May 1940, Churchill was happy for MacDonald to be the principal intermediary in talks with Dublin. These took place in June and July and it has been argued that MacDonald exceeded his brief in the concessions that he offered. Within the space of one week during these talks, the British side moved from rejection of Irish unity to a promise of a 'solemn undertaking' to achieve it, not in return for Eire joining the war but merely if the Royal Navy acquired renewed access to the treaty ports. Historians concerned to represent Churchill's role as simply presiding over Britain's decline tend, surprisingly, to accord little importance to this episode. John Charmley omits any reference to it in his book, *Churchill: The End of Glory*, but Clive Ponting, in his study of 1940, does incorporate a reference to it in the chapter he entitles 'Impotence'.[39]

Churchill's reward for even considering such concessions was de Valera's rejection of his government's overtures. The Irish leader did have his reasons. The case was not a strong one for trading off his state's neutrality for the mere promise of an end to partition from a government led by someone who seemed deeply hostile to him. Also, after the fall of France, any offers from an isolated Britain could seem simply academic, and senior voices both in the Fianna Fáil Cabinet and in the Catholic church hierarchy were already talking of an imminent German victory.

Much though he resented de Valera's response to these overtures in 1940, Churchill did not give up, as sources such as the Colville diaries and his published correspondence with Roosevelt make clear. A conspicuous example of this was his famous telegram to de Valera after the Japanese attack on Pearl Harbor, declaring: 'Now is your chance. Now or never. A Nation once again. Am very ready to meet you at any time.'[40] This was a typically Churchillian flourish, right down to borrowing the title of an Irish Home Rule party anthem. He meant that Eire could now in good conscience join the war as an ally of the United States, not just Britain, but Lord Cranborne, the new Dominions Secretary, had to point out how easily this telegram might be misinterpreted in Dublin. De Valera later laconically recalled the arrival of Churchill's message: 'I concluded that it was Mr. Churchill's way of intimating "now is the chance for taking action which would ultimately lead to the unification of the country." I indicated to Sir John Maffey [the British representative in Dublin] that I did not see the thing in that light.'[41]

With America in the war Churchill's concern with the treaty ports lessened, but he still believed access to them could have helped Britain in the sea war against Germany. Whether he would really have sanctioned a military operation to retake them is very doubtful. When his personal bodyguard put this possibility to him in private conversation, Churchill's reply was: 'No, that is the very thing against which we are fighting',[42] yet he could not be indifferent to Ireland's strategic importance any more than Hitler could. As Bromage put it: 'The decisions reached in London and in Berlin were the same: not to move unless Ireland gave specific invitations to do so or until the other moved first. Only if one of the belligerents tried to take Ireland would the other do so.'[43]

Contacts of the kind Churchill's government had made with de Valera in 1940 over the issue of the treaty ports and a possible reopening of the border question alarmed and enraged Ulster Unionists. Lord Craigavon, Northern Ireland's Prime Minister, reacted to them in language stronger than any he had used in twenty years to British ministers. 'To such treachery to Loyal Ulster I will never be a party',[44] he declared in a telegram to the Cabinet. This response to even exploratory London–Dublin talks driven by Britain's assessment of its strategic needs posed questions about Unionist priorities. As Robert Fisk has interpreted it: 'Craigavon and his ageing Cabinet placed the survival of the six counties as a first priority when Nazi Germany was threatening to destroy Britain, the Crown and all that to which Northern Ireland was allegedly loyal.'[45]

A further source of tension between Churchill and the Northern Ireland government was the disagreement with them which he had inherited from Chamberlain over whether conscription should be extended to the province. His predecessor's decision not to do this, endorsed by Churchill when he became Prime Minister, was based primarily on fear of the hostility conscription would cause within the nationalist community and on how the IRA might exploit this. Voluntary enlistment, while it did make a significant contribution to British manpower, was never as great as Unionists hoped it would be, not even from the Protestant majority they represented. The traumatic slaughter of Ulstermen on the Somme and the bitter years on the dole for many survivors saw to that, but as manpower problems worsened the debate over conscription in Northern Ireland was reopened.

In late May 1941, in the aftermath of the German Blitz on an under-defended and ill-prepared Belfast, the new Unionist Prime Minister, John Andrews, and four of his ministers arrived at Downing Street to put an agreed case for conscription. Opposition to it, however, was already building up on both sides of the Irish border. The idea was denounced in bitter terms by the Catholic Primate of All Ireland and Archbishop of Armagh, Cardinal MacRory, who was fiercely anti-British, if not actually pro-German, and de Valera made his own views known to John Dulanty, Eire High Commissioner in London. He passed these on to Churchill, who erupted into an angry diatribe against de Valera and an Irish people who had lost their soul and were faithless to the memory of their gallant compatriots in the First World War. Churchill shouted Dulanty down when he tried to explain the Dublin government's sentiments but he did agree that de Valera's objections to conscription had to be put to the Cabinet.

On 27 May 1941 it was announced that there would be no call-up in Northern Ireland, but a decisive factor was the intervention of the Royal Ulster Constabulary's Inspector General, as its senior officer was then called, Lieutenant-Colonel Charles Wickham. He accompanied the Stormont ministers to London and made the point forcefully that conscription, to be accepted, would have to apply fairly to both communities. This, he argued, would be hard to do when Protestants monopolised so much well-paid work in war industries which would be likely to remain 'reserved' occupations. He also stressed the dangers of giving a political initiative to the IRA over the issue, although in fact they renewed their attacks anyway on Crown forces in Northern Ireland the following year.[46]

Despite episodes such as these, Churchill never really moved beyond taking at face value Unionist Ulster's self-image of total loyalty to Britain. Before and during the war he wrote articles and made speeches echoing his acceptance of this and in a broadcast on 13 May 1945 he contrasted the help Britain and its allies had received from Northern Ireland with the 'deadly blow' struck by Eire's refusal of access to the treaty ports. In one passage in another broadcast he declared that 'had it not been for the loyalty and friendship of Northern Ireland we should have been forced to come to close quarters with Mr. de Valera or perish for ever from the earth'.[47] The military action against Eire which this implied had indeed been considered by Britain and contingency plans for retaking the treaty ports had been prepared, although their political symbolism was always greater than their strategic value after the fall of France.[48]

Three days later the Taioseach delivered his reply to Churchill via the same medium and one of his biographers has called it 'probably the most effective speech of his long career'.[49] He explained indulgently to Irish listeners that allowances must be made for Churchill's high emotions after victory in Europe but he went on:

> Mr. Churchill makes it clear that, in certain circumstances, he would have violated our neutrality and that he would justify his action by Britain's necessity. It seems strange to me that Mr. Churchill does not see that this, if accepted, would mean that Britain's necessity would become a moral code and that when this necessity became sufficiently great, other people's rights were not to count.[50]

De Valera continued, however, by commending Churchill for resisting the temptation to violate Eire's neutrality and so avoiding an act which could only have worsened what he described as 'the already blood-stained record of relations'[51] between Britain and Ireland. The exchange underlines for us the clear limits to Churchill's understanding of Ireland. These were a product of the essentially English nature of his Britishness and of his passionately held imperial vision. For him, de Valera in power, let alone de Valera asserting Irish neutrality, was a betrayal of the 1921 treaty which he had taken a key role in negotiating as a way of keeping any new Irish state within the Empire. Although the treaty could well have led to civil war, whatever de Valera's response to it, Churchill at the time and in later retrospect held him responsible and never related to the complexity of a leader whom he only met in 1953. By then de Valera was President of Ireland and Churchill recalled it as: 'A very agreeable occasion. I like the man.'[52]

In contrast to his fraught dealings with Dublin after the war his praise for the Stormont government was unstinting, yet he never could grasp the depth and destructive venom of sectarian divisions under Unionist rule. These were barely reported by the British media and the war years did little to soften them. The implications of Stormont's decision in 1944 not to assimilate the province's local council franchise, which permitted plural and property-based voting, to that used at Westminster elections, passed him by entirely.[53] Within a couple of years of his death, this would become a central issue in a civil rights campaign which would bring down Stormont and usher in decades of violence.

9

CHURCHILL AND THE BRITISH EMPIRE

Churchill's life, it has been pointed out, spanned a period in which the British Empire reached the apex of its power and yet also went into terminal decline.[1] He was the child of a high imperial age and this shaped many of his attitudes for much of his political career. The first public speech he ever made, to the Primrose League in Bath in 1897, finished with a ringing defence of Britain's imperial mission. He dismissed those who quoted the fall of Babylon and Rome: 'Do not believe these croakers but give the lie to their dismal croaking by showing by our actions that the rigour and vitality of our race is unimpaired and that our determination is to uphold the Empire that we have inherited from our fathers as Englishmen.'[2]

Forty-five years later, at the height of the Second World War, he would tell an audience at London's Mansion House that he had 'not become the King's First Minister in order to preside over the liquidation of the British Empire',[3] and near the end of his second term as Prime Minister he told the Bermuda Conference 'what a great misfortune it was when Great Britain cast away her duties in India'.[4] His concept of empire was always an emotional one, often expressed in racially blinkered and condenscending terms, and immensely damaging to him politically when he campaigned against the National Government's Indian policy in the 1930s. Yet in a long life, apart from army service in India and relatively short periods in Africa, he seldom visited the empire he extolled, giving preference for travel and recreation to France and the United States.

Posted to India with his regiment in late 1896, Churchill cared little for the British community he found there. In his first letter home he described how he saw 'a lot of horrid Anglo-Indian women' at the races.

157

'Nasty, vulgar creatures all, looking as though they thought themselves great beauties. I fear they are a very sorry lot.'[5] Apart from his military duties and playing polo, he spent his time educating himself with books sent out by his mother. However, he regarded tribal rebellion against British rule as an offence meriting the severest retribution and he took part with both bravery and relish in punitive campaigns on the North-West Frontier. In 1898, he utilised all his contacts to become assigned to Kitchener's campaign to reoccupy the Sudan in which, as in India, he created some friction in the army by combining the roles of combatant and press correspondent.

His eyewitness accounts still make compelling reading, and are also fiercely critical of the brutalities Kitchener sanctioned and of his wanton desecration of the tomb of the Mahdi, the religious leader of the defeated Islamic Dervish rebels. He was outraged, also, by events after the destruction by hugely superior British firepower of the rebel army. 'I shall merely say', he wrote to his mother, 'that the victory of Omdurman was disgraced by the inhuman slaughter of the wounded and that Kitchener was responsible for this.'[6] A new colonial crisis in South Africa made war imminent in the following year and Churchill was quick to get himself accredited by the *Daily Mail* to cover the fighting there.

His South African exploits as reporter, participant in some major military action, and prison escape earned him immediate celebrity status as well as a seat in Parliament representing Oldham in the July 1900 General Election. The Empire and the self-promotion which it, along with his own energy and courage, had made possible, had got him there and his belief in it as integral to British destiny had been confirmed by his experiences. He was not, however, attracted to Joseph Chamberlain's espousal of the cause of tariff reform as a way to create preferential trading relationships within the Empire, arguing that the bonds of empire could never be merely secular and commercial. This 'greedy gospel of materialism and expediency'[7] – as he called it in a speech in 1904 – could never be a substitute for the shared loyalties which had created and sustained the Empire, and his rejection of it was a major factor in his decision in May of that year to cross the floor of the House of Commons to the Liberal benches.

As cynics pointed out, the move was a timely one, as the Conservative government's divisions deepened, its authority crumbled and the Liberals' landslide victory in the January 1906 General Election carried him back into the House as their Member for north-west Manchester.

The opportunity to apply himself to imperial issues followed when the new government offered him the position of Parliamentary Under-Secretary for the Colonies. Churchill accepted with alacrity, perhaps not uninfluenced by the knowledge that his role in the Commons would be a major one since the Colonial Secretary was a peer, Lord Elgin, who also spent much time in Scotland with his ailing wife.

The major issue facing the Colonial Office in 1906 was South Africa's constitutional future. Well before the end of the Boer War, Churchill had been urging from the Conservative back benches the case for a peace based on reconciliation as the best way to secure long-term British interests. His early memorandum to Lord Elgin has been called 'a classic statement of the primary principle of political conduct of the Victorian and Edwardian ruling élite, the principle of timely concession to retain an ultimate control',[8] and Churchill indeed supported the case for a generous European franchise in the Transvaal in the mistaken belief that this would maximise representation of the English-speaking community. He spoke eloquently in Parliament on 31 July, prior to the vote which carried the Transvaal constitutional proposals, calling upon Conservative support by declaring that 'with all our majority we can only make it the gift of a Party; they can make it the gift of England'.[9]

The Orange River colony was also given responsible self-government but a 'gift relationship' between Britain and the Boers, while preparing the ground for the creation of the Union of South Africa in 1910, ignored the black African majority. Churchill's perception of a racial issue in South Africa was limited to Boer and British suspicions and the need to allay these. In one speech to Parliament early in 1906 he did speak of a 'black peril' in South Africa and described it as 'the one bond of union between the European races who live in the country, the one possibility of making them forget the bitter and senseless feuds that have so long prevailed'.[10] Talk like this, invoking the concept of equal rights for 'civilised' men, was common to political discourse in this period and even Socialist members of the House such as Keir Hardie were not absolute in their commitment to racial equality by today's standards.[11] All the same, there is irony in Churchill's role in creating a state that would later apply apartheid for decades, for a young Nelson Mandela greatly admired his wartime broadcasts from London.[12]

On the issue of Chinese labour imported into South Africa by the gold and diamond mining companies with the agreement of the former High Commissioner, Lord Milner, it fell to Churchill, as Parliamentary

Under-Secretary, to make the caase for phasing out a scheme which had been a brutal measure by the 'Randlords' to meet a labour crisis and which was a prelude to their worse exploitation of African workers.[13] 'Chinese slavery' had been an accusation made from many Liberal platforms during the General Election and Churchill told the House on 14 March that Milner, in allowing flogging in the Chinese compounds, had committed 'a gross dereliction of public duty and at the same time an undoubted infringement of the law'.[14] This enraged Opposition members, but a week later he outraged them by declaring that a discredited Milner should be ostracised by the House.[15] King Edward VII was driven to write to the Prince of Wales that Churchill was 'almost more of a cad in office than he was in opposition'.

In the autumn of 1907, Churchill set off on what turned out to be his last extended visit to Africa. It purported initially to be a private and sporting expedition through Uganda and up the Nile to Khartoum but became almost an official event, as Lord Elgin received a succession of memoranda and letters on African policy from his junior minister. Some of these were incorporated in a book, *My African Journey*, which also recorded big-game-hunting exploits over a four-month period. In it, he had much to say about the area's potential for economic development. His imperialism was a blend of romanticism and a perception of British self-interest and Wilfred Scawen Blunt, after meeting him in 1909, wrote that Churchill was 'championing an optimistic Liberal Imperialism whereby the British Empire was to be maintained, in part by concession, in part by force'.[16] By then, Churchill had left the Colonial Office, only returning in 1921 as Secretary of State after a peace settlement which had added substantially to its responsibilities.

The potential for development in Britain's African colonies was a major preoccupation, as indeed it had been in 1906 and 1907, and he worked hard to divert to them expenditure from what he saw as new commitments in the Middle East which were likely to be more costly than productive. Persuading the Cabinet of this proved beyond him, but in a Commons debate in July 1921 he drew a distinction between 'tractable and promising' African territories and a Middle East 'unduly stocked with peppery, pugnacious, proud politicians and theologians, who happen to be at the same time extremely well armed and extremely hard up'.[17] Whatever his reservations about the Arab states, Britain's post-war relations with them consumed much of his energy as, too, did its new responsibilities to administer Palestine and

Iraq (Mesopotamia) as territories 'mandated' to it by the League of Nations.

For several months after going to the Colonial Office, Churchill retained his responsibility for the new Royal Air Force (RAF) and quickly identified its importance in an 'air policing' role over Iraq, as post-war expenditure cuts began to bite into the budget needed for troops on the ground. Air power was a blunt instrument to use against simple desert and mountain tribes with few means of defence against it and Churchill became strongly critical of the way it was used, though he also for a time argued the dubious case for gas attacks to reduce loss of life on the ground. When, during 1921, he learned of aircraft continuing to fire on village people who had taken refuge in a lake from one punitive operation by the RAF, he was enraged enough to protest to Sir Hugh Trenchard, Chief of the Air Staff, declaring that: 'To fire wilfully on women and children taking refuge in a lake is a disgraceful act and I am surprised you do not order the officers responsible to be tried by court martial...by doing such things, we put ourselves on the lowest level.'[18]

Iraq and the new kingdom of Transjordan were converted into no more than British client states at a major Cairo conference over which Churchill presided, in March and April that year. Transjordan was created by what amounted to a partitioning of the territory of the proposed Jewish National Home in Palestine. This, in Churchill's view, was a safer way of securing British interests in the Middle East than assuming strategic advantage from a Jewish state. For the next twenty years the British were able, largely unimpeded, to impose and depose regimes in the area, install garrisons, crush rebellions and extract major oil concessions.

Zionism was a cause which Churchill had supported for many years and he believed that the 1917 Balfour Declaration in favour of a Jewish 'National Home' in Palestine must be honoured. He was, however, fearful of being drawn into the complex problems of administering Palestine, although the Declaration imposed no obligation on Britain to do so. Fortunately for him, Churchill was able to rely heavily upon Sir John Shuckburgh, Assistant Under-Secretary of State at the Colonial Office, who drafted a White Paper which in June 1922 set out a British view of Palestine's future. This stressed that not all of it would become a Jewish state, that Jewish settlement would not exceed the country's capacity for assimilation and that there would be no subordination of Arabs and their culture. It was still a bold document, given the level of anti-Zionism within both the Colonial Office and the Foreign Office. Churchill's commitment to the 'National Home' was genuine and remained so.

In Kenya, too, decisions of long-term importance had to be made and Churchill was concerned that it should achieve responsible self-government in due course. He was, however, less critical of the European settler community there than he had been fifteen years previously. Failure to persuade them to agree to a common electoral register with the colony's Indian population exposed Churchill to the charge of applying insufficient pressure to the settlers. African majority rights did not loom large in the arguments between him and his principal Cabinet critic Edwin Montagu, Secretary of State for India, who felt that Churchill was not consulting colleagues sufficiently about Kenya and that the India Office had a responsibility for people whose migration to East Africa it had earlier supported.

Indian affairs had in fact demanded Churchill's attention during his period as Secretary of State for War in July 1920. This concerned his support for the decision to censure General Richard Dyer for his action the previous year, when he ordered troops to fire upon an unarmed demonstration in Amritsar, resulting in almost 400 people being killed. Dyer had his defenders in the army and on the Conservative benches in the House of Lords and Montagu raised the temperature by the tone of his speech about Dyer's future in the Commons. Churchill followed him, taking the firm line that the War Office should refuse the General further employment and stressing that the Army Council was unanimously in favour of this. His measured case calmed the House, but the debate gave him a chance to set out his wider view of Britain's role in India.

Dyer's action, he argued, was fundamentally at odds with the historic legitimacy of British rule:

> Governments who have seized upon power by violence and by usurpation have often resorted to terrorism in their desperate efforts to keep what they have stolen but the august and memorable structure of the British Empire where lawful authority descends from hand to hand and generation after generation, does not need such aid. Such ideas are absolutely foreign to the British way of doing things.[19]

Churchill was talking not of repression but of how power, humanely exercised and in furtherance of agreed interests, could find wide acceptance. This power was now under challenge from Gandhi's Congress movement while in Britain itself, there was no longer unanimity on the future of the Raj. For Churchill there seemed no case for concessions to Indian nationalism, a conviction which was to consume much of his energy and eloquence in the inter-war period.

The paradox of what became such an obsession for Churchill lies in just how little interest he had taken in the subcontinent since his army service there. Prior to the crisis over the 1935 Government of India Bill, he had not revisited the country, and he never did. Yet he was ready to repudiate his party leadership and risk his own political isolation over his opposition to National Government policy. Clearly he was influenced by his great friend F. E. Smith, Lord Birkenhead, who as Secretary of State for India between 1924 and 1928 opposed almost all reform there and had a deep contempt for Indian nationalism, but the bitter confrontation which he led in 1935 stretched back to the Montagu–Chelmsford reforms of 1917–19. These conceded India some nominal measure of self-government but not enough to satisfy Gandhi's increasingly confident and militant Congress movement. Under the 1919 Act which put this reform package into effect, a Commission on its operation had to be set up within ten years. Birkenhead pressed ahead with this through fear of what another Labour government might do but also acquiesced in the appointment of a new Viceroy, Lord Irwin, later Lord Halifax.

This proved to be vital, because Irwin believed that a major conference was needed in order for Britain to concede that Dominion status had been an implicit part of the wartime reform proposals, and the Labour government in 1929 agreed to a declaration incorporating his assessment of what should be done. Baldwin, after initial uncertainty, came round to a position close to that of the Viceroy and the government. This was intolerable to Churchill, who rapidly emerged as an uncompromising opponent of any policy based on Dominion status. In January 1931, he resigned from the Opposition's front bench in protest at the Viceroy's decision to release Gandhi and other Congress leaders from prison so that they could take part in negotiations on constitutional change. Prior to this, he had sought in Parliament to rally support for 'British rights and British interests in India, and for two centuries of effort and achievement, lives given on a hundred fields, far more lives given and consumed in faithful and devoted service to the Indian people themselves.'[20]

Churchill's language became increasingly intemperate and suffused with disdain for the capacity of Indians to operate any form of self-government and he reserved some of his most virulent abuse for the Congress leadership. In February he told an Essex Conservative audience that he found it 'alarming and also distasteful to see Mr. Gandhi, a seditious Middle Temple lawyer, now posing as a fakir of a type well-known in the East, striding half-naked up the steps of the Viceregal Palace, while he is still organising and conducting a defiant campaign of civil disobedience, to parley on equal terms with the representative of the King-Emperor'.[21] That a Conservative-dominated National Government, after its overwhelming victory in the October 1931 General Election, could even consider moves to set up an Indian legislative body appalled him and his attacks were directed increasingly upon the new Secretary of State for India, Sir Samuel Hoare. Sometimes these attacks seemed to be part of growing doubts in Churchill's mind about the shortcomings of representative democracy itself. 'Why', he asked in October 1932, 'at this moment should we force upon the untutored races of India that very system?'[22]

These broodings were a mood which passed as Hitler's brutalities in Germany made democracy's virtues more apparent but privately, Hoare ascribed extravagantly sinister motives to Churchill: 'at the back of his mind he thinks that not only will he smash the Government but that England is going Fascist and that he, or someone like him, will eventually be able to rule India as Mussolini governs North Africa'.[23] Churchill's concern was to block government legislation and his chance came in the 1934–35 session of Parliament when Hoare presented his Government of India Bill, a hugely complex measure designed to set up an all-India federation with its own bicameral legislative body which would bring together the provinces and the princely states. Churchill's opposition to it was to be one of the most protracted and impassioned performances of his career.

A nucleus of around sixty Conservative backbenchers supported him, but as it became clear that all-party support for the Bill in Parliament was likely to carry it, Churchill turned increasingly to the party's constituency activists. Something of their demeanour was captured by the Parliamentary Under-Secretary at the India Office, R. A. Butler. Writing to the Governor of Bombay state, he described a recent encounter with them: 'At our last party conference the audience would have been a credit to the zoo or wild regions of the globe. No ray of enlightenment shone on a single face.'[24] Such zealots became

Churchill's allies in bodies such as the India Defence League, rallying to his accusations that Hoare and Baldwin had become the captives of an insidious Socialist agenda on India.

Many of Churchill's speeches on India were acknowledged by those who heard them as brilliant in style and delivery, though some observers thought he was carried along and mesmerised by his own eloquence. His case ranged across the communal anarchy which moves to self-government would unleash as Hindus began to exploit their majority power. He also invoked the likely ruination of Lancashire's export trade in cheap cotton goods. However, it was the threat to Britain's strategic interests and to the whole imperial structure, if its Indian keystone was removed, that drew out some of his most powerful oratory. The image of India as the jewel in the imperial crown, which he used in a speech to the Indian Empire Society four years earlier,[25] was never far from the more detailed arguments he sought to deploy against the Bill's many clauses and schedules.

It is questionable whether Churchill fully grasped the intentions of the 1935 Bill. He certainly seems to have misunderstood how, in the federation to be created by it, India's most conservative element, the princes and maharajahs, would have representation in the proposed legislative assembly large enough for them to act as a real counterweight to Gandhi's Congress. Once the Bill became law, however, they were quick to back away from the co-operation they had initially pledged, their doubts reinforced by Churchill's impassioned rhetoric. Thus, by the time war came in 1939, the subcontinent's future relationship to Britain was still unresolved.

It is difficult to dispute Butler's view that Churchill's campaign against the 1935 Act was 'a misfortune for Indian constitutional development and a tragedy in Churchill's own career'.[26] It was definitely the latter insofar as his break with Baldwin in January 1931 excluded him both from office and influence upon policy as the situation in Europe deteriorated and rapid British rearmament became a matter of urgency. Potential allies from the Conservative party's reformist and socially progressive wing, who came to agree with his foreign policy views, were alienated by the language with which he opposed even gradual moves to Indian self-government.

After Churchill took office in 1940, the Viceroy Lord Linlithgow and Leo Amery, the new Secretary of State for India, spent many months preparing a declaration which promised an expansion of the Viceroy's Executive Council to permit Indian representation, as well as

Dominion status, within a year of the war's end. Even though it seemed a long way off at this stage, Churchill was quick to veto the scheme, thus greatly contributing to the problems of Britain's representatives whose remit it was to maximise India's part in the war effort.

This negative posture was called into question when America entered the war. Roosevelt lost little time in putting the need to Churchill for new constitutional initiatives in India, modelled on American federal experience. This, the President argued, would be 'strictly in line with the world changes of the past half century and with the democratic processes of all who are fighting Nazism'.[27] Churchill's dismissive response is echoed in the fourth volume of his war history: 'This document [Roosevelt's communication on India] is of high interest because it illustrates the difficulties of comparing situations in various countries and scenes where almost every material fact is different, and the dangers of trying to apply any superficial resemblances which may be noticed to the conduct of war.'[28]

As 1942 wore on, Roosevelt became concerned with the importance of some special act to mark the Atlantic Charter's first anniversary. The implications of its third article, stressing the right of all subject peoples to self-determination, had not been lost upon Churchill when he signed the Charter,[29] and he remained wary of them where India was concerned. In August, when the President called for a special message based upon the Charter to be issued by the Allies, Churchill's response was guarded, warning him that the third article, if given undue emphasis, could cause 'grave embarrassment' to the defence of India.[30]

Reckless experimentation in the government of India, Churchill argued in further correspondence with Roosevelt, would endanger communal relations, thereby alarming Muslims with the prospect of Hindu majority rule. It would also, he claimed, undermine the morale of the Indian army by alienating the martial races, though he tended to overstate the proportion of soldiers who were Muslims. A million volunteers who had enlisted since 1939 were, he pointed out, loyal to their King-Emperor and fearful for their future in a self-governing state. In reality, the morale and political allegiances of Indian soldiers were a much more complex matter than he chose to recognise.[31]

By this time, American pressure pointed to the need for more flexibility on Indian policy, as did the dramatic advance of Japanese forces to India's Burmese border. Churchill accepted the proposals of the Cabinet's India Committee, chaired by Attlee, that in return for full co-operation in the war, an offer of independence to India would follow. Sir Stafford Cripps was sent there on a mission which Churchill hoped would fail.[32] Congress wanted more than Cripps could offer, and in response he told a press conference on 19 March that it might be possible to convert the Viceroy's Council into a Cabinet in which he could be overruled by Indian representatives. This antagonised Lord Linlithgow and played into Churchill's hands: he wanted to isolate Cripps by letting it seem to the Cabinet that he had exceeded his authority while in India. His telegram to Linlithgow stated that there could be no question of any convention limiting the Viceroy's powers.

This was the end of Cripps's role in India, though his popular standing in Britain remained high, but it also led directly to Gandhi's launching of the 'Quit India' campaign in August 1942. The militancy of this movement was the biggest challenge to British rule since the 1857 Mutiny and led to the arrest of Gandhi and thousands of his followers, which Churchill had always wanted. It also gave new momentum to Mohammed Ali Jinnah's Muslim League, whose activists the Viceroy wanted to form administrations in provinces where they had support, thus preparing the way for partition in 1947, an outcome Churchill certainly had not intended to bring about.

Gandhi's arrest and hunger strike in 1943 brought out an intransigent and ungenerous response from Churchill. He telegraphed to Halifax at the Washington embassy, telling him to make it clear to his contacts that British policy in India would not be influenced or diverted by the Mahatma's fast.[33] When this reached its sixteenth day, he sent a further telegram, this time to Smuts, the South African Prime Minister, disputing that Gandhi intended to take his fast to the point of death. 'What fools we should have been to flinch before all this bluff and sob-stuff', he wrote. 'It now seems almost certain that the old rascal will emerge all the better from his so-called fast.'[34]

There was no conception on Churchill's part of Gandhi's charisma and the powerful symbolism both of his incarceration and his prison fasts, but the Viceroy he appointed as Lord Linlithgow's successor that June was far more conversant with Indian politics and much more liberal than Churchill in his outlook. This was Field Marshal Wavell, as he had become after his dismissal by Churchill from his command in the Middle East. Since then he had served in India both as Commander-in-Chief and, for a time, with responsibility for the South-East Asian theatre. Churchill's motives in choosing him were not lost upon Wavell, and he later wrote: 'I am pretty sure that when he appointed me as Viceroy it was with the intention and expectation that I should simply keep things quiet in India till the war was over.'[35] Probably no Viceroy could have done this in 1943, but Wavell had views of his own. He argued as a practical soldier that Britain no longer had the resources or the will to rule India against its people's wishes. If independence was the only option then his instincts were to arrange the transition honourably by means which would leave the country united and an ally of Britain.

Churchill's attitudes drove Wavell close to despair. 'He has a curious complex about India and is always loath to hear good of it and appears to believe the worst. He has still at heart the cavalry subaltern's idea of India.'[36] He had an uphill task convincing Churchill that Gandhi's fast was anything other than a fraud and was shaken by Churchill's apparent conviction, at least for a time, that measures to relieve the terrible Bengal famine of 1943–44 might be seen as appeasement of the Congress movement. Mountbatten, appointed to the new South-East Asia Command, told Wavell of this the following September, adding that 'it was only the efforts of the Chiefs of Staff who realised the necessity for feeding India if it was to be a stable base for operations, which produced any food at all'.[37] By then, Gandhi had been released from prison on humanitarian grounds after his wife's death but Mountbatten reported that Churchill was 'quite furious' about this and 'quite impossible about India'.[38]

Almost a year earlier, Wavell had put it to Churchill, with the support of the Cabinet's India Committee, that talks might be reopened with Congress leaders on some parts of the abortive Cripps package. He encountered only hostility from the Prime Minister and when he later tried to raise the matter, he was ignored for a month before being told that no new policy initiatives were acceptable until after the war.

Churchill's sometimes dismissive view of Indian troops and allusions to their possible disloyalty were particularly hard for Wavell to accept: 'He accused me of creating a Frankenstein by putting modern weapons in the hands of Sepoys, spoke of 1857 [the year of the Indian mutiny] and was really childish about it.'[39]

Wavell's relations with the Prime Minister worsened as his recommendations for talks with the Congress leadership were blocked. Only in May 1945 was he permitted to bring Congress and Muslim League representatives on to his Executive Council and then to invite both parties to a special conference at Simla. By then Churchill had given in, knowing that the Viceroy had Amery's support as well as that of Labour ministers in the coalition who might use Indian policy against him in the forthcoming General Election. His prejudices, however, remained intact. On his way to the Yalta Conference in February 1945, he read a new book on India by the journalist Beverley Nichols which argued that partition was inevitable. Writing to his wife about it, Churchill declared: 'It certainly shows the Hindu in his true character and the sorry plight to which we have reduced ourselves by losing confidence in our mission.'[40]

The fact that this mission was no longer sustainable owed much to Churchill's own intransigence, but as a Labour government took over the responsibility for India's transition both to independence and partition, he attacked it in terms little different from those in which he had heaped obloquy on the Government of India Act ten years earlier. He quoted his own speeches and indeed one made by his father in 1886, praising the order and transquillity achieved under British rule.[41] Their creation and maintenance constituted 'the task which, with all our shortcomings and through all our ordeals, we have faithfully and loyally pursued since Queen Victoria assumed the Imperial Crown. That is the task which we have now declared ourselves willing to abandon completely.'[42]

Mountbatten, who agreed in February 1947 to go out to India as its last Viceroy, but with real plenipotentiary powers denied to his immediate predecessors, became for a time Churchill's target for particular vilification because he was ready to drive through the objectives of both independence and partition. In London that November for Princess Elizabeth's wedding, he was berated in ferocious terms by Churchill, who virtually called him a traitor. 'He accused me of having planned and organised the first victory of Hindustan (he refused to call it India) against Pakistan by sending in British-trained soldiers and British equipment to crush and oppress the Muslims in Kashmir.'[43]

Kashmir's status was one of many tortuous matters Mountbatten had to resolve during his time in India. He has been bitterly attacked for some of his decisions, particularly for driving so fast to partition and the related boundary awards that the new Indian and Pakistani armies could not contain the resulting communal violence.[44] Nonetheless, he had a vision of India's future and a respect for its new leader's aspirations which were beyond the reach of Churchill, whose responses to events there were preserved in the aspic of impressions and judgements formed very early in his life. He could never have achieved the generous empathy of J. A. Hobson when he analysed the hubris of Britain in the East: 'What Asia has to give, her priceless store of wisdom garnered from her experience of ages, we refuse to take; the much or little which we could give, we spoil by the brutal manner of our giving.'[45] Churchill continued to brood over what he saw as the loss of India, although he soon forgave Mountbatten for his part in it. As he grew older, however, he showed signs of introspection about British attitudes to India and its people. 'When you learn to think of a race as inferior beings it is difficult to get rid of that way of thinking', he told Lord Moran in January 1952, adding 'when I was a subaltern the Indian did not seem to me to equal the white man'.[46] Eighteen months later, Lord Moran recorded him talking of how 'some Indians had been treated with contempt. If we had made friends with them and taken them into our lives instead of restricting our intercourse to the political, things might have been very different.'[47]

More revealing is the way his attitudes altered towards Jawaharal Nehru, the first Prime Minister of independent India. Nehru had always admired Churchill, especially for his stand against the appeasement of Nazi Germany, and even when in prison during the latter part of the war thought of him as 'an honourable enemy'.[48] In 1949, once India's constitutional position within the Commonwealth had been resolved, Churchill arranged to meet Nehru in London. The Indian leader later recalled Churchill beginning their conversation with the words: 'Sir, I have done you great wrong. You are like the prodigal who has returned to the fold of the family.'[49] Once back in power in 1951, he treated Nehru's views with respect, and after the Queen's coronation service in 1953, he said to Nehru's daughter Indira: 'You must have hated the British for the treatment meted out to your father. It is remarkable how he and you have overcome that bitterness and hatred.'[50] Her reply was to deny that she had ever felt hatred of Britain, or indeed of Churchill himself.

Emotionally and politically, Australia and New Zealand mattered far less to Churchill than did India, though he often paid tribute to their military qualities. In both places he was viewed ambivalently because of the Gallipoli disaster. Lord Moran recalled him saying that 'Australians came of bad stock',[51] and he never showed much inclination to visit either country. At the height of the war he never accorded the respect to Australian leaders that he did to Jan Smuts of South Africa, yet in 1941 Robert Menzies, the Australian Prime Minister, spent some months in London pressing for the creation of an Imperial War Cabinet made up of British and Dominion statesmen which could

have substantially reduced the British Prime Minister's power. Churchill became alert to what Menzies had in mind and the plan went
nowhere.[52]

Menzies was critical of Churchill's attitudes, writing in May 1941 that
'he had no conception of the British Dominions as separate entities',[53]
but he was infinitely more pro-British than John Curtin, who replaced
him as Prime Minister after a party crisis three months later. Curtin
came from a Labour and Irish immigrant background which Churchill
distrusted. Their relationship was a tense one anyway, because as
Japan's posture became more threatening, Curtin felt he had to urge
upon Churchill the need for Australian troops to be brought back from
the Middle East and for the Singapore base to be reinforced. A full year
prior to this, Churchill's Chiefs of Staff had advised him of the problems of maintaining an effective British military and naval presence in
the Far East and he only agreed to more troops being sent to Singapore
when it was too late to save it.

In 1992, Paul Keating, Australia's Labour Prime Minister, claimed
that Churchill had placed his country in jeopardy by abandoning
Singapore without a real fight. One Australian historian, David Day,
has supported this view,[54] but governments prior to Curtin's, it has also
been pointed out, had done little to provide for their country's defence
or to respond to their military men's warnings both about Japanese
intentions and Singapore's weakness.[55]

Just three weeks after Pearl Harbor, Curtin declared, in the *Mel-
bourne Herald*, that Australia must look to support from the United
States against Japan 'free of any pangs as to our traditional links with
the United Kingdom'.[56] Churchill reacted badly to this, claiming later
in his history of the war that 'these outpourings of anxiety, however
understandable, did not represent Australian feeling'.[57] The fall of
Singapore served only to strengthen Curtin's reading of his country's
military situation even though, in May 1942, Churchill was still assuring Canberra of Britain's good faith and its readiness to help Australia
if Japan invaded, though from what military resources such help would
come was unclear.

Unlike their Prime Minister, some of Churchill's ministerial col-
leagues were able to perceive, in the 1941–42 military crisis in the
Far East, Australia's growing need for real self-assertion. Indeed,
they foresaw the likelihood of a major shift towards the United
States in the country's post-war defence policy. Lord Cranborne, the
Dominions Secretary, warned the War Cabinet against ignoring or

underestimating Australian feelings, arguing that 'a rot which started in
Australia might easily spread to other Dominions',[58] while King George
VI also passed on to Churchill his 'genuine alarm at the feeling which
appears to be growing in Australia'.[59]

Britain as an imperial power found itself stretched to breaking point
by the war and Churchill, on the eve of Singapore's surrender to the
Japanese, admitted this in a speech to Parliament:

> There never has been a moment, there never could have been a
> moment, when Great Britain or the British Empire, single-handed,
> could fight Germany and Italy, could wage the Battle of Britain, the
> Battle of the Atlantic and the Battle of the Middle East – and at the
> same time stand thoroughly prepared in Burma, the Malay Penin-
> sula and generally in the Far East.[60]

The pressure was political as well as military, especially once America
came into the war. *Life* magazine, in October 1942, ran an open letter
to the people of Britain calling upon them to 'stop fighting for the
British Empire and fight for victory',[61] while opinion polls in the
United States showed majorities hostile to Britain's continuing role as
an imperial power.[62]

In the same month there was evidence of the leftward shift in
wartime British politics putting the Empire under closer scrutiny.
Newspapers as different as Labour's *Daily Herald* and *The Times* posed
leading questions about whether Churchill's vision of Empire would be
sustainable in a post-war world. The historian Marjorie Perham, writing an editorial for *The Times*, argued that 'the pride and achievement
of the modern British Empire are that it has become in a certain
sense a self-liquidating concern...Its aims can be defined in terms
not of "have and hold" but of the Atlantic Charter and the "four
freedoms".'[63]

'Self-liquidation' was certainly not what Churchill had in mind for the
Empire's future once Germany and Japan were defeated, but the
election of a Labour government in 1945 persuaded him that the end
was in sight. 'It is with deep grief I watch the clattering down of the
British Empire with all its glories and all the services it has rendered to
mankind',[64] he told Parliament in 1947. His lamentation for the end of
Empire was premature. Withdrawals from India and Palestine did
represent a fairly dramatic contraction of British power, but they
have also been written of as 'a crisis of post-war adjustment... retrench-

ment after wartime overstretch'.[65] The Labour government which Churchill berated for the policy of 'scuttle' was in fact seriously divided over what Britain's overseas priorities should be, with Attlee arguing, for example, against a preoccupation with the need to maintain a presence in the Middle East.

The rapidity of Britain's post-war retreat from Empire can be exaggerated and is best understood as 'a cutting of losses in areas where the balance of burdens and benefits had tilted against Britain'.[66] This describes well enough the decision to grant independence to India and to Pakistan and to withdraw from Palestine. In the latter case Churchill, still bitter in his opposition to leaving India, came to feel that any useful role for Britain was over by 1948. Yet when he returned to office in 1951, he took responsibility for major colonial counter-insurgency operations in Malaya, Kenya and Cyprus which were neither opposed nor obstructed by the United States. A case has been made, by John Charmley in particular, that Churchill's wartime relationship with Roosevelt prepared the way for America to dismantle the British imperial system. After 1945, however, any residual American anti-imperialism was quickly subordinated to the need to contain the feared expansion of Soviet Communist power.

This was apparent in America's active approval when after October 1951, Churchill authorised an increased military effort against the Chinese Communist guerrillas in Malaya. Africa was also an area where Washington accepted a continued British presence. Churchill, like his Labour predecessors, supported hugely increased economic development there. He had no problems either, with the Truman or Eisenhower administrations over his backing for an ambitious though ultimately abortive federation in Central Africa to secure British interests and defer majority rule in Northern and Southern Rhodesia and Nyasaland.

Where Churchill misjudged American intentions was over Egypt and Britain's still huge Suez Canal base. In 1953, with his Foreign Secretary Eden indisposed, he took direct responsibility for British policy at a time of growing nationalist unrest and attacks on Britain's Suez garrison. He blamed the Foreign Office for its conciliatory stance and told Evelyn Shuckburgh that he 'never knew before that Munich was situated on the Nile'.[67] At this stage he hoped American support could gurantee the future of the Suez base within a Middle East regional defence organisation. Eisenhower was not willing to be drawn into overt support for a continuing British presence and made clear his belief in the need for a settlement of the issue without American involvement or undertakings. Churchill and his government had to present the best case they could for withdrawal in a debate in July 1954 which was marked by angry interventions from their own backbenchers.

When Egypt announced the nationalisation of the Suez Canal Company in 1956, Britain's withdrawal was complete and Churchill had been succeeded in office by Eden. His ill-fated attempt to reoccupy the Suez Canal zone in collusion with the governments of Israel and France deeply divided British opinion as well as antagonising both the United Nations and the United States. Eden still has his defenders, Charmley arguing that he simply 'sinned against the Churchillian wisdom of accepting a satellite relationship of Britain to the United States',[68] but this is part of an intellectually crude denigration of Britain's wartime and post-war alliance with America.

Immediately prior to British and French operations against Port Said being launched, Eden, it has been claimed, expressed the hope that Churchill might return to the Cabinet as a minister without portfolio.[69] Nothing came of this but on 3 November 1956, Churchill did make public a message to his constituency association in which he described the government's action as a regrettable necessity if peace and stability were to be maintained in the Middle East.[70] He further stressed that the American alliance remained the keystone of British policy, and there has always been speculation as to whether he would have embarked upon such a course of action without the promise of American support. It seems unlikely, though Anthony Montague Brown, his last Private Secretary, has quoted him as saying 'I would never have done it without squaring the Americans and once I'd started I would never have dared stop.'[71]

The Suez crisis, it has been said, 'demonstrated with brutal frankness that Britain was no longer in the great power league, was no longer capable of playing by its rules and simply looked absurd when it tried to cheat'.[72] It destroyed Eden, which upset Churchill, and it was a bitter postscript to a career in which, over half a century, a major imperial world role was something he had believed in and taken for granted. At times he expressed this belief in racial and Social Darwinian terms that now grate on many ears, but which, during much of his political lifetime, were simply the common currency of political discourse. His vision of empire was also often a benign and paternalistic one. Only four years before the Suez crisis, he was urging the view that

British influence in Egypt could help the cause of land reform and thus ease the plight of the fellahin (peasants) which had angered him as a young officer fifty years earlier.[73] In his retirement, Churchill's principal literary endeavour was to complete and publish his *History of the English Speaking Peoples*. 'Almost no-one reads it as history,' it has been said, 'only as one great Englishman's vision of the nation he served',[74] and that vision comes through strongly, even in his final years, as still inseparable from a British, not merely an English, imperial destiny. For much of his life this vision ran with the grain of a British popular culture steeped in imperial beliefs disseminated through schools, youth organisations, films, books and many other sources.[75] In his greatest 1940 broadcast, there was no incongruity for his listeners in his invocation of an Empire's defiance of Hitler, not just that of the British Isles.

In his final years, Churchill suffered increasing spells of depression during one of which he told his cousin, Clare Sheridan, that his life's work 'had been all for nothing ... The Empire I believed in has gone.'[76] While this was a morbid devaluation of what he had achieved, the Empire as he had known it was already, like Churchill himself, beginning to slip into history. This is perhaps why it was right that his funeral, on 30 January 1965, gave the world one of its last chances to watch a British imperial spectacle. Of the hundred nations represented, twenty had once, and in many cases quite recently, been ruled from the very city through whose streets the cortège paraded: 'Melancholy though the occasion was, intuitively though the British felt its deeper significance, they did it, as Churchill wished, in the high old style.'[77]

EPILOGUE

On a grey London day on 30 January 1965, amid muffled drums and slow, marching troops, the gun-carriage with Churchill's flag-draped coffin on it was borne out of view from the many thousands who had come to pay their final respects. Something else was already disappearing, however, and that was Churchill's Britain. The Beatles already had a huge following; immigration from the 'new Commonwealth' was turning large areas of London and other English cities into multiracial communities; and military conscription, the shared experience of a whole generation who had often garrisoned an Empire existing on borrowed time, had been phased out. A sceptical and irreverent era had taken shape in which old certainties were being questioned. Many subscribed to the view expressed by Jimmy Porter, anti-hero of John Osborne's 1956 play *Look Back in Anger*, that there were no brave causes left.

Yet at the time of Churchill's death and even now, Britain's defiance of Hitler in 1940 remains such a cause and he will always symbolise it. As Prime Minister, it has been said, he 'did not have to conjure national unity out of thin air. He had only to sense and evoke it, to find the tones, the style of leadership to which it would respond.'[1] The high tide of democratic patriotism to which his leadership gave voice had to subside and it has left a residue compounded of pride, nostalgia and some resentment as Britain's world role has diminished. Churchill believed victory could be won over Hitler without that happening, but in his final years he seems to have accepted it. By then, his work was done. His youngest daughter Mary Soames described him movingly in his twilight years: 'Remembering him thus,' she has written, 'I recall Landor's lines: "I warmed both hands before the fire of life, it sinks and I am ready to depart".'[2]

176

NOTES

Preface

1. I. Berlin, *Mr Churchill in 1940* (London, 1949), p. 16.

1 Churchill the Warrior

1. V. Bonham Carter, *Winston Churchill As I Knew Him* (London 1965), p. 262.
2. M. Gilbert, *Winston S. Churchill: Vol. III, 1914–1916* (London 1971), p. 31.
3. W. S. Churchill, *The Story of the Malakand Field Force* (London 1898), p. 88.
4. Winston S. Churchill, *My Early Life* (London 1930), p. 208.
5. A. Marder, *From Dreadnought to Scapa Flow* (London 1961), Vol. I, p. 435.
6. M. Howard, 'Churchill and the First World War', in R. Blake and William Roger Louis, *Churchill: A Major New Assessment of His Life in War and Peace* (Oxford 1993), p. 130.
7. Bonham Carter, *Winston Churchill*, p. 334.
8. *Morning Post*, 13 October 1914.
9. Lord Beaverbrook, *Politicians and the War 1914–1916* (London 1928), p. 78.
10. G. Moorhouse, *Hell's Foundations: A Town, Its Myths and Gallipoli* (London 1992).
11. Lord Beaverbrook, *Politicians*, p. 124.
12. R. Rhodes James, *Gallipoli* (London 1965), p. 352.
13. Ibid., p. 353, also R. Rhodes James, *Churchill: A Study in Failure, 1900–1939* (London, 1970), pp. 74–7. See also J. Keegan, *The First World War* (London 1998), pp. 253–69 for a concise treatment of this campaign.
14. A. J. P. Taylor, *English History, 1914–1945* (Oxford 1965), p. 25.
15. Lord Beaverbrook, *Men and Power, 1917–1918* (London 1956), p. 122.
16. M. Gilbert, *Winston S. Churchill: Vol. IV, 1917–1922* (London 1975), p. 912.
17. G. J. De Groot, *Douglas Haig 1861–1928* (London 1988), pp. 339–40.
18. D. Jablonsky, *Churchill, the Great Game, and Total War* (London 1991), p. 52.
19. De Groot, *Douglas Haig*, pp. 401–2.
20. R. Rhodes James, *Churchill: A Study in Failure* (London 1970), p. 107.
21. Gilbert, *Winston S. Churchill: Vol. IV*, pp. 246–7.

22. K. Jeffrey (ed.), *The Military Correspondence of Field Marshal Sir Henry Wilson 1918–1922* (London 1985), pp. 103–4.
23. Gilbert, *Winston S. Churchill: Vol. IV*, p. 311.
24. Ibid.
25. Ibid., pp. 418–21.
26. Rhodes James, *Churchill*, pp. 122–3.
27. Jeffrey, *Correspondence*, p. 316.
28. P. Gretton, *Former Naval Person: Winston Churchill and the Royal Navy* (London 1968), p. 244.
29. M. Howard, *The Continental Commitment: The Dilemma of British Defence Policy in the Era of Two World Wars* (London 1972), pp. 89–90. See also P. O'Brien, 'Churchill and the US Navy 1919–29', in R. A. C. Parker (ed.), *Winston Churchill: Studies in Statesmanship* (London 1995), pp. 22–41. Here it is argued that Churchill believed that the spending cuts he was pressing for were compatible with Britain's maintenance of its maritime supremacy, especially over America, whose intentions he distrusted at this time.
30. See Chapter 5.
31. M. Carver, 'Churchill and the Defence Chiefs', in Blake and Louis (eds), *Churchill*, pp. 353–4.
32. W. S. Churchill, *The Second World War, Vol. I: The Gathering Storm* (London 1948), pp. 62–3.
33. J. Charmley, *Churchill: The End of Glory* (London 1993), p. 292.
34. M. Gilbert, *In Search of Churchill* (London 1994), pp. 128–30.
35. Ibid., pp. 134–5.
36. Rhodes James, *Churchill*, pp. 238–9.
37. Ibid., p. 240.
38. Ibid., pp. 248–54.
39. W. S. Churchill, *The Second World War, Vol. II: Their Finest Hour* (London 1949), p. 346.
40. Jablonsky, *Churchill*, p. 151.
41. R. Fisk, *In Time of War: Ireland, Ulster and the Price of Neutrality 1939–1945* (London 1983), pp. 116–18, 125–7.
42. S. Roskill, *Churchill and the Admirals* (London 1977), p. 95.
43. F. Kersaudy, *Norway 1940* (London 1990), pp. 225–7.
44. M. Gilbert, *Finest Hour: Winston S. Churchill: Vol. VI, 1939–1941* (London 1983), p. 294.
45. R. Rhodes James (ed.), *'Chips': The Diaries of Sir Henry Channon* (London 1967), p. 246.
46. G. Orwell, *Collected Essays, Journalism and Letters, Vol. 2: My Country Right or Left 1940–1943* (London 1968), p. 87.
47. A. J. P. Taylor, *English History*, p. 473.

2   National Leader, 1940–1945

1. Churchill, *Gathering Storm*, pp. 523–4; Gilbert, *Finest Hour*, pp. 301–2; A. Roberts, *The Holy Fox, A Life of Lord Halifax* (London 1991), pp. 204–7.

2. Ibid., p. 208.
3. Churchill, *Gathering Storm*, pp. 526–7.
4. J. Colville, *The Fringes of Power: Downing Street Diaries 1939–1945* (London 1985), p. 122.
5. J. Colville, in J. Wheeler-Bennett (ed.), *Action This Day: Working With Churchill* (London 1968), p. 49.
6. Ibid., pp. 49–50.
7. R. V. Jones, *Most Secret War* (London 1978), p. 107.
8. Churchill, *Their Finest Hour*, p. 342.
9. P. M. S. Blackett, *Studies of War* (London 1962), p. 238.
10. Jablonsky, *Churchill*, pp. 144–6.
11. C. Andrew, 'Churchill and Intelligence', in M. Handel (ed.), *Leaders and Intelligence* (London 1989), p. 18. See also D. Stafford, *Churchill and Secret Intelligence* (London 1977), for a very full exploration of Churchill's dealings with the intelligence services.
12. J. Connell, *Wavell: Scholar and Soldier* (London 1964), pp. 233–5, 278–9, 287–9, 362–5.
13. See I. Beckett on Wavell and P. Warner on Auchinleck in J. Keegan (ed.), *Churchill's Generals* (London 1991), pp. 70–89, 130–48.
14. Jablonsky, *Churchill*, pp. 138–9.
15. J. Kennedy, *The Business of War* (London 1957), p. 241.
16. Ibid., p. 274
17. W. S. Churchill, *The Second World War, Vol. III: The Grand Alliance* (London, 1950), pp. 705–6, also *Vol. VI: Triumph and Tragedy* (London 1954), p. 615.
18. T. Wilson, *Churchill and the Prof.* (London, 1995), pp. 100–3; also A. Roberts, *Eminent Churchillians* (London 1994), Ch. 2.
19. W. S. Churchill, *History of the Second World War: Vol. IV, The Hinge of Fate* (London 1951), p. 459.
20. B. Loring Villa, *Unauthorised Action: Mountbatten and the Dieppe Raid 1942* (Oxford 1989), pp. 44–5.
21. Ibid., p. 40.
22. R. Rhodes James (ed.), *Churchill Speaks 1897–1963* (London 1981), pp. 798–802.
23. D. Day, *The Great Betrayal: Britain, Australia and the Onset of the Pacific War 1939–42* (London 1988), p. 261.
24. Gilbert, *Road to Victory*, pp. 47–8.
25. Churchill, *Hinge of Fate*, p. 43.
26. Orwell, *My Country*, pp. 246–7.
27. Gilbert, *Winston S. Churchill: Vol. VII, Road to Victory 1941–1945* (London, 1986), pp. 125, 141. P. Addison, *The Road to 1945: British Politics and the Second World War* (London 1975), pp. 206–10.
28. Gilbert, *Road to Victory*, p. 208.
29. S. Ambrose, 'Churchill and Eisenhower in the Second World War', in Blake and Louis, *Churchill*, pp. 399–401.
30. J. Ellis, *Brute Force: Allied Strategy and Tactics in the Second World War* (London 1990), p. 293.

31. W. S. Churchill, *The Second World War, Vol. V: Closing the Ring* (London: 1952), p. 437.
32. Lord Moran, *Winston Churchill: the Struggle for Survival* (London 1966), pp. 157–8.
33. C. D'Este, *Fatal Decision: Anzio and the Battle for Rome* (London 1991), pp. 94–5.
34. Ibid.
35. Ibid., p. 99.
36. D. Fraser, 'Alanbrooke', in J. Keegan (ed.), *Churchill's Generals*, p. 98.
37. D. Eisenhower, *Crusade in Europe* (London 1948), p. 214.
38. W. Kimball (ed.), *Churchill and Roosevelt: The Complete Correspondence*, Vol. III (Princeton 1984), pp. 225–6.
39. Eisenhower, *Crusade*, p. 312.
40. J. Keegan, 'Churchill's Strategy', in Blake and Louis, *Churchill*, pp. 334–6.
41. Keegan, *Churchill's Generals*, p. 350.
42. Churchill, *Grand Alliance*, p. 54.
43. Rhodes James (ed.), *Churchill Speaks*, p. 764.
44. Charmley, *Churchill: The End of Glory*, pp. 455–6.
45. J. Lukacs, *The Duel: Hitler v. Churchill 10 May–31 July 1940* (London 1990), p. 232.
46. C. de Gaulle, *War Memoirs: Salvation 1944–1946* (London 1960), pp. 56–7.
47. Colville, *Fringes of Power*, p. 186.
48. Gilbert, *Finest Hour*, p. 803.
49. Gilbert, *Road to Victory*, p. 179.
50. A. Harris, *Bomber Offensive* (London 1947), pp. 88–9. See also R. Overy, *Why the Allies Won* (London 1995), pp. 127–31, for a forceful statement of the case for strategic air power having a decisive role in Germany's defeat.
51. A. Montague Brown, *Long Sunset: Memoirs of Winston Churchill's Last Private Secretary* (London 1995), p. 201.
52. Sir C. Webster and N. Frankland, *The Strategic Air Offensive Against Germany 1939–1945, Vol. I* (London 1961), p. 184.
53. J. Charmley, *Churchill's Grand Alliance: The Anglo-American Special Relationship 1940–1957* (London 1995), pp. xiv–xv.
54. C. Ponting, *1940: Myth and Reality* (London 1990), pp. 109–110, also p. 118.
55. P. Hennessy, *Never Again: Britain 1945–1951* (London 1992), p. 28.
56. Roberts, *Holy Fox*, pp. 231–6.
57. T. Harrison, *Living Through the Blitz* (London 1976), pp. 280–91.
58. Colville, *Fringes of Power*, pp. 373, 441–2.
59. M. Gilbert, *Never Despair: Vol. VIII, Winston Churchill 1945–1965* (London 1988), p. 1075.
60. Rhodes James (ed.), *Churchill Speaks*, p. 73.
61. C. Barnett, *The Audit of War: The Illusion and Reality of Britain as a Great Nation* (London 1986), pp. 159–61.
62. Hennessy, *Never Again*, p. 33.
63. Jablonsky, *Churchill*, p. 123.
64. Gilbert, *Road to Victory*, p. 847.
65. Ibid., pp. 846–7; also M. Gilbert, *Auschwitz and the Allies* (London 1981).

3 Churchill and the United States

1. K. Halle (ed.), *The Irrepressible Churchill* (London 1985), p. 223; also Gilbert, *Never Despair*, pp. 196–7.
2. Randolph S. Churchill, *Winston S. Churchill: Vol. I, Youth 1874–1900* (London 1966), p. 543.
3. N. Rose, *Churchill: An Unruly Life* (London 1994), p. 36.
4. Rhodes James (ed.), *Churchill Speaks*, p. 212.
5. Churchill, *Gathering Storm*, p. 20.
6. Kimball (ed.), *Churchill and Roosevelt: The Complete Correspondence*, Vol. I, p. 23.
7. R. A. Callaghan, *Churchill: Retreat from Empire* (Delaware 1984), p. 49.
8. Churchill, *Gathering Storm*, p. 199.
9. Kimball, *Churchill and Roosevelt: The Complete Correspondence*, Vol. I, pp. 24–5.
10. Ibid., pp. 37–8.
11. Charmley, *Churchill's Grand Alliance*, p. 23.
12. Ponting, *1940: Myth and Reality*, p. 10.
13. Kimball, *Churchill and Roosevelt: The Complete Correspondence*, Vol. I, p. 80.
14. Ibid., pp. 108–9.
15. Charmley, *Churchill's Grand Alliance*, pp. 94, 120–1.
16. W. Roger Louis and R. Robinson, 'The Imperialism of Decolonization', *Journal of Imperial and Commonwealth History*, 22 (1994), pp. 462–511.
17. Kimball, *Churchill and Roosevelt: The Complete Correspondence*, Vol. I, p. 121.
18. C. Ponting, *Churchill* (London 1994), p. 510.
19. D. Reynolds, *Britannia Overruled: British Policy and World Power in the 20th Century* (London 1979), pp. 151, 991.
20. W. Averell Harriman and E. Abel, *Special Envoy to Churchill and Stalin 1941–1946* (London, 1976), p. 22.
21. Gilbert, *Finest Hour*, p. 988.
22. H. Thomas, *The Armed Truce: The Beginnings of the Cold War 1945–1946* (London 1986), p. 116.
23. Gilbert, *Finest Hour*, pp. 1163–4; also C. Thorne, *Allies of a Kind: The United States, Britain and the War Against Japan 1941–1945* (London 1978), pp. 160–1.
24. Gilbert, *Finest Hour*, pp. 1176–7.
25. R. Sherwood, *The White House Papers of Harry L. Hopkins: An Intimate History, Vol. I* (London 1948), pp. 374.
26. Rhodes James, *Churchill Speaks*, p. 816.
27. Kimball, *Churchill and Roosevelt: The Complete Correspondence*, Vol. I, pp. 344–5.
28. Reynolds, *Britannia Overruled*, p. 152.
29. Kimball, *Churchill and Roosevelt: The Complete Correspondence*, Vol. I, pp. 447–8.
30. Thorne, *Allies of a Kind*, pp. 244–45, also Reynolds, *Britannia Overruled*, p. 152.
31. Moran, *Winston Churchill*, pp. 82–3.

32. A. Bryant, *Alanbrooke, War Diaries, Vol. II* (London 1965), pp. 506–8.
33. J. Erickson, *The Road to Berlin: Stalin's War with Germany, Vol. 2* (London 1983), p. 160.
34. Moran, *Winston Churchill*, p. 136.
35. Kimball, *Churchill and Roosevelt: The Complete Correspondence*, Vol. III, p. 17.
36. Harriman and Abel, *Special Envoy to Churchill and Stalin 1941–1946*, pp. 355–8.
37. Ibid.
38. Churchill, *Triumph and Tragedy*, pp. 197–9.
39. T. H. Anderson, *The United States, Britain and the Cold War 1944–1947* (Columbia and London 1981), pp. 17–18.
40. Churchill, *Triumph and Tragedy*, p. 417.
41. D. Reynolds, 'Roosevelt, Churchill and the Wartime Anglo-American Alliance 1939–1945', in W. Roger Louis and H. Bull (eds) *The Special Relationship: Anglo-American Relations Since 1945* (Oxford 1986), p. 40.
42. Gilbert, *Road to Victory*, p. 415.
43. M. Gowing, 'Nuclear Weapons and the "Special Relationship"', in Louis and Bull (eds), *Special Relationship*, p. 119.
44. Gilbert, *Road to Victory*, p. 416.
45. Ibid., p. 970.
46. Churchill, *Triumph and Tragedy*, p. 553.
47. J. Morgan (ed.), *The Backbench Diaries of Richard Crossman* (London 1981), p. 305.
48. D McCullough, *Truman* (New York, 1992), p. 412.
49. Gilbert, *Never Despair*, p. 167.
50. Thomas, *Armed Truce*, pp. 486–9.
51. Rhodes James, *Churchill Speaks*, p. 881.
52. Ibid., p. 883.
53. McCullough, *Truman*, pp. 489–90.
54. Ibid., also Gilbert, *Never Despair*, pp. 205–6.
55. Anderson, *United States*, p. 114.
56. *The Times*, 9 March 1946.
57. P. Weiler, *Ernest Bevin* (Manchester, 1993), pp. 175–6.
58. H. B. Ryan, *The Vision of Anglo-America: the US–UK Alliance and the Emerging Cold War 1943–1946* (Cambridge, 1987), pp. 26–7, 31–2.
59. F. Harbutt, *The Iron Curtain: Churchill, America and the Origins of the Cold War* (Oxford 1987), p. 165.
60. Reynolds, 'Wartime Anglo-American Alliance', in Louis and Bull (eds), *Special Relationship*, p. 37.
61. McCullough, *Truman*, pp. 874–5.
62. Moran, *Winston Churchill*, pp. 356–7.
63. R. H. Ferrell, *The Eisenhower Diaries* (New York 1981), p. 223.
64. Montague Brown, *Long Sunset*, pp. 153–5.
65. Gilbert, *Never Despair*, p. 811.
66. Ibid., p. 830.
67. Colville, *Fringes of Power*, p. 683.
68. Ibid, p. 685.

69. Moran, *Winston Churchill*, p. 508.
70. Gilbert, *Never Despair*, p. 944.
71. R. A. Butler, *The Art of the Possible: The Memoirs of Lord Butler* (London 1971), p. 173.
72. P. Hennessy, *Muddling Through: Power, Politics and the Quality of Government in Post-War Britain* (London 1996), p. 191.
73. Gilbert, *Never Despair*, p. 1025, also Reynolds, *Britannia Overruled*, p. 184.
74. Gilbert, *Never Despair*, p. 1026.
75. Ibid., p. 1027.
76. E. Shuckburgh, *Descent to Suez: Diaries 1951–1956* (London 1986), pp. 221–4.
77. Hennessy, *Never Again*, pp. 194–5.
78. Ibid., p. 197; also J. Young, *Winston Churchill's last Campaign: Britain and the Cold War 1951–1955* (Oxford 1996).
79. D. Cameron Watt, 'Demythologizing the Eisenhower Years', in Louis and Bull (eds), *Special Relationship*, p. 72.
80. Quoted in Hennessy, *Never Again*, p. 195.

4 Churchill and the Soviet Union

1. M. Djilas, *Conversations With Stalin* (London 1962), p. 61.
2. Gilbert, *Never Despair*, p. 1008.
3. Gilbert, *Winston S. Churchill: Vol. IV*, p. 278.
4. I. McLean, *The Legend of Red Clydeside* (Edinburgh 1983), p. 125.
5. Gilbert, *Winston S. Churchill: Vol. IV*, p. 227.
6. Rose, *Churchill*, p. 369.
7. Ibid., p. 147.
8. Gilbert, *Winston S. Churchill: Vol. IV*, p. 293.
9. D. Lloyd George, *War Memoirs*, Vol. I (London 1938), p. 953.
10. Gilbert, *Winston S. Churchill: Vol. IV*, p. 246.
11. Ibid., p. 241.
12. Ibid., pp. 253–4.
13. Jeffery, *Correspondence*, pp. 122–3.
14. Gilbert, *Winston S. Churchill: Vol. IV*, p. 383.
15. Ibid., pp. 370–1.
16. Charmley, *Churchill: The End of Glory*, pp. 152–3.
17. Rhodes James, *Churchill: A Study in Failure*, p. 107.
18. Ibid., p. 122.
19. Gilbert, *Winston S. Churchill: Vol. IV*, p. 440.
20. P. Addison, *Churchill on the Home Front 1900–1955* (London 1992), p. 211.
21. Rhodes James, *Churchill Speaks*, p. 402.
22. Ibid.
23. Gilbert, *Winston S. Churchill: Vol. IV*, p. 377.
24. Churchill, *Gathering Storm*, p. 306.

25. Ibid.
26. Ibid., p. 307.
27. Gilbert, *Finest Hour*, p. 44.
28. Ibid., p. 50.
29. I. Maisky, *Memoirs of a Soviet Ambassador* (London 1967), p. 32.
30. Churchill, *Gathering Storm*, p. 429.
31. R. Macleod and D. Kelly (eds), *The Ironside Diaries 1937–1940* (London 1962), pp. 182–4.
32. Kersaudy, *Norway 1940*, pp. 17–18.
33. J. Erickson, *The Road to Stalingrad: Stalin's War with Germany*, Vol. I (London 1975), p. 74.
34. Ibid., p. 93.
35. Rhodes James, *Churchill Speaks*, pp. 762–3.
36. Colville, *Fringes of Power*, p. 404.
37. Ibid., pp. 405–6.
38. H. Ismay, *The Memoirs of General Lord Ismay* (London 1960), pp. 223–5.
39. I. McLaine, *Ministry of Morale: Home Front Morale and the Ministry of Information in World War II* (London 1979), pp. 196–7.
40. Ibid., p. 200.
41. Charmley, *Churchill: The End of Glory*, pp. 455–6.
42. Ibid., p. 200.
43. M. Kitchen, 'Winston Churchill and the Soviet Union During the Second World War', *Historical Journal*, XXX: 2 (1987), pp. 415–36.
44. Gilbert, *Road to Victory*, p. 111.
45. Churchill, *Hinge of Fate*, pp. 447–8.
46. Churchill, *Closing the Ring*, p. 330; also, Gilbert, *Road to Victory*, pp. 580–1.
47. Gilbert, *Road to Victory*, p. 586.
48. O. Rzheshevsky, *Operation Overlord* (Moscow 1984), p. 41.
49. L. Woodward, *British Foreign Policy* (London, 1971), Vol. II, p. 547.
50. Kitchen, 'Winston Churchill', p. 427.
51. Ibid.
52. Erickson, *Road to Berlin*, pp. 279–82.
53. Kimball (ed.), *Churchill and Roosevelt: The Complete Correspondence, Vol. III*, p. 295.
54. Ibid., pp. 350–1.
55. Rose, *Churchill*, p. 313.
56. Ibid.
57. Churchill, *Triumph and Tragedy*, p. 351.
58. Colville, *Fringes of Power*, p. 562.
59. Gilbert, *Road to Victory*, pp. 1329–30.
60. Churchill, *Triumph and Tragedy*, p. 498.
61. Gilbert, *Never Despair*, p. 1192.
62. Ibid., p. 200.
63. See Chapter 3.
64. Hennessy, *Never Again*, p. 388.
65. Shuckburgh, *Descent to Suez*, pp. 91–2.
66. Montague Browne, *Long Sunset*, pp. 157–9.

67. See Chapter 3.
68. Gilbert, *Never Despair*, p. 1100.

5 Churchill and Appeasement

1. Churchill, *Gathering Storm*, p. 14.
2. Rhodes James, *Churchill: A Study in Failure* p. 221.
3. J. Ramsden, ' "That Will Depend on Who Writes the History": Winston Churchill as his own Historian', Inaugural Lecture, Queen Mary and Westfield College, London 1996.
4. R. H. Powers, 'Winston Churchill's Parliamentary Commentary on British Foreign Policy 1935–1938', *Journal of Modern History*, XXVI: 2 (1954), pp. 179–83.
5. D. C. Watt, *Personalities and Policy* (London 1965), p. 131.
6. A. J. P. Taylor, *The Origins of the Second World War* (London 1961), p. 189.
7. Ibid., pp. 92, 125.
8. P. W. Schroeder, 'Munich and the British Tradition', *Historical Studies*, XIX: 1 (1976), pp. 223–43; also P. Kennedy, 'The Tradition of Appeasement in British Foreign Policy 1865–1939', in his *Strategy and Diplomacy* (London 1983), pp. 13–39.
9. W. K. Hancock and J. Van der Poel (eds), *Selections from the Smuts Papers* (Cambridge 1966), p. 87.
10. Gilbert, *Winston S. Churchill: Vol. IV*, pp. 608–9.
11. S. Roskill, *Naval Policy Between the Wars: Vol. I, 1919–1929* (London 1968), p. 446.
12. Howard, *Continental Commitment*, pp. 89–90.
13. K. Middlemas and J. Barnes, *Baldwin: A Biography* (London 1969), pp. 368–71.
14. D. Marquand, *Ramsay MacDonald* (London 1977), p. 517.
15. Rhodes James, *Churchill: A Study in Failure*, p. 168.
16. G. A. Craig, 'Churchill and Germany', in Blake and Louis, *Churchill*, p. 33.
17. Churchill, *Gathering Storm*, p. 59.
18. Ibid., pp. 59–60; see also Gilbert, *Winston S. Churchill: Vol. V*, pp. 447–8.
19. Churchill, *Gathering Storm*, p. 457.
20. Gilbert, *Winston S. Churchill: Vol. V*, 1922–1939, (London, 1976), p. 457.
21. D. Hamilton, *JFK: Reckless Youth* (London 1992), p. 468.
22. Rhodes James, *Churchill: A Study in Failure*, p. 278.
23. Charmley, *Churchill: The End of Glory*, p. 292.
24. See P. Kennedy, *The Realities Behind Diplomacy: Background Influences on British External Policy 1865–1980* (London 1981), pp. 230–6.
25. Gilbert, *Winston S. Churchill: Vol. V*, pp. 726–7.
26. Ibid., p. 796.
27. Charmley, *Churchill: The End of Glory*, p. 293.
28. Churchill, *Gathering Storm*, p. 110.

29. R. MacLeod and D. Kelly, *Ironside Diaries*, pp. 40–1.
30. Ibid.
31. Ibid., p. 90.
32. Gilbert, *Winston S. Churchill: Vol. V*, p. 226.
33. Ibid., p. 677.
34. Rhodes James, *Churchill: A Study in Failure*, pp. 258–9.
35. A. J. P. Taylor, *English History 1914–1945* (Oxford 1965), p. 385.
36. Churchill, *Gathering Storm*, p. 144.
37. Rhodes James, *Churchill Speaks*, p. 622.
38. Ibid.
39. Churchill, *Gathering Storm*, p. 152.
40. Quoted in D. Dutton, *Anthony Eden, A Life and Reputation* (London 1997), p. 67.
41. K. Feiling, *Life of Neville Chamberlain* (London 1946), p. 193.
42. Churchill, *Gathering Storm*, p. 156.
43. Rhodes James, *Churchill: A Study in Failure*, p. 263.
44. Rose, *Churchill*, p. 238.
45. R. A. C. Parker, *Chamberlain and Appeasement: British Policy and the Coming of the Second World War* (London 1993), pp. 65–6.
46. Addison, *Churchill on the Home Front*, p. 320.
47. Rhodes James, *Churchill Speaks*, p. 631.
48. Ibid.
49. Ibid., p. 623.
50. Addison, *Churchill on the Home Front*, p. 321.
51. Churchill, *Gathering Storm*, p. 167.
52. H. Thomas, *The Spanish Civil War* (London 1979 edition), pp. 822–3; also Rhodes James, *Churchill Speaks*, pp. 650–1.
53. A. Hitler, *Mein Kampf* (new edition, London 1969, ed. D. C. Watt), p. 1.
54. Rhodes James, *Churchill Speaks*, p. 642.
55. Ibid., p. 643.
56. Gilbert, *Winston S. Churchill: Vol. V*, pp. 939–40.
57. *Ibid.*; see also Churchill, *Gathering Storm*, p. 223.
58. Roberts, *Holy Fox*, pp. 113–20.
59. Rhodes James (ed.), *'Chips': The Diaries of Sir Henry Channon*, p. 171.
60. H. Nicolson, *Diaries and Letters 1930–1939* (London 1966), p. 371. see also Charmley, *Churchill: The End of Glory*, pp. 349–50.
61. Parker, *Chamberlain*, p. 184.
62. Rhodes James, *Churchill Speaks*, p. 654.
63. Ibid., pp. 655–62.
64. Parker, *Chamberlain*, p. 184.
65. Gilbert, *Winston S. Churchill: Vol. V*, p. 1012.
66. Katherine, Duchess of Atholl, *Working Partnership* (London and Edinburgh 1958), p. 229; also N. Thompson, *The Anti-Appeasers* (Oxford 1971), p. 193.
67. R. Cockett, *Twilight of Truth: Chamberlain, Appeasement and the Manipulation of the Press* (London 1989), p. 189.
68. Parker, *Chamberlain*, p. 189.

69. Thompson, *Anti-Appeasers*, pp. 212–13.
70. Ibid., p. 293.
71. Charmley, *Churchill: The End of Glory*, pp. 287–8.
72. Rose, *Churchill*, pp. 244–6.
73. Kennedy, *Realities*, pp. 276–301.
74. Thompson, *Anti-Appeasers*, p. 2.

6   Churchill and Europe

1. Colville, *Fringes of Power*, p. 272.
2. Ibid., p. 264.
3. Rhodes James, *Churchill Speaks*, p. 909.
4. Gilbert, *Winston S. Churchill: Vol. IV*, pp. 170–1.
5. G. A. Craig, 'Churchill and Germany', in Blake and Louis, *Churchill*, p. 29.
6. Churchill, *Gathering Storm*, p. 7.
7. Gilbert, *Winston S. Churchill: Vol. IV*, pp. 607–9.
8. Gilbert, *Winston S. Churchill: Vol. V*, p. 51.
9. Ibid.
10. J. Lukacs, *The Duel 10 May–31 July 1940: The Eighty Day Struggle Between Churchill and Hitler* (London 1991), pp. 53–4.
11. Ibid., p. 42.
12. Ibid., p. 48.
13. R. E. Herzstein, *The War that Hitler Won: The Most Infamous Propaganda Campaign in History* (London 1979), pp. 336–9.
14. R. Vansittart, *Black Record: Germans Past and Present* (London 1941).
15. Colville, *Fringes of Power*, p. 329.
16. Churchill, *Triumph and Tragedy*, pp. 138–9.
17. Moran, *Winston Churchill*, p. 179; also Wilson, *Churchill and the Prof.*, pp. 188–90.
18. Wilson, *Churchill and the Prof.*, pp. 190–2.
19. A. Horne, *Macmillan 1894–1956* (London 1988), p. 316.
20. H. Schwarz, *Churchill and Adenauer* (Ilford 1994), p. 16.
21. Lord Normanbrook, in Wheeler-Bennett (ed.), *Action This Day*, p. 41.
22. P. G. Boyle, *The Churchill–Eisenhower Correspondence 1953–1955* (Chapel Hill and London 1990), p. 175. See also W. Krieger, 'Churchill and the Defence of the West 1951–1955', in Parker (ed.), *Winston Churchill*, pp. 183–200.
23. Gilbert, *Never Despair*, p. 1055.
24. Ibid., p. 1056.
25. Boyle, *Churchill–Eisenhower Correspondence*, p. 44.
26. Gilbert, *Never Despair*, pp. 829–32.
27. Schwarz, *Churchill and Adenauer*, pp. 26–7.
28. Ibid., p. 27.
29. Ibid., pp. 28–9.

30. Ibid., p. 31.
31. Gilbert, *Never Despair*, p. 1197.
32. Ibid., p. 247.
33. F. Kersaudy, *Churchill and de Gaulle* (London 1981), pp. 25–33.
34. D. Johnson, 'Churchill and France', in Blake and Louis, *Churchill*, p. 49.
35. Ibid., p. 50.
36. Gilbert, *Winston S. Churchill: Vol. V*, pp. 121–5.
37. Ibid.
38. Kersaudy, *Churchill and de Gaulle*, p. 32.
39. Colonel Macleod and Kelly (eds), *Ironside Diaries*, p. 51.
40. R. W. Thompson, *Churchill and Morton* (London 1976), p. 72.
41. Churchill, *Gathering Storm*, pp. 441–2.
42. Ibid.
43. N. Harman, *Dunkirk: The Necessary Myth* (London 1980), pp. 122–3, 189.
44. Gilbert, *Finest Hour*, pp. 498–515.
45. Ibid., p. 506.
46. E. Spears, *Assignment to Catastrophe* (Composite Volume of Memoirs, London 1956), p. 589.
47. Churchill, *Their Finest Hour*, pp. 180–1.
48. Ibid., p. 138.
49. Ibid., p. 643.
50. W. Tute, *The Deadly Stroke* (London 1973), p. 17.
51. Kersaudy, *Churchill and de Gaulle*, pp. 84–6.
52. V. Rothwell, *Anthony Eden: A Political Biography 1931–1957* (Manchester 1992), pp. 80–4.
53. Gilbert, *Finest Hour*, pp. 630–1.
54. Kersaudy, *Churchill and de Gaulle*, pp. 187–92.
55. Ibid., pp. 222–4.
56. D. Stafford, *Churchill and Secret Intelligence*, p. 250.
57. Kersaudy, *Churchill and de Gaulle*, p. 279.
58. Ibid., pp. 343–5.
59. Gilbert, *Road to Victory*, p. 789.
60. De Gaulle, *War Memoirs*, pp. 53–4.
61. H. Footitt and J. Simmonds, *France 1943–1945* (Leicester 1988), pp. 206–7.
62. De Gaulle, *War Memoirs*, p. 148.
63. A. Bryant, *Triumph in the West: The Allanbrooke Diaries* (London 1959), p. 374.
64. Churchill, *Triumph and Tragedy*, p. 245.
65. Kersaudy, *Churchill and de Gaulle*, pp. 390–1.
66. Gilbert, *Never Despair*, p. 407.
67. Horne, *Macmillan*, pp. 320–1.
68. Earl of Kilmuir, *Political Adventure* (London 1964), pp. 186–8.
69. Horne, *Macmillan*, p. 348. See also A. Seldon, *Churchill's Indian Summer: The Conservative Government 1951–1955* (London 1981), pp. 413–14.
70. Montague Browne, *Long Sunset*, p. 275.
71. Ibid., p. 273. See also Gilbert, 'Churchill and the European Idea', in Parker (ed.), *Winston Churchill*, pp. 201–16.

7 Churchill, Party Politics and Social Policy

1. K. Robbins, *Churchill* (London 1992), p. 28.
2. W. S. Churchill, *A History of the English Speaking Peoples: Vol. III – Age of Revolution* (London 1957), p. 109.
3. T. Paterson, *Churchill: A Seat for Life* (Dundee 1980), p. 156.
4. Churchill, *Their Finest Hour*, p. 134.
5. S. David, *Churchill's Sacrifice of the Highland Division* (London 1994).
6. Paterson, *Churchill*, p. 103.
7. Ibid., pp. 173–4.
8. H. Nicolson, *Diaries and Letters 1939–1945* (London 1967), p. 449.
9. Addison, *Churchill on the Home Front*, p. 403.
10. C. Harvie, *Scotland and Nationalism* (London 1977), p. 170.
11. Ibid.
12. A. Marr, *The Battle for Scotland* (London 1992), pp. 95–8.
13. Charmley, *Churchill's Grand Alliance*, p. 360.
14. Gilbert, *Winston S. Churchill: Vol. IV*, p. 891.
15. See W. M. Walker, *Juteopolis: Dundee and its Textile Workers 1885–1923* (Edinburgh, 1979), pp. 107–9.
16. W. M. Walker, 'Dundee's Disenchantment with Churchill', *Scottish Historical Review*, 49 (1970), pp. 85–108.
17. Ibid.
18. Gilbert, *Winston S. Churchill: Vol. IV*, pp. 879–80.
19. *Scotland on Sunday*, 10 May 1998.
20. M. Gilbert, *Churchill: A Life* (London 1991), p. xix.
21. Pelling, *Churchill* (London 1974), p. 73.
22. N. and J. MacKenzie (eds), *Diary of Beatrice Webb: Vol. II, 1892–1905* (London 1986), p. 327.
23. Rhodes James, *Churchill Speaks*, pp. 110–11.
24. P. Clarke, *Liberals and Social Democrats* (Cambridge 1978), pp. 116–17.
25. Ibid.
26. N. and J. MacKenzie (eds), *The First Fabians* (London 1977), p. 355.
27. B. Drake and M. Cole (eds), *Our Partnership by Beatrice Webb* (London 1948), p. 147.
28. Addison, *Churchill on the Home Front*, p. 74.
29. Ibid., pp. 80–1.
30. E. David (ed.), *Inside Asquith's Cabinet: From the Diaries of Charles Hobhouse* (London 1977), p. 73.
31. Ibid.
32. Rhodes James, *Churchill Speaks*, p. 176.
33. Ibid.
34. Ibid. p. 174.
35. Ibid., p. 175.
36. P. Clarke, *Hope and Glory: Britain 1900–1990* (London 1996), p. 65.
37. R. S. Churchill, *Winston S. Churchill: Vol. II, Young Statesman 1901–14* (London 1967), pp. 340–1.
38. Bonham Carter, *Winston Churchill As I Knew Him*, pp. 196–7.

39. Ibid.
40. Ponting, *Churchill*, p. 101.
41. J. Rosen, *Marie Stopes and the Sexual Revolution* (London 1992), p. 134.
42. Churchill, *Young Statesman*, pp. 373–8.
43. Addison, *Churchill on the Home Front*, p. 146.
44. Ibid., p. 145.
45. Marquand, *Ramsay MacDonald*, p. 145.
46. L. Masterman, *C. F. G. Masterman: A Biography* (London 1939), p. 208.
47. Rose, *Churchill*, p. 80.
48. Gilbert, *Winston S. Churchill: Vol. IV*, p. 898.
49. K. O. Morgan, *Consensus and Disunity: The Lloyd George Coalition Government 1918–1922* (Oxford 1979), pp. 102–3.
50. F. Brockway, *Towards Tomorrow* (London 1977), p. 68.
51. Middlemas and Barnes, *Baldwin*, p. 280.
52. P. Clarke, 'Churchill's Economic Ideas', in Blake and Louis, *Churchill*, p. 89.
53. Moran, *Winston Churchill*, p. 297.
54. Ponting, *Churchill*, p. 297.
55. Taylor, *English History 1914–1945*, pp. 244–5.
56. P. Renshaw, *The General Strike* (London 1975), p. 162.
57. R. Rhodes James (ed.), *Memoirs of a Conservative: J. C. C. Davidson's Memoirs and Papers 1910–1937* (London 1969), pp. 232–50.
58. I. McIntyre, *The Expense of Glory: A Life of John Reith* (London 1993), p. 142.
59. Middlemas and Barnes, *Baldwin*, p. 436. See also Addison, *Churchill on the Home Front*, pp. 264–8.
60. Addison, *Churchill on the Home Front*, pp. 268–70.
61. Ponting, *Churchill*, pp. 306–15.
62. Gilbert, *In Search of Churchill*, pp. 256–8.
63. P. Addison, 'Churchill and Social Reform', in Blake and Louis, *Churchill*, p. 70.
64. A. Marwick, 'Middle Opinion in the Thirties', *English Historical Review*, LXXIX:ccx (1964), pp. 285–98; also Addison, *Road to 1945*, pp. 38–40.
65. Churchill, *Hinge of Fate*, p. 862.
66. Addison, *Churchill on the Home Front*, pp. 366–7.
67. G.Orwell, *Collected Essays, Journalism and Letters, Vol. 2*, p. 318.
68. Wilson, *Churchill and the Prof.*, p. 145.
69. Addison, *Road to 1945*, pp. 150–1.
70. A. Calder, *The People's War* (London 1965), pp. 288–9.
71. M. Soames, *Clementine Churchill* (London 1979), p. 382.
72. Gilbert, *Never Despair*, pp. 35–6.
73. Churchill, *Triumph and Tragedy*, p. 583.
74. Addison, *Churchill on the Home Front*, p. 383.
75. Addison, *Road to 1945*, p. 126.
76. Rhodes James (ed.), *'Chips': the Diaries of Sir Henry Channon*, p. 409.
77. Gilbert, *Never Despair*, p. 109.
78. J. D. R. Blake, *The Conservative Party from Peel to Churchill* (London 1970), p. 258.

79. Seldon, *Churchill's Indian Summer*, p. 420.
80. Ibid., p. 262.
81. Ibid., pp. 416–17.
82. Ibid., pp. 206–7.
83. Roberts, *Eminent Churchillians*, pp. 252–77.
84. Montague Browne, *Last Sunset*, pp. 129–31.
85. Roberts, *Eminent Churchillians*, pp. 276–7.
86. Addison, *Churchill on the Home Front*, p. 412.
87. K. Morgan, *The People's Peace* (Oxford 1992). (This is the title of Chapter 4 in this book.)

8 Churchill and Ireland

1. Churchill, *My Early Life*, p. 16.
2. Churchill, *Winston S. Churchill: Vol. I*, p. 318.
3. W. S. Churchill, *Lord Randolph Churchill* (London, Odham's Press edition, 1951), p. 439.
4. M. Bromage, *Churchill and Ireland* (Notre Dame, 1964) Introduction, p. xi.
5. Churchill, *Young Statesman*, pp. 470–1.
6. Ibid.
7. Ibid., pp. 480–4.
8. A. T. Q. Stewart, *Edward Carson* (Dublin 1981), p. 87.
9. W. S. Churchill, *The World Crisis 1911–1914* (London 1923), p. 182.
10. Rhodes James, *Churchill Speaks*, p. 271.
11. Ibid., p. 273.
12. I. F. W. Beckett (ed.), *The Army and the Curragh Incident 1914* (London 1981), pp. 124–5, 288.
13. A. T. Q. Stewart, *The Ulster Crisis* (London 1967), p. 171.
14. Ibid.
15. Ibid., p. 172.
16. Beckett, *Army*, p. 74.
17. David (ed.), *Inside Asquith's Cabinet*, p. 155.
18. Bonham Carter, *Winston Churchill As I Knew Him*, pp. 298–300.
19. Ibid.
20. Rose, *Churchill* p. 16.
21. Ibid.
22. Author's recollection.
23. Jeffrey, *Correspondence*, p. 180.
24. Gilbert, *Winston S. Churchill: Vol. IV*, p. 471.
25. Ibid., p. 676. See also T. P. Coogan, *Michael Collins* (London 1990), p. 276.
26. Ibid., p. 692.
27. Ibid., pp. 711–12.
28. Bromage, *Churchill and Ireland*, p. 67.

29. M. Farrell, *Arming the Protestants: The Formation of the Ulster Special Constabulary and the Royal Ulster Constabulary 1920–1927* (London 1983), p. 134.
30. Coogan, *Michael Collins*, pp. 379–80.
31. Gilbert, *Winston S. Churchill: Vol. IV*, p. 746.
32. E. Staunton, 'The Boundary Commission Debacle 1925: Aftermath and Implications', *History Ireland*, 4:2 (1996), pp. 42–6.
33. Ibid.
34. Bromage, *Churchill and Ireland*, pp. 105–7.
35. Ibid., p. 110.
36. *Daily Mail*, 29 March 1932.
37. Ibid., 15 February 1933. Also quoted in Fisk, *In Time of War*, pp. 64–5.
38. Fisk, *In Time of War*, p. 30.
39. Ponting, *1940: Myth and Reality*, pp. 189–94.
40. Fisk, *In Time of War*, p. 323.
41. Earl of Longford and T. P. O'Neill, *Eamon de Valera* (London 1970), p. 393.
42. W. H. Thompson, *I Was Churchill's Shadow* (London 1951), p. 196.
43. Bromage, *Churchill and Ireland*, p. 154.
44. Fisk, *In Time of War*, p. 207.
45. Ibid., p. 209.
46. Ibid., p. 517.
47. Ryle Dwyer, *Eamon de Valera* (Dublin 1980), p. 127.
48. Ibid., p. 124.
49. Ibid., p. 127.
50. Ibid.
51. Ibid.
52. Moran, *Winston Churchill*, p. 473.
53. B. Barton, *Northern Ireland in the Second World War* (Belfast 1995), p. 130.

9 Churchill and the British Empire

1. E. J. Hobsbawm, *Age of Extremes: The Short Twentieth Century 1914–1991* (London 1994), p. 7.
2. Rhodes James, *Churchill Speaks*, p. 24.
3. Gilbert, *Road to Victory*, p. 254.
4. Gilbert, *Never Despair*, p. 934.
5. Churchill, *Winston S. Churchill: Vol. I*, p. 297.
6. Ibid., pp. 254–5. See also T. Royle, *The Kitchener Enigma* (London 1985), p. 133.
7. Rhodes James, *Churchill Speaks*, p. 61.
8. R. Hyam, *Elgin and Churchill at the Colonial Office, 1905–1908* (London 1968), p. 116.
9. Churchill, *Young Statesman*, p. 155.
10. Ibid., p. 164.
11. I. McLean, *Keir Hardie* (London 1975), p. 131.

12. N. Mandela, *Long Walk to Freedom* (London 1994), p. 58.
13. S. Marks and S. Trapido, 'Lord Milner and the South African State', *History Workshop*, 8 (1979) pp. 50–80.
14. Churchill, *Young Statesman*, p. 174.
15. A. M. Gollin, *Proconsul in Politics: A Study of Lord Milner* (London 1964), pp. 82–4.
16. W. S. Blunt, *My Diaries*, Vol. II (London 1965), p. 283.
17. Rose, *Churchill*, p. 154.
18. D. E. Omissi, *Air Power and Colonial Control: The Royal Air Force 1919–1939* (Manchester 1990), p. 174.
19. Gilbert, *Winston S. Churchill: Vol. IV*, p. 409.
20. Gilbert, *Winston S. Churchill: Vol. V*, p. 382.
21. *The Times*, 24 February 1931.
22. Rhodes James, *Churchill: A Study in Failure*, p. 213.
23. G. J. Douds, 'The Indian Princes: Britain's Fifth Column', *South Asia*, XI:2 (1988), pp. 57–69.
24. Butler, *Art of the Possible*, p. 53.
25. Rhodes James, *Churchill Speaks*, pp. 517–18.
26. Butler, *Art of the Possible*, p. 40.
27. Kimball, *Churchill and Roosevelt, the Complete Correspondence*, Vol. I, p. 403.
28. Churchill, *Hinge of Fate*, p. 90.
29. See Chapter 3.
30. Gilbert, *Finest Hour*, p. 1164.
31. Douds, 'Indian Princes'.
32. B. Lapping, *The End of Empire* (London 1985), p. 53.
33. Gilbert, *Road to Victory*, pp. 350–1.
34. Ibid.
35. P. Moon, *The Viceroy's Journal* (London 1973), p. 159.
36. Ibid., pp. 3–4.
37. Ibid., p. 89.
38. Ibid.
39. Douds, '"Matters of Honour": Indian Troops in the North African and Indian Theatres', in P. Addison and A. Calder (eds), *Time to Kill: The Soldier's Experience of War in the West 1939–1945* (London 1997), pp. 115–29.
40. Gilbert, *Road to Victory*, p. 1166.
41. Gilbert, *Never Despair*, p. 293.
42. Ibid.
43. P. Ziegler, *Mountbatten: The Official Biography* (London, 1985), p. 461.
44. Roberts, *Eminent Churchillians* pp. 81–132.
45. J. A. Hobson, *Imperialism: A Study* (London 1902), p. 327.
46. Moran, *Winston Churchill* p. 370.
47. Ibid. pp. 449–50.
48. S. Wolpert, *Nehru: A Tryst with Destiny* (Oxford 1996), p. 333.
49. S. Gopal, 'Churchill and India', in Blake and Louis, *Churchill*, pp. 468–9.
50. Ibid.
51. Moran, *Winston Churchill*, p. 21.

52. D. Day, *Menzies and Churchill at War* (Oxford 1993), pp. 166–7, 225–6, 239.
53. Thorne, *Allies of a Kind*, p. 63.
54. D. Day, *The Great Betrayal: Britain, Australia and the Onset of the Pacific War 1939–42* (London 1988), pp. 10, 255–6, 354–8.
55. R. O'Neil, 'Japan and British Security in the Pacific', in Blake and Louis (eds), *Churchill*, pp. 285–6.
56. Reynolds, *Britannia Overruled*, p. 149.
57. Churchill, *Hinge of Fate*, p. 8.
58. Thorne, *Allies of Kind*, p. 257.
59. Ibid.
60. Reynolds, *Britannia Overruled*, p. 149.
61. Thorne, *Allies of a Kind*, p. 209.
62. Ibid.
63. *The Times*, 21 November 1942, also quoted in Thorne, *Allies of a Kind*, p. 211.
64. Gilbert, *Never Despair*, p. 301.
65. Reynolds, *Britannia Overruled*, p. 169.
66. Ibid.
67. Shuckburgh, *Descent to Suez*, p. 75.
68. Charmley, *Churchill's Grand Alliance*, pp. 346–7.
69. Montague Brown, *Long Sunset*, pp. 210–11.
70. Gilbert, *Never Despair*, pp. 1220–1.
71. Montague Brown, *Long Sunset*, p. 213.
72. Clarke, *Hope and Glory*, p. 263.
73. W. R. Louis, 'Churchill and Egypt', in Blake and Louis, *Churchill*, p. 476.
74. Callaghan, *Churchill: Retreat from Empire*, p. 265.
75. J. MacKenzie, *Propaganda and Empire* (Manchester 1984).
76. A. Leslie, *Clare Sheridan* (New York 1977), pp. 304–5.
77. J. Morris, *Farewell the Trumpets: An Imperial Retreat* (London 1978), pp. 556–7.

Epilogue

1. M. Howard, *The Lessons of History* (Oxford 1991), p. 158.
2. Parker, *Winston Churchill*, p. 4.

Select Bibliography

General

Anyone writing on Churchill has now to do so in the shadow of the huge official biography of him by his son Randolph and magisterially completed by Martin Gilbert. The first volume of this came out in 1966 and the final one in 1988. There are eight in total, and there are also companion volumes of documents. Along with Churchill's own voluminous writings, they constitute a daunting but necessary preparation for even beginning to grasp the magnitude and drama of Churchill's life. Many shorter biographies have been written and among these are H. Pelling, *Churchill* (London 1974), K. Robbins, *Churchill* (London 1992), J. Charmley, *Churchill: The End of Glory* (London 1993), C. Ponting, *Churchill* and N. Rose, *Churchill: An Unruly Life* (both London 1994). The Charmley and Ponting books are 'revisionist' and, in some important respects, hostile to their subject. The same could also be said of A. Roberts, *Eminent Churchillians* (London 1994).

The essays in A. J. P. Taylor (ed.), *Churchill: Four Faces and the Man* (London 1969) range over different aspects of Churchill the man and what he achieved. R. Rhodes James, *Churchill: A Study in Failure* (London 1970) and the same author's edited compendium of speeches, *Churchill Speaks 1897–1963* (London 1981) are both indispensable. So too is the collection of essays edited by R. Blake and W. Roger Louis, *Churchill: A Major New Assessment of His Life in Peace and War* (London 1993) and also R. A. C. Parker (ed.), *Winston Churchill: Studies in Statesmanship* (London 1995).

Superb and path-breaking work has been done by P. Addison in *The Road to 1945: British Politics and the Second World War* (London 1975) and *Churchill on the Home Front 1900–1955* (London 1992). The same author has written extensively on Churchill's beliefs. His article, 'The Political Beliefs of Winston Churchill', *Transactions of the Royal Historical Society*, Fifth Series, 30 (1980), pp. 23–47, should not be missed, nor should his 'Destiny, history and providence: the religion of Winston Churchill', in M. Bentley (ed.), *Public and Private Doctrine: Essays in British History Presented to Maurice Cowling* (Cambridge 1993), pp. 236–50.

Anecdotal and very personal accounts of Churchill can be found in M. Gilbert, *In Search of Churchill* (London 1994), A. Montague Brown, *Long Sunset: Memoirs of Winston Churchill's Last Private Secretary* (London 1995) and in the diaries of

Lord Moran and Sir John Colville, which are referred to elsewhere in this review of the available literature on Churchill.

1 Churchill the Warrior

Churchill wrote vividly about his early military service in *The Story of the Malakand Field Force* (London 1898), *The River War* (London 1899), *Ian Hamilton's March* and *London to Ladysmith* (both London 1900) and *My Early Life* (London 1930). *Marlborough, His Life and Times* (4 vols, London 1934–38) is a major work of military history. All the biographical writing on Churchill covers his army service as well as his often contentious role as a war correspondent. D. Jablonsky, *Churchill, the Great Game and Total War* (London 1991) can be strongly recommended for its treatment of its subject's relationship to the conduct of war and defence policy. D. Stafford, *Churchill and Secret Intelligence* (London 1997), is a very important work.

R. Hough, *Former Naval Person: Churchill and the Wars at Sea* (London 1985) and S. Roskill, *Churchill and the Admirals* (London 1977) are splendid on his dealings with the Royal Navy. Churchill's great work, *The World Crisis 1911–1918* (2 vols, London 1923) offers a hugely dramatic account of the First World War and his part in it, while its successor work, *The Aftermath* (London 1924), surveys events after the Armistice. K. Jeffrey, *The British Army and the Crisis of Empire 1918–1922* (Manchester 1984) gives a general review of many post-war military issues with which Churchill had to deal.

Debates on defence policy in the inter-war period are thoroughly covered by M. Gilbert in *Winston S. Churchill: Vol. V, 1922–1939* (London 1976) and by many specialist works such as M. Howard, *The Continental Commitment: The Dilemma of British Defence Policy in the Era of the Two World Wars* (London 1972), P. Cosgrave, *Churchill at War Vol. I: Alone 1939–1940* (London 1974) and F. Kersaudy, *Norway 1940* (London 1990), which also should be consulted on the military and naval events which helped to bring Churchill to power as Prime Minister.

2 National Leader, 1940–1945

Churchill's climactic years as Prime Minister after 1940 come pulsatingly alive in his own history of the Second World War, though his version of events has now to be re-examined and at many points modified in the light of the access historians now have to government papers and to so many other sources not available to Churchill. Martin Gilbert, in two of the finest of his volumes, *Winston S. Churchill: Vol. VI, Finest Hour 1939–1941* (London 1983) and *Winston*

S. Churchill: Vol. VII, Road to Victory 1941–1945 (London 1986), covers the period in unstinting detail.

There are also illuminating books by those close to Churchill, such as Lord Moran, *Winston Churchill 1940–1955: The Struggle for Survival* (London 1966) and J. Colville, *The Fringes of Power: Downing Street Diaries 1939–1955* (London 1985). J. Wheeler-Bennett (ed.), *Action This Day: Working with Churchill* (London, 1968) draws upon the recollections of senior civil servants and Cabinet Office staff who worked closely with Churchill. A. Bryant (ed.), *The Turn of the Tide* (London 1957) and *Triumph in the West* (London 1959), broke important ground with the access he had to the Allanbrooke diaries. These give a compelling picture of Churchill's often turbulent relations with his Chiefs of Staff.

R. Lewin has written fine studies of Churchill's conduct of the war in *Churchill as Warlord* (London 1973) and *Churchill as War Leader: Right or Wrong?* (London 1991). J. Lukacs, *The Duel: Hitler v. Churchill 10 May–31 July 1940* (London 1990) is a fascinating work. C. Ponting, *1940: Myth and Reality* (London 1990) is a rather snide work. R. Overy, *Why the Allies Won* (London 1996) gives an incisive and far better balanced assessment of Churchill's role, as do several contributions to the collection of essays already referred to by R. Blake and W. Roger Louis and published in 1993. J. Keegan (ed.), *Churchill's Generals* (London 1991) is immensely useful and so too is the 1995 volume of essays, *Winston Churchill: Studies in Statesmanship*, edited by R. A. C. Parker in 1995.

There is little likelihood of work on Churchill's role in the conduct of the war drying up. The same is true on the political aspects of his war leadership, where P. Addison's work, referred to elsewhere here, has been of seminal importance, as has Angus Calder's classic *The People's War* (London 1969), now deservedly reprinted. See also M. Howard, 'Churchill and the Era of National Unity' in his *The Lessons of History* (Oxford 1991), pp. 152–66.

3   Churchill and the United States

In his own writing on the two world wars, Churchill reveals much of his attitudes to the United States and its leaders. He never lost his affection and admiration for it even as the balance of power shifted away from Britain, a process carefully documented in D. Reynolds, *Britannia Overruled: British Policy and World Power in the Twentieth Century* (London 1991). The genesis of this admiration is very clear in Churchill's *History of the English Speaking Peoples* (4 vols, London 1956–58).

Indispensable reading on the advent of the American alliance in the Second World War is provided by W. Kimball (ed.), *Churchill and Roosevelt: The Complete Correspondence* (3 vols, Princeton, 1984) and in the same author's *Forged in War: Churchill, Roosevelt and the Second World War* (London 1997). W. Averell Harriman and E. Abel, *Special Envoy to Churchill and Stalin 1941–1946* (London 1976) is an enthralling account of the wartime alliance in action, while J. Charmley,

Churchill's Grand Alliance: The Anglo-American Special Relationship 1940–1957 (London 1995) is a sustained attack on wartime American policy and what is claimed to be Churchill's acquiescence in it. C. Thorne, *Allies of a Kind: The US, Britain and the War Against Japan 1941–1945* (Oxford 1978) explores inter-allied tensions generated by the war in the Far East.

Churchill's influence upon Britain's relations with America in the Cold War period is covered in many books. Among the best of these are H. Thomas, *The Armed Truce: The Beginnings of the Cold War 1945–46* (London 1986); F. Harbutt, *The Iron Curtain: Churchill, America and the Origins of the Cold War* (Oxford 1987); T. H. Anderson, *The United States, Britain and the Cold War 1944–1947* (Columbia and London 1987); W. Roger Louis and H. Hull (eds), *The Special Relationship: Anglo-American Relations Since 1945* (Oxford 1986) and J. Young, *Winston Churchill's Last Campaign: Britain and the Cold War 1951–1955* (Oxford 1996).

4   Churchill and the Soviet Union

M. Gilbert, in *Winston S. Churchill: Vol. IV, 1916–1922* (London 1975), covers in great detail Churchill's hostility to the new Soviet state and his tenacious support for military intervention against it. In *Winston S. Churchill: Vol. VII, Road to Victory 1941–1945* (London 1986), he gives a vivid account of Churchill's wartime relations with Stalin. Churchill's own account of these in his history of the war is not to be missed.

M. Kitchen, 'Winston Churchill and the Soviet Union During the Second World War', *Historical Journal*, XXX:2 (1987), pp. 415–36, is an article of major importance. Paul Addison's *The Road to 1945: British Politics and the Second World War* (London 1975) and his *Churchill on the Home Front 1900–1955* (London 1992), have important insights into the politics of Britain's wartime Soviet alliance. I. Maisky, *Memoirs of a Soviet Ambassador* (London 1967) should be consulted, as should I. McLaine, *Ministry of Morale: Home Front Morale and the Ministry of Information in World War II* (London 1979). The latter book looks, among many other matters, at the dilemmas for British wartime propaganda which were created by Russia's entering the war on Britain's side. J. Erickson, *The Road to Stalingrad: Stalin's War with Germany Vol. 1* (London 1975) and *The Road to Berlin: Stalin's War with Germany Vol. 2* (London 1983) are enormous and magnificent works which cover very fully Churchill's dealings with Stalin.

Many books explore the onset of the Cold War and Churchill's response to it, e.g. T. H. Anderson, *The United States, Britain and the Cold War 1944–1947* (Columbia and London 1981); also H. Thomas, *Armed Truce: the Beginnings of the Cold War 1945–46* (London 1986). J. Young, *Winston Churchill's Last Campaign: Britain and the Cold War 1951–1955* (Oxford 1996) should be consulted on Churchill's attempts in his last years in office to revive his wartime personal contacts with the Soviet leadership after Stalin's death.

5   Churchill and Appeasement

For many years, debate on this issue was dominated by *The Gathering Storm*, the first volume of Churchill's great history of the Second World War. Possibly the first serious questioning of his treatment of the appeasement years came in a short research article by R. H. Powers, 'Winston Churchill's Parliamentary Commentary on British Foreign Policy 1935–1938', *Journal of Modern History* XXVI:2 (1954), pp. 179–82. D. C. Watt, in *Personalities and Policy* (London 1965), took this approach further, as did R. Rhodes James in his *Churchill: A Study in Failure* (London 1970). N. Thompson, *The Anti-Appeasers* (Oxford 1971) remains an excellent source on Churchill's role in foreign policy debates. P. W. Schroeder, 'Munich and the British Tradition', *Historical Journal* XIX:1 (1976), pp. 223–43 gives a thoughtful appraisal of appeasement as a concept. P. Kennedy, *Realities Behind Diplomacy: Background Influences on British External Policy 1865–1980* (London 1981) explores with great care what choices British governments had in the 1930s. J. Charmley, in *Chamberlain and the Lost Peace* (London 1989), offers a critique of Churchill's attacks on appeasement which he has repeated in other books. J. Ramsden, *That Will Depend on Who Writes the History: Winston Churchill as his Own Historian*, inaugural lecture, Queen Mary and Westfield College, London 1996, makes entertaining but perceptive points on the appeasement debate.

6   Churchill and Europe

The changes and sometimes contradictions in Churchill's thinking about Europe in general and about steps towards its post-1945 economic and political integration emerge in his own writings, speeches and private observations. These are fully documented by Martin Gilbert in the official biography. G. A. Craig, 'Churchill and Germany', D. Johnson, 'Churchill and France' and M. Beloff, 'Churchill and Europe' are also essential reading in the collection of essays referred to already, edited by R. Blake and W. Roger Louis. In a more recent volume edited by R. A. C. Parker, *Winston Churchill: Studies in Statesmanship* (London 1993), there are illuminating chapters: M. Vaisse, 'Churchill and France 1951–55', H. P. Schwarz, 'Churchill and Adenauer', W. Krieger, 'Churchill and the Defence of the West' and M. Gilbert, 'Churchill and the European Idea'. F. Kersaudy, *Churchill and de Gaulle* (London 1981), is still the best treatment of an always volatile and troubled relationship. A. Seldon, *Churchill's Indian Summer: The Conservative Government 1951–1955* (London 1981), is very thorough on European policy, as is V. Rothwell's excellent *Anthony Eden: A Political Biography 1931–1957* (Manchester 1992). Political memoirs of the post-1945 period also throw light on Churchill's European role, e.g. H. Macmillan's autobiography, *Vol. III, Tides of Fortune 1945–55* (London 1969) and the Earl of Kilmuir, *Political Adventure* (London 1964). A. Horne's official biography, *Macmillan 1894–1956, Vol. I* (London 1988) is also useful on Churchill's second spell in Downing Street and his attitudes to Europe.

7 Churchill, Party Politics and Social Policy

All the major biographies of Churchill contain much of value on his domestic political career and on his contribution to social policy. P. Addison still dominates this area with his two brilliant books, *The Road to 1945: British Politics and the Second World War* (London 1975) and *Churchill on the Home Front 1900–1955* (London 1992).

P. Clarke, *Liberals and Social Democrats* (Cambridge 1978), is very good on social policy debates before 1914 and Churchill's part in them. The same author's *Hope and Glory: Britain 1900–1990* (London 1996) assesses Churchill's importance within the broader history of twentieth-century Britain. K. Morgan, *The People's Peace* (Oxford 1992), is well worth referring to for the post-Second World War context to Churchill's time in opposition and his second term as Prime Minister. A. Seldon, *Churchill's Indian Summer: The Conservative Government 1951–1955* (London 1981), is faultless in its detail. A. Roberts, *Eminent Churchillians* (London 1994), is an acerbic book which blames Churchill's second government for what its author claims was its appeasement of trade unions and its failure to control immigration from the Asian and Caribbean countries of the British Commonwealth. Two general histories of the Conservative Party which seek to assess Churchill's complex relationship to it are R. Blake, *The Conservative Party from Peel to Churchill* (London 1970) and A. Clark, *The Tories: Conservatives and the Nation State 1922–1997* (London 1998).

There is a predictable lack of books on Churchill and Scotland. C. Harvie, *No Gods and Precious Few Heroes: Scotland Since 1914* (London 1981) and A. Marr, *The Battle for Scotland* (London 1992) deal in a concise and very readable way with the politics of Scottish self-government and independence. T. Paterson, *Churchill: A Seat For Life* (Dundee 1980), is a disappointingly superficial look at Churchill's time representing a Scottish constituency in Parliament. Infinitely better on this are W. M. Walker, *Juteopolis: Dundee and its Textile Workers 1885–1923* (Edinburgh 1979) and the article by the same author, 'Dundee's Disenchantment With Churchill', *Scottish Historical Review*, 49 (1970), pp. 85–108.

8 Churchill and Ireland

Churchill's involvement with the Irish question is covered in detail in the relevant volumes of the official biography, i.e. by Randolph Churchill in *Winston S. Churchill: Vol. II, Young Statesman 1901–1914* (London 1967) and by Martin

Gilbert's *Winston S. Churchill: Vol. IV, 1917–1922* (London 1975) and *Winston S. Churchill: Vol. V, 1922–1939* (London 1976).

The best general treatment of his attitudes to Ireland is probably still by the American M. Bromage, *Churchill and Ireland* (Notre Dame 1964). A. T. Q. Stewart, *The Ulster Crisis* (London 1967) and *Edward Carson* (Dublin 1981) are indispensable background reading for understanding Churchill's role before 1914.

T. P. Coogan, *Michael Collins* (London 1990) and M. Farrell, *Arming the Protestants: The Formation of the Ulster Special Constabulary and the Royal Ulster Constabulary 1920–1927* (London 1983) both offer useful insights into Church-ill's response to the Irish war of independence and the treaty and partition which followed it. T. Ryle Dwyer, *Eamon de Valera* (Dublin 1981) and the Earl of Longford and T. P. O'Neill, *Eamon de Valera* (London 1990) are also useful on Churchill's view of a key figure in the creation and early history of the new Irish state.

R. Fisk, *In Time of War: Ireland, Ulster and the Price of Neutrality 1939–1945* (London 1983), is an outstanding work and much can be learned from it about the way Churchill saw issues like Irish neutrality in the Second World War and the position of Northern Ireland. B. Barton, *Northern Ireland in the Second World War* (Belfast 1995), is a short but excellent book which puts into perspective some of the decisions Churchill had to make over the province and Britain's relations with it during the war.

9   Churchill and the British Empire

Churchill's early military writings, e.g. *The Story of the Malakand Field Force* (London 1898) and *The River War* (London 1899), his *My African Journey* (London 1908) and *My Early Life* (London 1930), all offer revealing insights into his belief in Britain's imperial role. The collection of essays edited by R. Blake and W. Roger Louis includes R. Hyam, 'Churchill and the British Empire', S. Gopal, 'Churchill and India' and W. Roger Louis, 'Churchill and Egypt 1946–1956'. All of these are well worth consulting. So too are R. A. Callaghan, *Churchill: Retreat from Empire* (Delaware 1984) and B. Lapping, *The End of Empire* (London 1985).

R. Rhodes James, in his *Churchill: A Study in Failure*, explores Churchill's hostility to the National Government's Indian policy, and P. Moon (ed.), *The Viceroy's Journal* (London 1973), draws on Wavell's writings to show how little the war altered the Prime Minister's views on India. C. Thorne, in his *Allies of a Kind: The United States, Britain and the War Against Japan 1941–1945* (Oxford 1978), has much of value to offer on how Churchill's conception of Britain's imperial role affected his conduct of the war in the Far East. D. Day, *The Great Betrayal: Britain, Australia and the Onset of the Pacific War 1939–42* (London 1988), and the same author's *Churchill and Menzies at War* (Oxford 1993), are impor-tant for the way they examine Churchill's very ambivalent view of Australia.

W. Kimball, in his edited volumes of Churchill's wartime correspondence with Roosevelt, which have been referred to already, makes clear the tensions created by Churchill's conviction that an imperial role for Britain was compatible with its wartime alliance with the United States. D. Reynolds, in *Britannia Overruled: British Policy and World Power in the Twentieth Century* (London 1991), also deals with this topic. The author shows the extent to which the Cold War and the imperatives it created did for some time induce the United States to accept a significant role for Britain in the Middle East, Africa and Asia.

INDEX